World Poverty and Human Rights

For Ling

八千日夜雲和月

World Poverty and Human Rights

Cosmopolitan Responsibilities and Reforms

Thomas W. Pogge

polity

First published in 2002 by Polity Press in association with Blackwell Publishing Ltd.

Reprinted 2003, 2004, 2005

Polity Press
65 Bridge Street
Cambridge CB2 1UR, UK

Polity Press
350 Main Street
Maldon, MA 02148, USA

ISBN 0-7456-2994-6
ISBN 0-7456-2995-4 (pbk)

A catalogue record for this book is available from the British Library and has been applied for from the Library of Congress.

Typeset in 10.5 on 12 pt Times New Roman
by Graphicraft Limited, Hong Kong
Printed and bound in Great Britain by Marston Book Services Limited, Oxford

This book is printed on acid-free paper.
For further information on Polity, please visit our website: http://www.polity.co.uk

Contents

General Introduction

> Everyone has the right to a standard of living adequate for the health and well-being of himself and of his family, including food, clothing, housing and medical care.
>
> Everyone is entitled to a social and international order in which the rights and freedoms set forth in this Declaration can be fully realized.
>
> *UDHR*, Articles 25 and 28[1]

The eight essays collected in this volume were written between 1990 and 2001. They develop different aspects of a normative position on global justice. The General Introduction states this position in a unified and non-technical way. With this overview, chapters can be read selectively and in any order. Chapters 1–3 are the most philosophical, discussing universal justice, human rights, and moral theorizing. Chapters 3–5 show that the common moral acceptance of the existing global order is incoherent with firmly entrenched moral convictions about interpersonal morality and domestic justice. Chapters 6–8 propose modest and feasible, but significant, global institutional reforms

This General Introduction has been improved by very helpful comments from Robert Amdur, Christian Barry, Charles Beitz, Danielle Celermajer, Mona El-Ghobashy, Andy Kuper, Andy Nathan, and Ling Tong. I also want to thank Daniela Mitrovich for her substantial help in harmonizing the eight chapters and in constructing the index.

that would better align our international order with our moral values. These last three chapters offer the most accessible entry to the book.

I Some cautions about our moral judgments

During the last 220 years, moral norms protecting the weak and the vulnerable have become increasingly restrictive and increasingly effective. Forms of conduct and social organization that were accepted and practiced in the eighteenth and nineteenth centuries and for millennia before – domestic violence, slavery, autocracy, colonialism, genocide – are now proscribed, outlawed, and displayed as paradigms of injustice. On the face of it, at least, there has been tremendous moral progress.

Yet, how well are the weak and vulnerable faring today? Some 2,800 million or 46 percent of humankind live below the World Bank's $2/day poverty line – precisely: in households whose income per person per day has less purchasing power than $2.15 had in the US in 1993. On average, the people living below this line fall 44.4 percent below it. Over 1,200 million of them live on less than half, below the World Bank's better-known $1/day poverty line. People so incredibly poor are extremely vulnerable to even minor changes in natural and social conditions as well as to many forms of exploitation and abuse. Each year, some 18 million of them die prematurely from poverty-related causes. This is one-third of all human deaths – 50,000 every day, including 34,000 children under age five.[2]

Such severe and extensive poverty persists while there is great and rising affluence elsewhere. The average income of the citizens of the affluent countries is about 50 times greater in purchasing power and about 200 times greater in terms of market exchange rates than that of the global poor. The latter 2,800 million people together have about 1.2 percent of aggregate global income, while the 903 million people of the "high-income economies" together have 79.7 percent. Shifting merely 1 percent of aggregate global income – $312 billion annually[3] – from the first group to the second would eradicate severe poverty worldwide.

In reality, however, the shift in global income goes the other way. Inequality continues to mount decade after decade as the affluent get richer and the poor remain at or below the subsistence minimum. Over a recent, closely studied five-year period, real growth in global average *per capita* income was a respectable 5.7 percent. The top quintile (fifth) of the world's population got all of the gain – and then some: real incomes declined in all other income segments. "The bottom 5 percent of the world grew poorer, as their real incomes decreased between 1988 and 1993 by 1/4 while the richest quintile grew richer. It gained 12 percent in real terms, that is it grew more than twice as much as mean world income (5.7 percent)."[4]

This juxtaposition of great progress in our moral norms and conduct with a rather catastrophic moral situation on the ground raises two questions:

1 How can severe poverty of half of humankind continue despite enormous economic and technological progress and despite the enlightened moral norms and values of our heavily dominant Western civilization?
2 Why do we citizens of the affluent Western states not find it morally troubling, at least, that a world heavily dominated by us and our values gives such very deficient and inferior starting positions and opportunities to so many people?[5]

Answers to the second question help answer the first. Extensive, severe poverty can continue, because we do not find its eradication morally compelling.[6] And we cannot find its eradication morally compelling until we find its persistence and the relentless rise in global inequality troubling enough to warrant serious moral reflection. To be sure, many among us know only the bare outlines of the problem. But this is mostly because those who do know more of the relevant data – economists and other academics, journalists, politicians – find them not morally disturbing enough to highlight, publicize, and discuss. They do not see global poverty and inequality as morally important issues for us. To understand why this is so, one must examine their conscious and semi-conscious reasons for seeing things the way they do: the justifications they give themselves and others, or would give if pressed. Beginning with section II, next, much of this book is such an examination.

To answer our two questions fully, one must also explore other causal factors that influence how our social world and moral values develop in interaction with each other. A rather too neat account of such other causal factors is Marx's historical materialism, claiming that dominant conceptions of justice are shaped by the dominant group's shared interests, which in turn are shaped by its specific role in controlling the means of economic production (capital, technologies, labor power, land, and natural resources). Thus, historical materialists refuse to see the history of the last 220 years as a success of moral effort and enlightenment: colonialism, slavery, and the subjection of women, together with the moralities condoning them, disappeared because they obstructed newly accessible, more effective ways of combining the factors of production through market institutions. Our shifting morality merely trails the shifting interests of those who own capital, technologies, land, and natural resources. Any protection and relief moral norms afford the weak and the poor is merely incidental.[7]

Historical materialism is surely too thin a theory to explain all changes in moral norms and values, or even just the major historical shifts. But it is undeniable that one's interests and situation influence what one finds morally salient (worthy of moral attention) and what notions of justice and ethics one finds appealing and compelling. Consider whether it is unjust to deny basic health care to citizens on account of their inability to pay. A poor person is rather more likely than a rich one to find this question important and more likely also conscientiously to believe the affirmative. Such discrepancies may be greater when groups live in mutual isolation and lack vivid awareness of each other's circumstances, experiences, and perspectives on the world. We live in extreme isolation from severe poverty. We do not know people scarred by the experience of losing a child to hunger, diarrhea, or measles, do not know anyone earning less than $10 for a 72-hour week of hard, monotonous labor. If we had such people as friends or neighbors, many more of us would believe that world poverty demands serious moral reflection and many more of us would hold that we should all help to eradicate this problem.

One's interests and situation also affect the concrete judgments one derives from one's moral values. Unconsciously, at least, people tend to interpret their moral values in their own favor and tend to select, represent, and connect the facts so as to facilitate the desired concrete judgments. This rationalizing tendency is stronger in people surrounded by others whose relevant interests coincide. Here each person's desire to see the pursuit of these interests as morally defensible is reinforced by her peers' expressed moral judgments and like conduct. Regular direct contact with outsiders could show the members of such a group that its values – applied perhaps in light of a better or fuller understanding of the relevant facts – support different moral judgments. But few citizens of the affluent countries have such outside contacts which might interfere with their embrace of two going moral prejudices: that the persistence of severe poverty abroad does not require our moral attention, and that there is nothing seriously wrong with our conduct, policies, and the global economic institutions we forge in regard to world poverty.

By showing how these widely shared judgments are promoted by the causal factors sketched in the last two paragraphs, I have not refuted these judgments in any way. But those influences do suggest that these judgments require further thought, that we should not allow incipient doubts about them to be overwhelmed by the manifest unconcern of nearly all our politicians, academics, and mass media.

Let me turn to another set of causal factors, which bear only on the first question of how so much misery can persist despite great progress in moral norms, unprecedented technological advances, and solid global economic growth. Moral norms, designed to protect the livelihood and dignity of the vulnerable, place burdens on the strong. If such norms are compelling enough, the strong make an effort to comply. But they also, consciously or unconsciously, try to get around the norms by arranging their social world so as to minimize their burdens of compliance. Insofar as agents succeed in such norm avoidance, they can comply and still enjoy the advantages of their dominance. Such success, however, generally reduces not merely the costs and opportunity costs of moral norms for the strong, but also the protection these norms afford the weak.

This phenomenon is familiar from more formal, legal rules such as those constituting the tax code. Clever accountants for wealthy individuals and corporations are endlessly searching for loopholes and other methods of tax avoidance which keep their clients in compliance with the law and yet thwart legislative efforts at fine-tuning the distribution of tax burdens. Moral norms elicit similar strategic responses: corporations, concerned about harsh working conditions in a foreign plant, sell it and then buy its products from its new local owner. The developing world has been similarly transformed from colonies into independent states. Many people there are still desperately poor and oppressed, and we still get the natural resources we need. But we now pay native rulers and "elites" for such imports and therefore are – or at least feel – morally disconnected from the misery of the locals.

So a suspicion, elaborated in chapter 3, is that the celebrated historic transformation of our moral norms has mostly produced cosmetic rearrangements. Imagine some visionary European statesman, in 1830 say, posing the question of how the advanced states of Europe and North America can preserve and, if possible, expand their economic and political dominance over the rest of the world even while bringing themselves into compliance with the core norms of Enlightenment morality. Find the best solution to this task you can think of and then compare it to the world today. Could the West have done any better?

The actual transformation was not, of course, the result of such a deliberate plan or grand conspiracy. It would probably have been far less successful for us if it had been pursued according to a plan. It came about through the uncoordinated activities of many influential players – each seeking its own advantage, learning from its errors, processing new data, and strategically adjusting itself to compelling moral norms by seeking to find and to exploit moral loopholes and other methods of morality avoidance. An invisible hand, rather less benign than the one acclaimed by Adam Smith, ensures that the world, driven by these self-seeking efforts, equilibrates toward a mode of organization that gives the strong as much as possible while still allowing them to be in compliance with their moral norms. Such a process gravitates toward the worst of all possible worlds to which the strong can morally reconcile themselves.

The affluent Western states are no longer practicing slavery, colonialism, or genocide. But they still enjoy crushing economic, political, and military dominance over the rest of the world. And a large proportion of humankind still can barely obtain enough to survive. The extent and severity of the deprivations they suffer, contrasted with our vastly higher standard of living, suggest caution against thoughtless approval of our conduct, policies, and global institutions. Moreover, how we assess ourselves depends on objective features: on the structure of the human world and on our role within it, as well as on subjective features: on how we direct our moral attention, on our conceptions of justice and ethics, and on how we apply these conceptions to the human world and to our role within it. Reflection on the causal influences that affect these five features suggests more caution against a hasty embrace of the two common prejudices. Given what is at stake, we cannot embrace them without examining their plausibility. Such an examination involves reflection on our conscious and semiconscious *reasons* for these judgments.

II Four easy reasons to ignore world poverty

What reasons do people in the developed West have for being unconcerned with the persistence of severe poverty abroad? The inquiry into this question faces a difficulty: those who judge an issue not worthy of moral attention cannot have an elaborate defense for this judgment because such a defense presupposes the very attention they fail to summon. And yet, there must be something in their moral outlook that explains why the basic data about poverty, which are known, do not seem morally salient to them. If something of this magnitude does not strike people as worth serious inquiry and reflection, one would expect them to have at least a superficial reason. What superficial reasons do they have for not deeming vast global poverty and inequality important, and how well do these reasons stand up to critical reflection?

One easy assumption is that preventing poverty deaths is counterproductive because it will lead to overpopulation and hence to more poverty deaths in the future.[8] This assumption does not square with the facts. In the last few decades, the rise in the human population has been overwhelmed by enormous efficiency gains in food production, reflected in a 32 percent drop in real prices of basic foodstuffs over the 1985–2000 period (n. 144). More importantly, there is now abundant evidence that birth rates tend to fall dramatically wherever poverty is alleviated and women gain better economic opportunities, more control within their households, and better access to reproductive information and technologies. Accelerated progress against poverty and the subordination of women may actually be the best strategy *against* overpopulation and toward an early leveling-off of the human population around 10 billion.[9] In any case, the available evidence does not support the conclusion that efforts to reduce severe poverty must multiply human suffering and deaths over time.

A second easy assumption is that world poverty is so gigantic a problem that it simply cannot be eradicated in a few years, at least not at a cost that would be bearable for the rich societies. This assumption is widespread. Richard Rorty, for instance, doubts that we are able to help the global poor by appealing to the claim that "a politically feasible project of egalitarian redistribution of wealth, requires there to be enough money around to insure that, after the redistribution, the rich will still be able to recognize themselves – will still think their lives worth living."[10] What Rorty presumes seems obvious: ending the poverty of 2,800 million human beings would sap our arts and culture and our capacity to achieve social justice at home. It would greatly damage our lives and communities and thus is clearly politically unfeasible.

Yet this presumption ignores the enormous extent of global inequality. The aggregate shortfall of all these people from the $2 PPP a day poverty line amounts to some $300 billion annually or just 1.2 percent of the aggregate annual gross national incomes of the high-income economies. On any credible account of Rorty's recognitional capacities, and ours, he and the rest of us could still recognize ourselves quite easily after accepting reforms that entail a 1.2 percent reduction in our incomes for the sake of eradicating severe poverty worldwide. Indeed, in a sense of the word Rorty would not allow, we might recognize ourselves for the very first time.

Moreover, the second easy assumption, even if it were true, cannot justify neglect of poverty. World poverty appears as one overwhelming – Herculean or rather Sisyphean – task to which we, as individuals, cannot meaningfully contribute. One makes a disaster-relief contribution after an earthquake and finds that, two years later, the damaged city has been largely rebuilt, with our help. One makes a contribution to poverty relief and finds that, two years later, the number of people living and dying in extreme poverty is still unimaginably large. The former contribution seems meaningful because we think of the task as limited to one disaster – rather than including the effects of all natural disasters, say. The latter contribution appears pointless. But such appearances arise from our conventional sorting categories. Seeing the global poor as one vast homogeneous mass, we overlook that saving ten children from a painful death by hunger does make a real difference, *all* the difference for these children, and that this difference is quite significant even when many other children remain hungry.

A third easy assumption is that, as the history of failed attempts at development assistance illustrates, world poverty cannot be eradicated by "throwing money at the problem." Now it may be true that official development assistance (ODA) has done little for development. But this is not evidence for the prized conclusion because most such aid is not aimed at promoting development. Rather, our politicians allocate it to benefit those who are able and willing to reciprocate: export firms in the donor countries and political-economic elites of strategically important developing states. This diagnosis is supported by a detailed study of the aid allocations made by the various "donor" countries.[11] It is also supported by the fact that ODA was sharply reduced after the end of the Cold War (n. 143), when our need for political support from developing states declined (whereas the needs of the global poor and our capacity to help did not). The diagnosis is further supported by the fact that only 19 percent of all ODA goes to the 43 least developed countries and only 8.3 percent is targeted toward meeting basic needs.[12] The unimpressive results of ODA fail to show, then, that money cannot be used effectively for poverty reduction. In fact, the appropriately targeted portion of ODA has done a lot of good.

To be sure, good intentions do not always lead to success. Even the most dedicated anti-poverty organizations sometimes waste money and effort. But, if anything, this is a reason to think harder about world poverty and ways of attacking it, rather than less. Where corruption is an obstacle, we can try to reduce it, circumvent it, or focus our efforts elsewhere. If foreign donations of food depress demand, prices, and hence incentives for production in the target country, we can instead enhance the income of the poor. Where direct transfers to poor households create dependency, we can, targeting children especially, fund vaccination programs, basic schooling, school lunches, safe water and sewage systems, housing, power plants and networks, banks and microlending, and road, rail, and communication links. Such projects augment poor people's capacity to fend for themselves and their access to markets while also stimulating local production. Such projects, publicly funded, played an important role in the eradication of poverty in the (now) developed world. And in the developing world, too, such projects have been successfully realized by UN agencies, NGOs, and individual donor states.

With regard to any such project, to be sure, there may always be some expert ready to speculate whether it may not have some unobvious bad effects elsewhere or later that neutralize the apparent good – and ready to argue perhaps that, appearances notwithstanding, public spending domestically (e.g. in Franklin D. Roosevelt's New Deal) or internationally (e.g. in the Marshall Plan) did not contribute to the eradication of poverty in today's affluent countries. Such arguments deserve a hearing, and one should try to learn from them how to identify, and to preempt and correct, unintended adverse effects. But they cannot possibly justify the quick and convenient conclusion that all possible such poverty eradication projects would be wholly ineffective in each and every poor country.

Moreover, our financial contribution to overcoming world poverty need not take the form of spending and transfers. We could agree to restructure the global order to make it more hospitable to democratic government, economic justice, and growth in the developing countries and we could drive less hard a bargain against these countries in negotiations about international trade, investment, and taxation. Making such concessions, we would, for the sake of reducing world poverty, bear opportunity costs by not using our superior bargaining power to insist on terms more favorable to ourselves. Such options, discussed throughout chapters 4–7, further undermine the easy assumption that the Western states simply cannot influence the global income distribution so as to reduce world poverty.

A fourth easy assumption is that world poverty is disappearing anyway. The popularity of this assumption in the developed world has less to do with actual trends than with people being eager to believe and with organizations such as the World Bank taking good care to define and measure poverty so as to show improvement.[13]

At the last World Food Summit in Rome, organized by the UN Food and Agriculture Organization (FAO) in November 1996, the 186 participating governments agreed to "pledge our political will and our common and national commitment to achieving food security for all and to an on-going effort to eradicate hunger in all countries, with an immediate view to reducing the number of undernourished people to half their present level no later than 2015."[14] Such strong words, denying the second and third easy assumptions, encourage the belief that a major effort is underway to annihilate world poverty.

But the pledge cannot justify setting this problem aside: Our governments' plan envisages that, even in 2015, there will still be 420 million undernourished human beings and, assuming rough proportionality, 9 million annual poverty deaths. Are these levels we can condone? With a linear decline, implying a 474,000 annual reduction in the number of poverty deaths, the plan envisages 250 million deaths from poverty-related causes over the 19-year plan period. Is so huge a death toll acceptable because these deaths would be occurring at a declining rate?

There is little assurance, moreover, that the plan is actually being carried out. The US immediately disowned responsibility, publishing an "Interpretive Statement" to the effect that "the attainment of any 'right to adequate food' or 'fundamental right to be free from hunger' is a goal or aspiration to be realized progressively that does not give rise to any international obligations."[15] There is also some effort to fudge the target. Rather than aim to halve the *numbers* of poor and undernourished, one can halve their *percentage* of the world's rising population[16] or of the faster-rising population of the developing countries. As the last formulation defines the most modest target, it will probably win out. Since the aggregate population of the developing world is projected to grow from 4,860 million in 1996 to an estimated 6,217 million in 2015, we would then aim to reduce the numbers of poor and undernourished by merely 36 (rather than 50) percent. Five years into the plan, even this reduced target seems unrealistic as the reported decline in the number of undernourished people – from 840 to 826 million[17] – is tiny. The plan is far behind schedule and the death toll from poverty over the 19 years may well exceed 300 million. In fact, present trends suggest there will be *more* poverty and malnutrition in 2015 than in 1996.[18] So we can certainly not rest assured that this problem merits no attention because it is disappearing.

The four easy assumptions I have briefly discussed provide superficial reasons that incline many in the affluent countries to disregard world poverty. None of these reasons can survive even a little reflection. They survive by discouraging such reflection. The survival of such flimsy reasons confirms the cautions of section I: we cannot take for granted that our unreflective moral judgments regarding world poverty are well-founded or reliable.

III Defending our acquiescence in world poverty

If the reasons for ignoring world poverty as not meriting moral attention are bad reasons, then the sheer magnitude of the problem requires that we give it careful thought. Doing so, we examine the second prejudice: that there is nothing seriously wrong with our conduct, policies, and the global economic institutions we forge in regard to world poverty. A skillful defense of this judgment will invoke the common belief that people may give priority to their compatriots, especially in the context of a system of competing states: it is permissible for us and our representatives vigorously to pursue our interests within an adversarial system in which others and their representatives can vigorously pursue their interests.

Variants of such views are discussed especially in chapters 3–5. I argue that the existence of an adversarial system can help justify the vigorous pursuit of individual or group interests only if there is minimal fairness of the institutional framework within which individuals or groups compete and give priority to their near and dear over outsiders. When agents competitively pursue their interests within a framework of rules, these rules themselves and their adjudication typically become objects of their competition and may then be deformed by stronger parties to the point where the framework becomes manifestly unfair. Such cases are familiar from domestic contexts: powerful corporations lobby for rules that stifle emergent competitors, incumbent political parties revise the electoral laws to perpetuate their reign, wealthy litigants vastly outspend their opponents on jury specialists, expert witnesses, and complex motions. Although they emerge from the competitive pursuit of group interests within an adversarial system, some such outcomes, and efforts to achieve and to perpetuate them, are nonetheless morally condemned.

Implicit in our moral thinking and practice there is, then, an important distinction – albeit not precisely formulated or well justified – between matters legitimately subject to change through competing group interests, on the one hand, and certain basic features of the institutional order requisite to preserve the fairness of the competition, on the other. I extend and apply this fundamental distinction to the global institutional order, arguing that *any* coercive institutional order must meet certain minimal conditions, which chapters 1–2 formulate in terms of human rights. I also argue that the existing global institutional order falls short of meeting these conditions, on account of excessive inequalities in bargaining power and of the immense poverty and economic inequality it avoidably produces.

The priority-for-compatriots idea is similarly limited in scope. We may well have less reason to benefit foreigners than to confer equivalent benefits on our compatriots. But we have as much reason not to harm foreigners as we have not to inflict equivalent harms on compatriots. The priority for compatriots can thus help justify our conduct, policies, and the global economic institutions we forge only insofar as we are not through them harming the global poor. A skillful defense of the second prejudice will claim that we are indeed not harming the poor abroad.

Such a defense will concede that we could prevent much desperate poverty through more foreign aid or other redistributive mechanisms. But it takes such preventability to indicate not that we cause poverty, but that we fail to contribute as much as we might to poverty eradication. This distinction is thought to have great moral significance: as individuals, we could do more to protect foreigners from life-threatening poverty than we are doing in fact. But failing to save lives is not morally on a par with killing. To be sure, it is morally better to do more. But if we do less or even nothing, we are not therefore the cause of, or responsible for, any poverty deaths we might have prevented. The same holds for the conduct of our governments. And an analogous point is thought to apply also to the global economic order: We affluent Western states could redesign this order to be more promoting of poverty eradication (perhaps by including some redistributive tax scheme like the Tobin Tax). It would be good of us to do so. But a global order that fails to include an effective such redistributive mechanism is not therefore causally or morally responsible for any poverty it might have prevented.

This defense combines two claims. Its factual claim asserts that we are not harming the global poor by causing severe poverty, but merely failing to benefit them by not eradicating as much severe poverty as we might. Its moral claim asserts that, while it is seriously wrong to harm the global poor by causing severe poverty, it is not seriously wrong to fail to benefit them by not eradicating as much severe poverty as we might.

Challenging the moral claim, one might argue that the distinction between causing poverty and failing to reduce it has little or no moral importance. Allowing hunger to kill people whom one could easily save, even mere foreigners, is morally on a par with killing them or at any rate little better.[19] At least this is true for economic institutions: What matters for the moral assessment of an economic order under which many are starving is whether there is a feasible institutional alternative under which such starvation would not occur. It does not matter, or does not matter much, in what kind of causal relation the relevant economic order stands to the starvation in question.

This challenge can draw support from consequentialist ideas and veil-of-ignorance reasoning à la Rawls. But I reject such heavily recipient-oriented approaches and agree, on this point, with libertarians and defenders of the second prejudice: I agree that the distinction between causing poverty and merely failing to reduce it is morally significant.[20] And I grant at least for argument's sake that, notwithstanding the enormous complexity of modern economic interaction, such a distinction can be applied, at least roughly, to the global order. My argument conceives, then, both human rights and justice as involving solely negative duties: specific minimal constraints – more minimal in the case of human rights – on what harms persons may inflict upon others.

My response to the skillful defense challenges its factual claim about, in particular, the global institutional order for which our governments, hence we, bear primary responsibility. I challenge the claim that the existing global order is not causing poverty, not harming the poor. This dispute is about the explanation of the persistence of severe poverty: why is global economic inequality increasing so rapidly that, despite an impressive rise in human affluence overall, hundreds of millions still barely survive from one day to the next?

There is much work, by economists, historians, and others, on the causes of poverty. Nearly all of it examines how poverty has evolved in various countries and regions and tries to determine which of the internationally diverse local factors explain relative successes and failures. Such work is of great significance for learning why poverty persists in some environments and not in others. It also lends credibility to the factual claim of the skillful defense: if one can identify factors that are active in developing countries where poverty persists and absent in ones where poverty is disappearing, then, it seems, one has shown that poverty is caused by these factors – and not by elements of the global institutional order.

However welcome and influential, this line of thought is fallacious. That research into poverty turns up national or local factors is due not to the world but to how these inquiries are focused: on the differential evolution of poverty in various developing countries and regions. Comparative investigations can pinpoint special factors that contribute to the outbreak and destructiveness of fires. Oxygen, if equally present in all investigated scenarios, will not be pinpointed in such investigations. Still, it would be a gross mistake to infer that oxygen is not a causal contributor to fires. It would be an analogous gross mistake to conclude, from the fact that comparative poverty research uncovers national and local factors, that the existing global economic order is not a causal contributor to poverty.

False inferences of this kind overlook how causes often act together: spark, powder, and oxygen together caused the explosion – no two of them would have sufficed. Similarly, poverty can be caused by a combination of global and local factors: by a country's low foreign exchange reserves in conjunction with global currency markets that allow speculators to short-sell its currency. Drawing this conclusion also overlooks that causes themselves have causes. A short-circuit was caused by a defective wire which in turn had been corroded by humidity. Similarly, poverty may be caused by cuts in domestic social spending which in turn are necessitated by increasing global interest rates that raise the country's debt service obligations.

There are good methodological reasons for the research bias toward national and local causes: there being only this one world to observe, it is hard to obtain solid evidence about how the overall incidence of poverty would have evolved differently if this or that global factor had been different. By contrast, solid evidence about the effects of national and local factors can be gleaned from many developing countries that differ in their natural environment, history, culture, political and economic system, and government policies. To be sure, such evidence does not produce agreement: libertarian economists – holding up Japan, Hong Kong, Taiwan, Singapore, and South Korea as their success stories – argue that the best way to expel human misery is economic growth, and the best way to achieve economic growth is to foster free enterprise with a minimum in taxes, regulations, and red tape. More left-leaning development economists dispute that those success stories really exemplify *laisser-faire* social institutions and policies. Some of them, like Amartya Sen, draw attention to Kerala, a poor state in India whose socialist policies led to exceptional advances in health, education, and life expectancy.[21] Though such disputes are not easily settled, they are nonetheless rendered more interesting, useful, and intellectually satisfying by the availability of solid evidence.

Lively disputes about national and local factors (inadvertently?) withdraw attention from foreign and global influences on the evolution of poverty. The heavy concentration of development economics on *national* development encourages the view, widespread in the developed countries, that world poverty today can be fully explained in terms of national and local factors. This view, which I discuss under the label *explanatory nationalism*,[22] is further reinforced by our reluctance to see ourselves as causally connected to severe poverty and by the general cognitive tendency to overlook the causal significance of stable background factors in a diverse and changing situation.

If true, explanatory nationalism would defeat my challenge, would vindicate the factual claim that the existing global order is not causing poverty, not harming the poor. A moment's reflection reveals, however, that explanatory nationalism cannot be strictly true, that there are significant international interdependencies and cross-border externalities some of which clearly aggravate the situation of the global poor.[23] Let me bypass such international externalities, however, and return to the skillful defense and its factual claim that the existing global order is not harming the poor. If this claim falls, then so does explanatory nationalism.

IV Does our new global economic order really not harm the poor?

There is much discussion about whether the new global economic order, instituted with the World Trade Organization (WTO), benefits, or at least does not harm, the poor. There is also confusion about the meaning of this claim and of its notions of harm and benefit. A proper evaluation of the claim requires that its different interpretations be disentangled.

Harm and benefit are comparative notions suggesting that our new global economic order makes the poor, respectively, worse or better off. But worse or better off than what? One might invoke some earlier time as a baseline. In this vein it is often suggested that the global order must be benefiting the poor because poverty is declining. But this argument is invalid. That the winds are benefiting you in your journey is not shown by your getting closer to your destination – your progress may be slowed badly by strong headwinds. Similarly, our global order may be exacerbating poverty even while, thanks to other causal factors, world poverty is in decline.

This thought reveals that one needs here not diachronic comparisons, but subjunctive ones. Whether the winds are harming or benefiting you turns on how much better or worse your journey *would* be progressing if you were not encountering these winds. In this simple example, one may find it unproblematic to define the subjunctive baseline as zero wind and easy to determine what things would then be like. But what subjunctive baseline is to be associated with the claim that the new global order benefits the poor? Here one might hold present national borders, populations, and technologies constant and then imagine minimal mutual interaction among states or some global institutional order different from ours. Or one might imagine alternative histories that led to only minimal interaction among organized national societies or else preserved a state of nature worldwide. Each of these four (and other) possibilities might be specified in different ways, yielding many quite distinct candidate baseline scenarios. How can one, in a nonarbitrary way, select the one to which the status quo should be compared? And how can one determine what the state of world poverty would be in this most appropriate baseline scenario?

One may think that it is unnecessary to reflect deeply upon such complex hypotheticals because our present world is clearly superior to all of them. This may be true for most citizens of the affluent countries. But the relevant comparison concerns poverty. Causing a third of all human deaths, world poverty now is so severe and so extensive that one cannot even say with confidence that poverty would be worse in a global Lockean state of nature in which all human beings have access to a proportional share of the world's natural resources.[24]

There may be no convincing way of clarifying the factual claim and evaluating it on empirical grounds. This impasse may suggest a narrower inquiry: is our new global economic order worse or better for the poor than a continuation of its predecessor would have been? This narrower question is easier to make precise. And it is what people often have in mind when they discuss whether our new global economic order is harming or benefiting the poor. So let me examine this narrower question.

Suppose poverty and poverty deaths are actually less now than they would now be if the WTO Treaty had not been concluded. It is tempting to infer that the new regime is then benefiting the poor, since it treats them better than the old one would have done. But this reasoning fails by unjustifiably taking continuation of the old (pre-WTO) regime as a neutral baseline, as not harming the poor. By analogous reasoning one could argue that the headwind you are facing today must be benefiting you because it is not as strong as yesterday's headwind.

The narrower question thus raises a new, distinct issue. It focuses not on the effects of the new global economic order on world poverty, but on the effects of the *change to* this new order. For some background, let me quote from *The Economist*, a magazine that, laboring to outdo all other news media in its defense of the WTO and in its vilification of protesters against it as enemies of the poor, can certainly not be accused of anti-WTO bias:

> Rich countries cut their tariffs by less in the Uruguay Round than poor ones did. Since then, they have found new ways to close their markets, notably by imposing anti-dumping duties on imports they deem "unfairly cheap". Rich countries are particularly protectionist in many of the sectors where developing countries are best able to compete, such as agriculture, textiles, and clothing. As a result, according to a new study by Thomas Hertel, of Purdue University, and Will Martin, of the World Bank, rich countries' average tariffs on manufacturing imports from poor countries are four times higher than those on imports from other rich countries. This imposes a big burden on poor countries. The United Nations Conference on Trade and Development (UNCTAD) estimates that they could export $700 billion more a year by 2005 if rich countries did more to open their markets. Poor countries are also hobbled by a lack of know-how. Many had little understanding of what they signed up to in the Uruguay Round. That ignorance is now costing them dear. Michael Finger of the World Bank and Philip Schuler of the University of Maryland estimate that implementing commitments to improve trade procedures and establish technical and intellectual-property standards can cost more than a year's development budget for the poorest countries. Moreover, in those areas where poor countries could benefit from world trade rules, they are often unable to do so. . . . Of the WTO's 134 members, 29 do not even have missions at its headquarters in Geneva. Many more can barely afford to bring cases to the WTO.[25]

This report makes clear that some of the agreements reached in the Uruguay Round are very costly for the developing countries and their people. These agreements exacerbate poverty and bring about additional deaths from poverty-related causes.

Defenders of the WTO can retort that, while the poor do not benefit from the adoption of each and every new rule and provision, they do benefit from the adoption of the WTO Treaty taken as a whole. But, even if this is true of "the poor" conceived as a pool, it is clearly false of "the poor" conceived as individuals. Many of those who have died from poverty-related causes after the WTO Treaty came into force would have survived if this treaty had not been concluded.

WTO defenders can reply that these deaths, however regrettable, must not be held against the WTO Treaty. Had it not been concluded, then there would have been even more poverty, and even more poverty deaths, if the old regime had continued. It follows that the harms caused by the switch to the new regime (e.g. people dying of poverty who would have survived had the old regime endured) are justifiable because they are outweighed by the benefits of this switch (people surviving who would have died had the old regime endured).

Suppose there is indeed less poverty under the new regime than there would have been had the old one continued. The reply then makes sense when advanced in behalf of a Third World government that faced a stark choice between a smaller number of poverty deaths after accepting the new regime and a larger number of poverty deaths after declining to join. But this reply cannot plausibly be advanced in behalf of our governments. They did not face such a stark choice between continuing the old regime and pressing for *this* WTO Treaty. They could have agreed that tariffs on manufacturing imports faced by poor countries should be no higher than those faced by rich countries, rather than four times as high. They could have agreed to open their markets to agricultural, textile, and footwear imports from the poor countries. They could have agreed to reduce their farm subsidies which, in 2000, amounted to \$245 billion.[26] Our governments' successful insistence on the protectionist exemptions had a huge impact on employment, incomes, economic growth, and tax revenues in the developing world where many live on the brink of starvation. The magnitude of this impact is suggested by the \$700 billion annual loss in export revenues. This figure is 12.5 times annual ODA from all donor countries combined, or 11 percent of the aggregate annual gross national incomes of all developing countries.

With hundreds of millions undernourished and barely surviving, the dramatic changes brought by the WTO Treaty had a significant impact on who would live and who would die. Millions who would have lived had the old regime continued have in fact died from poverty-related causes. These people were killed, and others harmed in other ways, by the change-over to the new regime. Perhaps even more millions who would have died from poverty-related causes had the old regime continued have in fact survived. But our governments cannot use this benefit to justify the harm they caused, because they could have avoided most of this harm, without losing the benefit, by making the WTO Treaty less burdensome on the developing countries. They did not do this because they sought to maximize our gains from the agreement. But our material gains cannot justify the harm either.

The point is obvious in small-scale contexts. Suppose you can do something that would gain you $10,000 while foreseeably saving three and killing two innocent persons. It would be clearly impermissible to do this if instead you could do something else that would gain you $5,000 while foreseeably saving three and killing no innocent persons. The case of introducing *this* WTO Treaty rather than a less burdensome alternative is analogous. That we do not even see how our governments' choice of the first option can be morally problematic shows that we implicitly think of the global poor as a pool, as one homogeneous mass like coffee cream in the office fridge: one may take some out provided that, over time, one takes out no more than one puts in. So we are content when some creative accounting by well-paid economists helps us believe that there would have been even more poverty and poverty deaths under a continuation of the old regime than there are now. Good, we are not taking out more poor people than we save.

But think of the global poor as individual children, women, and men, for whom a few dollars more or less can make the difference between life and death, and the pleasant belief becomes irrelevant. It is undeniable that our governments, by pressing this WTO Treaty on the rest of the world, have foreseeably taken out millions of poor persons who would have survived without the treaty. Most of these deaths would have been avoided, had our governments not, for the sake of minor material gains for us, insisted on the protectionist exemptions and other onerous commitments by the developing countries. There is no justification of our governments' choice to cause those deaths for the sake of these gains.

Many critics of the WTO regime are, and many more are dismissed as, opponents of open markets, free trade, or globalization. It is worth stressing then that my critique involves no such opposition. My complaint against the WTO regime is not that it opens markets too much, but that it opens *our* markets *too little* and thereby gains for us the benefits of free trade while withholding them from the global poor. I see the appalling trajectory of world poverty and global inequality since the end of the Cold War as a shocking indictment of one particular, especially brutal path of economic globalization which our governments have chosen to impose. But this is no reason to oppose any and all possible designs of an integrated global market economy under unified rules of universal scope. Indeed, chapters 6–8 outline not an alternative of greater mutual isolation, but a different path of globalization, involving political as well as economic integration, which would fulfill human rights worldwide and afford persons everywhere an opportunity to share the benefits of global economic growth.

There is a simple two-part explanation for why our new global economic order is so harsh on the poor. The details of this order are fixed in international negotiations in which our governments enjoy a crushing advantage in bargaining power and expertise. And our representatives in international negotiations do not consider the interests of the global poor as part of their mandate. They are exclusively devoted to shaping each such agreement in the best interest of the people and corporations of their own country. To get a vivid sense of the zeal with which our politicians and negotiators pursue this task, you need only recall to what incredible length the US government has gone to shift some of its share of the UN general budget onto other countries.[27] This hard-fought victory saves the US $35 million annually, 12 cents per US citizen each *year* – or 58 cents when one adds the similarly reduced US share of the cost of UN peacekeeping operations.[28] This is one example, chosen only because it is so well known. There are plenty of cases illustrating similar zeal by the representatives of other affluent states. Our new global economic order is so harsh on the global poor, then, because it is shaped in negotiations where our representatives ruthlessly exploit their vastly superior bargaining power and expertise, as well as any weakness, ignorance, or corruptibility they may find in their counterpart negotiators, to shape each agreement for our greatest benefit. In such negotiations, the affluent states will make reciprocal concessions to one another, but rarely to the weak. The cumulative result of many such negotiations and agreements is a grossly unfair global economic order under which the lion's share of the benefits of global economic growth flows to the most affluent states.

V Responsibilities and reforms

In many cases, our negotiators must know that the better they succeed, the more people will die of poverty. Our foreign and trade ministers and our presidents and prime ministers know this and so do many journalists and academics as well as the experts at the World Bank, which bills itself as the official champion of the global poor even while its management and decision-making are heavily dominated by the affluent states. After the terrorist attacks of September 11, 2001, the President of the World Bank publicized his estimate "that tens of thousands more children will die worldwide and some 10 million people are likely to be living below the poverty line of $1 a day . . . because the attacks will delay the rich countries' recovery into 2002." Where do we find similar estimates about our tariffs, anti-dumping duties, agricultural subsidies, and enforcement of property rights in seeds and drugs? Or at least a reasoned denial that we are causing grievous harms or that these harms are unjustifiable?

When some 800,000 Tutsis and moderate Hutus were slaughtered in Rwanda in early 1994, the world took notice. The massacres were widely discussed in academia and the media, with many discussants expressing dismay at the decisions by Western governments to avoid both the word "genocide" and a peacekeeping operation.[29] They believe that we should have stopped the massacres, even if this would have meant risking the lives of our soldiers and spending a few hundred million dollars or more. We all felt a bit responsible, but bearably so. The deaths, after all, were brought about by clearly identifiable villains, and we were clearly not among them and also did not benefit from the killings in any way. Deaths caused by global economic arrangements designed and imposed by our governments are a different matter: these governments are elected by us, responsive to our interests and preferences, acting in our name and in ways that benefit us. This buck stops with us.

One lesson from the comparison with the Rwandan genocide is that we might feel more comfortable about the topic of world poverty if we could connect it to some foreign villains. There are indeed such villains, and I apologize for denying them the early and prominent stage appearance they have come to expect in Western treatments of world poverty. Let me try to make up.

As sketched thus far, my position on world poverty can be charged with leaving out the most important factor: the incompetence, corruption, and tyranny entrenched in the governments, social institutions, and cultures of many developing countries. This factor – much stressed by Rawls (n. 238) and other explanatory nationalists – may seem to undercut much of my argument: if the vital interests of the global poor are neglected in international negotiations, it is because their own governments do not vigorously represent these interests. And even if our governments had nonetheless agreed to reduce protectionist barriers against exports from the developing countries, this would have done far more toward enriching their corrupt elites than toward improving conditions for the poor. The main responsibility for the persistence of world poverty lies, then, with the leaders and elites of the developing countries rather than with our governments and ourselves.

This objection is right about the responsibilities of Third World rulers and elites. Many governments of the developing countries are autocratic, corrupt, brutal, and unresponsive to the interests of the poor majority. They are greatly at fault for not representing the interests of the poor in international negotiations and for consenting to treaties that benefit themselves and foreigners at the expense of their impoverished populations. But can we plausibly tell the poor that, insofar as the global economic order is unfair to them, they only have their own leaders to blame for this? They can surely point out in response that they did not authorize the clique that rules them in anything resembling free and fair elections and that their interests can be sold out by this clique only because *we* treat it as entitled to consent in behalf of the people it manages to subjugate.

This response can be extended to show that we share responsibility not only for the damage authoritarian rulers can do to the interests of "their" people in international negotiations, but also for authoritarianism and corruption being so widespread in the developing world. In this vein it is often mentioned that our governments have instigated the violent installation of many oppressive rulers in the developing world, are selling juntas and autocrats the weapons they need to stay in power,[30] and have fostered a culture of corruption by permitting our firms to bribe foreign officials and by blessing such bribes with tax deductibility (n. 243). Still more significant, in my view, are the resource and borrowing privileges that our global order confers upon those who manage to bring a country under their control. Such rulers are internationally recognized as entitled to sell natural resources and to borrow money in the name of the country and its people. These international privileges facilitate oppressive rule and greatly encourage coup attempts and civil wars in the developing countries.

The extensive treatment, in chapters 4 and 6, of the two international privileges is meant to illustrate three insights. First, the national social factors we most like to blame for the persistence of severe poverty – bad governments and corruption in the developing countries – are not wholly native ingredients of a lesser culture, but sustained by core features of our present global order. A reliable market supply of natural resources is important to the affluent consumer societies, and we therefore benefit from a rule that allows buyers to acquire legally valid ownership rights in such resources from anyone who happens to control them. But this rule fosters bad government in the resource-rich developing countries by giving repressive rulers a source of revenues and by providing incentives to try to seize political power by force.

The second insight follows directly. The two international privileges benefit us and Third World elites and autocrats at the expense of the poor populations of resource-rich developing countries. This shows how thinking about global justice must not be confined to international relations. When we ask whether we are treating developing countries unfairly when we buy their resources at going world market prices, we will answer in the negative. In doing so, we are liable to overlook the far more important question whether we are treating the poor populations of developing countries unfairly when we purchase their natural resources from their oppressors. The question is not what are we doing to the developing countries? The crucial question is what are we and the rulers and elites of the developing countries *together* doing to their impoverished populations?

The third insight is that we must stop thinking about world poverty in terms of helping the poor. The poor do need help, of course. But they need help only because of the terrible injustices they are being subjected to. We should not, then, think of our individual donations and of possible institutionalized poverty eradication initiatives – like the Tobin Tax, or the Global Resources Dividend proposed in chapter 8 – as helping the poor, but as protecting them from the effects of global rules whose injustice benefits us and is our responsibility. And we should not only think about such remedial measures, but also about how the injustice of the global order might be diminished through institutional reforms that would end the need for such remedial measures. Chapter 7 discusses some such reforms, and chapter 6 contains a detailed proposal concerning the reform of the two international privileges in particular.

Some critics of our complacency about world poverty argue that the existing global distribution of income and wealth is fundamentally unjust. Others criticize our individual consumption choices as sustaining exploitation and dispossession. I see what they point to as mere symptoms of a deeper injustice: the imposition, by our governments in our name, of a coercive global order that perpetuates severe poverty for many who cannot resist this imposition. In behalf of the global poor, my criticism is not that they are worse off than they might be, but that we and our governments participate in depriving them of the objects of their most basic rights. This critique is Lockean in spirit: "Men being . . . by Nature, all free, equal and independent, no one can be put out of his Estate, and subjected to the Political Power of another, without his own Consent."[31] This principle forbids the developed countries' substantial contribution to subjecting the global poor, without their consent, to their local rulers and to the rules of the world economy and to reducing the global poor, without their consent, below a proportional share of natural resources or its equivalent. This principle also challenges the benefits we derive from their subjection and deprivation, in particular through the cheap appropriation of global natural resources (cf. nn. 264–5).

Mine is not, then, a leftist critique. The political right, too, condemns poverty caused by an unjust coercive institutional order – for instance, the severe poverty and dependence engendered by feudal regimes or by the collectivized agriculture imposed by Stalin in 1928. They agree that such poverty is unjust and that those causing it are responsible for it and also have a responsibility to eradicate it. Their moral and political outlook is thus quite consistent with my claim that we have a duty to help eradicate severe poverty in the developing countries. If they deny this claim, it is because they – along with most Westerners anywhere on the political spectrum – assume too easily that we, and the global order we impose, do not substantially contribute to severe poverty abroad.

Seeing how much depends on this assumption, it is disheartening to find how easily people in the West accept it – carried along by powerful personal motives and massive propaganda that ought to make them more vigilant rather than less. To be sure, it is rarely denied that many in the developing world are born into desperate poverty that leads to their early death or else to permanently diminished physical and mental functioning and sparse opportunities for escaping poverty. Nor is there much doubt that unjust social rules coercively imposed upon the poor through no fault of their own substantially contribute to their poverty. But people do not see, and do not want to see, that we and the governments acting in our name are substantially involved in supporting such unjust rules and their coercive imposition.

So what are we responsible for? Am I seriously accusing those who represent us in WTO negotiations and at the International Monetary Fund (IMF), and also governments and corporations that sustain corrupt and oppressive elites in the developing countries with aid, loans, arms sales, and resource purchases, of being hunger's willing executioners? Would I describe us all as accomplices in a monumental crime against humanity? Questions like these are often posed as a *reductio ad absurdum* – not to continue the dialogue, but to break it off. Such interlocutors recognize that individuals and small groups, sociopaths and pedophiles, can be horribly mistaken in their moral judgments. But they find it inconceivable that we all, the civilized people of the developed West, could be so fundamentally wrong.

Why do they find this inconceivable, totally out of the question? There are surely enough poverty deaths for a full-sized crime against humanity: as many every seven months as perished in the Nazi death camps. So how can they be so absolutely certain that they have no responsibility for these deaths and thus no need for further dialogue and reflection? Some trust the collective wisdom of our culture. They trust that others among us must have thought long and hard about world poverty and must have concluded that our conduct and policies are basically alright. They trust that any good reasons to doubt this conclusion would be seriously and prominently debated by politicians, academics, and journalists. Sections I and II have given preliminary reasons for thinking that such trust may be misplaced.

Others feel that there is no need to think long and hard about our shared moral world view because there are no objective moral truths it might misrepresent. Our moral judgments are the data that any moral conception must explain and reaffirm, the "fixed points" that count as more certain than any complex philosophical arguments to the contrary. This convenient thought can be used to shut oneself off from arguments aiming to show that there is, other things being equal, little moral difference between failing to rescue people and killing them. But my arguments do not challenge the morality prevalent in the West. On the contrary, I invoke a central element of this morality: that it is wrong severely to harm innocent people for minor gains. What I challenge is a common factual claim: that we are not harming the poor, that the developed countries and the global economic order they sustain are not substantial contributors to life-threatening poverty suffered by billions in the developing world. However attached one may be to one's moral convictions, one can hardly appeal to them in support of one's beliefs about world poverty and the causes of its persistence.

Is there any chance that we or our governments will decide to end world poverty? One might hope that one of the more powerful countries will produce a moral leader who will make us realize our responsibilities and represent them forcefully along with our interests. But it seems less unlikely that the impetus for reform will come from us citizens. This scenario presupposes that some of us recognize the harms we are involved in producing or the benefits we derive from these harms, find the case for ending poverty morally compelling, and act on this moral judgment. As things are, this moral stance is rarely considered, very rarely attained, and hard to maintain.

When Hume's reflections confronted him with the baselessness of all human reasoning and belief, he found it most fortunate that "nature herself" ensures that he would not long linger in such dark skepticism: "I dine, I play a game of back-gammon, I converse, and am merry with my friends; and when after three or four hours' amusement, I wou'd return to these speculations, they appear so cold, so strain'd, and ridiculous, that I cannot find it in my heart to enter into them any farther."[32]

When Parfit's reflections led him to a reductionist view of personal identity, he found it *un*fortunate that one cannot long maintain this view of the world, which removes the glass wall between oneself and others and makes one care less about one's own death. Focusing on his arguments, one can only briefly stun one's natural concern for one's own future by reconceiving oneself in accordance with the reductionist view.[33]

Our world is arranged to keep us far away from massive and severe poverty and surrounds us with affluent, civilized people for whom the poor abroad are a remote good cause alongside the spotted owl. In such a world, the thought that we are involved in a monumental crime against these people, that we must fight to stop their dying and suffering, will appear so cold, so strained, and ridiculous, that we cannot find it in our heart to reflect on it any farther. That we are naturally myopic and conformist enough to be easily reconciled to the hunger abroad may be fortunate for us, who can "recognize ourselves," can lead worthwhile and fulfilling lives without much thought about the origins of our affluence. But it is quite unfortunate for the global poor, whose best hope may be our moral reflection.

1

Human Flourishing and Universal Justice

1.0 Introduction

The question of human flourishing elicits an extraordinary variety of responses,[34] which suggests that there are not merely differences of opinion at work, but also different understandings of the question itself. So it may help to introduce some clarity into the question before starting work on one answer to it.

That human persons are flourishing means that their lives are good, or worthwhile, in the broadest sense. Thus, the concept of human flourishing, as I understand it, marks the most comprehensive, "all-in" assessment of the quality of human lives. This concept is broader than many other concepts that mark more specific such assessments – including those of pleasure, wellbeing, welfare, affluence, and virtue as well as those denoting various excellences and accomplishments. Understanding the conceptual relations in this way, one need not deny the substantive claim that the most comprehensive assessment of

Many thanks to Marko Ahtisaari, Christian Barry, Ellen Frankel Paul, Peter Koller, Angelika Krebs, Jonathan Neufeld, Brian Orend, and the members of the Columbia University Seminar for Social and Political Thought for many very helpful critical comments and suggestions. This essay first appeared in *Social Philosophy and Policy* 16, 1 (Winter 1999): 333–61. It is reproduced with minor revisions by permission of Cambridge University Press.

human lives is exhausted by one of the more specific assessments, that pleasure, say, is all there is to human flourishing. For this claim, that human flourishing is nothing more than pleasure (or virtue, or affluence, or any of the others), does not entail that the *concept* of human flourishing is no broader than the *concept* of pleasure. This latter conclusion would follow only if the contrary claim, that human flourishing is more than just pleasure, were self-contradictory, which, on my understanding of the concepts, it clearly is not.

Let me try to give some more structure to the concept of flourishing. A straightforward distinction, which goes back at least to Plato, is that between *components* of flourishing, good for their own sake, and *means* to flourishing, good for the sake of their effects.[35] Something (e.g. happiness, wisdom) is a component of flourishing if and only if it is constitutive of flourishing, part of what flourishing does or can consist in. Something (e.g. affluence, education) is a means to flourishing if and only if it tends to enhance the components of flourishing on balance. These two categories of what one might broadly call *contributors* to flourishing are not mutually exclusive: A component of flourishing may also be a means to other components.[36] It is evident that the first of these categories has a certain priority: we cannot determine whether something is a means to flourishing until we have a sense of what flourishing consists in.

What, then, constitutes human flourishing, a comprehensively good or worthwhile life for human persons? Even this narrower question still elicits an overwhelming diversity of responses. One obvious reason for this is that we have diverse substantive conceptions, which differ in what they single out as components of human flourishing and in how they weight and relate these components. As a first step toward clarifying these differences, one might distinguish between *personal* value, a life being good for the person living it, and *ethical* value, a life being worthy or ethically good in the broadest sense. There are surely features of human lives (e.g. friendship, knowledge, art, or love) that contribute to both its personal and its ethical value. But – though the ancients resisted this insight – it is manifest that the two measures weight even these features differently and also diverge strongly in regard to other features. Pains from chronic gout, for instance, detract from the personal but not from the ethical value of a life[37] – while, conversely, menial and solitary labors for good causes tend to contribute to its ethical but not to its personal value. Given such divergences, substantive conceptions of human flourishing differ in how they relate the overall quality of a human life to its personal and ethical value.

The two more specific notions are themselves complex. Thus, personal value is related to a person's *experiences*: to their being, for instance, enjoyable, intense, interesting, rich, and diverse. But personal value would also seem to be related to a person's *success* in the world. These two ideas easily come apart: persons may not know about some of their successes and failures; and, even when they do, their inner lives may be dulled by successes and much enriched by failures.

The notion of ethical value also suggests two main ideas. It is associated with the idea of good *character*, of a person having admirable aims and ambitions, virtuous maxims and dispositions, noble feelings and emotions. But it is also associated with ethical *achievement*, with the ethical significance of the person's conduct.[38] These two ideas, as well, come apart easily: how one's character manifests itself in the world is significantly affected by one's social starting position and talents as well as by circumstances and luck. And worthy achievements may well result from base motives.

Distinguishing these four dimensions – experience, success, character, and achievement – may give some structure to the concept of human flourishing. Within this structure, one can then ask further whether these dimensions are jointly exhaustive, how and how much each of them contributes to human flourishing, and what more specific components of flourishing should be distinguished within each of them: different ways in which experiences may be good and undertakings successful, different character traits and kinds of achievement. The complexities indicated by these questions are one major reason for the diversity of views about what constitutes human flourishing.

Another important reason is the multiplicity of perspectives on human flourishing, which make this notion appear to us in various ways. It makes a difference whether one poses the question of flourishing *from within*, in regard to one's own life, or *from without*, in reference to the lives of others. And it matters also whether the question is posed *prospectively*, with practical intent and in search of normative guidance for how to use one's power to shape one's own life and the lives of others, or *retrospectively*, in the spirit of mere evaluation.

The relevance of these distinctions can be appreciated by noting that the choice of perspective has a substantial bearing on (at least our perception of) the relative importance of the dimensions of human flourishing distinguished above. It seems appealing, for example, to give more weight to ethical (relative to personal) value when one reflects prospectively on one's own life than when one reflects prospectively on the life of one's child. We are more likely to approve of someone who sees a large part of her child's future flourishing in this child's happiness than of someone who sees an equally large part of her own future flourishing in her own happiness.[39] Similarly, it seems appealing to give more weight to experience and character (relative to success and achievement) when we think about another's life prospectively (with practical intent) than when we assess it retrospectively. We may conclude in the end that these are perspectival distortions that should be explained away en route to a unified conception of human flourishing. But in order to reach any such adequate conception, we must first notice that human flourishing appears differently to us depending on the perspective we take.

The perspective in which we encounter the question of human flourishing also makes an important difference in another way. When one thinks prospectively (with practical intent) about the life of another person, a certain deference seems to be called for. It is widely agreed, nowadays, that the autonomy of adult persons ought to be respected and that the measure of a person's flourishing – the specification of its various dimensions, their relative weights, and their integration into *one* measure of the comprehensively good life – is then, to some extent, to be posited by this person herself. This is not just the trivial thought that, if one wants to make another person happy, one must give her what she enjoys and not what one would enjoy oneself. For this thought still assumes an underlying common currency – happiness or joy – in terms of which the personal value of *any* life can be assessed. To respect the autonomy of another means, however, to accept *her* measure of human flourishing. If she cares about knowledge rather than happiness, for example, then one should give her a good book for her birthday. This is likely to make her happy – both because the book will enhance her knowledge and also because one has chosen one's gift with care. Nevertheless, if one truly respects her autonomy, then one will give her the book not for the sake of her expected joy but for the sake of enriching her knowledge. One is respecting another's autonomy insofar as one takes her flourishing to consist in whatever *she* takes it to consist in.

This is certainly not tantamount to the introduction of autonomous living as a universal currency on a par with how the classical utilitarians conceived of happiness. To respect another as autonomous does not mean seeing him as someone whom one should try to goad toward free and deep reflections about his own life. It does not even mean accepting him as someone who has managed, through free and deep reflections, to develop his own measure of the value of his life. To the contrary: I respect someone's autonomy only insofar as I accept *his* measure of his flourishing as well as *his* way of arriving at this measure – without demanding that he must have come to it on some path I approve as sufficiently reflective. This notion of autonomy is connected not to self-legislation, to the *giving* of directives to oneself, but, more simply and more literally, to *having* one's own directives: a purpose of one's own.

1.1 Social justice

The idea of human flourishing is central not only to our personal and ethical reflections about our own lives and the lives of those around us, but also to our political discourse about our social institutions and policies. Here it is, in particular, our idea of justice that affords yet another perspective on the question of human flourishing. In its ordinary meaning, the word "justice" is associated with the morally appropriate and, in particular, equitable treatment of persons and groups. Its currently most prominent use is in the moral assessment of social institutions, understood not as organized collective agents such as the US government or the World Bank, but rather as a social system's practices or "rules of the game," which govern interactions among individual and collective agents as well as their access to material resources. Such social institutions define and regulate property, the division of labor, sexual and kinship relations, as well as political and economic competition, for example, and also govern how collective projects are adopted and executed, how conflicts are settled, and how social institutions themselves are created, revised, interpreted, and enforced. The totality of the more fundamental and pervasive institutions of a social system has been called its institutional order or basic structure (Rawls).[40] Prominent within our political discourse is, then, the goal of formulating and justifying a criterion of justice, which assesses the degree to which the institutions of a social system are treating the persons and groups they affect in a morally appropriate and, in particular, even-handed way.[41] Such a criterion of justice presupposes a measure of human flourishing, and one specially designed for the task of evaluating how social institutions treat the persons they affect. This task differs significantly from other tasks for which a measure of human flourishing is likewise needed, and its solution may therefore require a distinct conception of human flourishing.

When we think of how social institutions treat persons, we generally have in mind the persons living under those institutions, the persons to whom these institutions apply. But this focus on present participants may be too narrow in two respects. First, social institutions may have a significant impact on present non-participants. The political and economic institutions of the US, for example – through their impact on foreign investment, trade flows, world market prices, interest rates, and the distribution of military power – greatly affect the lives of many persons who are neither citizens nor residents of this country. We should allow, then, that the justice of an institutional order may in part depend on its treatment of outsiders. Second, social institutions may also affect the flourishing of past and future persons – through their impact on pollution, resource depletion, and the development of religions, ways of life, and the arts, for example.

Here it may be objected that social institutions cannot possibly affect the flourishing of past persons in any way. Already Aristotle showed, however, that this thought is at least disputable.[42] To dispute it, one might argue as follows. It is relevant to a person's flourishing whether her confidence in her successes and ethical achievements is mistaken. This is so when her confidence concerns the present (the love she ascribes to her husband or the knowledge she ascribes to herself are not real) and also when it concerns the future (she wrongly believes that her invention will lead to great future benefits). But it seems arbitrary to hold that the – to her, in any case, unknown – true impact of her life is relevant to her flourishing only up to the time of her death. A person's flourishing may therefore depend in part on the long-term success and ethical achievement of her life. It may thus be in a person's interest that her last will be followed, that her creative productions remain available, or that her projects be continued by others. And social institutions can then arguably be unjust by avoidably causing the non-realization of such interests.[43]

In thinking about the justice of social institutions, we should not, then – as is so often done – ignore, or exclude in advance, the interests of past and future persons or those of present non-participants. Recognizing these interests does not preclude us from acknowledging the special status of present participants, who generally are more significantly affected by social institutions and also, by continuing and supporting them, tend to bear a greater moral responsibility for their shape.

It makes no sense to try to assess the justice of social institutions one by one. Doing so, we would detect various supposed injustices that turn out to be illusory when examined in a broader context. Compulsory male military service, for instance, is not unjust so long as men are not disadvantaged overall in comparison to women. Doing so, we would also be likely to overlook comparisons and reforms that involve discrepancies in regard to several institutions: even if each of our social institutions is perfectly just so long as all the others are held constant, it may still be possible to render them more just by redesigning several of them together.[44]

Assessing the social institutions of each country together as one scheme is, in the modern world, only a partial solution to this challenge. For both the formation and the effects of such national basic structures are heavily influenced by foreign and supranational social institutions. This is especially evident in the case of politically and economically weaker countries, where the feasibility and effectiveness of national institutions (meant to secure, perhaps, the rule of law, or access to adequate nutrition for all) depend on the structure of the international order and also on that of the national institutions of more powerful states. We need, then, a holistic understanding of how the living conditions of persons are shaped through the interplay of various institutional regimes, which influence one another and intermingle in their effects.

These interdependencies are of great significance – and are nonetheless frequently overlooked by moral philosophers, social scientists, politicians, and the educated public. We tend to assess a country's domestic institutional order, and also the policies of its rulers, by reference to how they treat its citizens, thereby overlooking their often quite considerable effects upon foreigners. Similarly, we tend to overlook the effects of the global institutional order, which may greatly affect national basic structures and their effects on individuals.

These institutional interconnections – an important aspect of so-called globalization – render obsolete the idea that countries can peacefully agree to disagree about justice, each committing itself to a conception of justice appropriate to its history, culture, population size and density, natural environment, geopolitical context, and stage of development. In the contemporary world, human lives are profoundly affected by non-domestic social institutions – by global rules of governance, trade, and diplomacy, for instance. About such global institutions, at least, we cannot agree to disagree, as they can at any time be structured in only one way. If it is to be possible to justify them to persons in all parts of the world and also to reach agreement on how they should be adjusted and reformed in light of new experience or changed circumstances, then we must aspire to a *single*, *universal* criterion of justice which all persons and peoples can accept as the basis for moral judgments about the global order and about other social institutions with substantial international causal effects.

Both moral and pragmatic reasons demand that we should try to formulate this universal criterion of justice so that it can gain universal acceptance. This desideratum suggests that respect of autonomy should be extended beyond persons to include societies and cultures as well. While a shared criterion of justice will of course impose important constraints, it should also be compatible with a significant diversity of national institutional schemes and ways of life. Here, again, the wider, more literal sense of "autonomy": *having* one's own way of life, is appropriate rather than the narrower one: *choosing* one's own way of life. What matters is that a society's institutional order and way of life be endorsed by those to whom they apply – they need not be endorsed in a way others find sufficiently reflective. The shared criterion of justice we seek should not, then, hold that cultures have an autonomy worthy of respect only insofar as they sustain supracultural reflection, discourse, and choice in matters of human flourishing.[45] In fact, it must not make this demand, if it is to be widely acceptable worldwide and thus immune to the complaint that it manifests an attempt to impose Western Enlightenment values upon other cultures.

1.2 Paternalism

Respect of autonomy was first mentioned above in the context of relating to an adult whose ideas about flourishing differ from our own. Rather than promote his good as we see it, we should often promote his good as he defines it for himself (while sometimes perhaps also engaging him in a discussion of this subject). It is tempting to advocate a like deference in the domain of justice, defining each person's flourishing as whatever this person takes it to be. Such a nonpaternalistic strategy fails, however, in this domain, and that for at least two separate reasons.

First, since there is not one set of social institutions that best meets the values and aspirations of all persons affected, and since persons always differ in how they define flourishing for themselves, we must, in deciding between two institutional alternatives, compare the relative gains and losses in flourishing of different persons or groups. Such comparisons evidently presuppose a common measure. If we are not to go beyond how the relevant persons themselves define a good life for themselves, then this common measure can only be the *degree* to which particular social institutions meet the disparate values and aspirations of the persons affected by them. Such a measure can indeed be constructed for simple cases where persons have divergent preference rankings over outcomes.[46]

But the conceptions persons have of their own flourishing are not simple preference orderings over states of the world. They involve deeper issues, which block any straightforward conversion of preferences and facts into a numerical value on a one-dimensional flourishing scale. One such deep issue concerns the question whether what matters is the fulfillment or the satisfaction of aspirations and desires,[47] where *fulfillment* is the actual realization of a person's desire in the world, while *satisfaction* is her belief that her desire is so realized.[48] Here one might respond that a nonpaternalistic strategy should go with each person's own desires regarding fulfillment versus satisfaction – that is, we should go by where she herself would place the outcomes *fulfilled but not satisfied* (she is loved but believes that she is not) and *satisfied but not fulfilled* (she believes falsely that she is loved) between *fulfilled and satisfied* (she correctly believes that she is loved) and *neither fulfilled nor satisfied* (she correctly believes that she is not loved). But this amendment runs into awesome complications. Is there, for each desire of every person, a fact of the matter regarding the relative weight this person would attach to the fulfillment versus the satisfaction of that desire? How can such relative weights be ascertained in an objective way? And how feasible is a social-justice calculus whose operation requires that such fulfillment-versus-satisfaction weights be ascertained for every desire of every person?

Another deep issue concerns how we should deal with a person's desires about desires – for instance, with her desires concerning her own desires. A person may desire active enjoyment over passive contemplation, yet regret this desire – and then again wish she did not have this regret. Such tensions across levels are commonplace when persons seek to define a good life for themselves. And it is not clear how, when there are such tensions, the degree to which a particular institutional order meets a person's values and aspirations is to be measured. Should we go with her first-order desires,[49] with the first-order desires she would prefer to have, with the first-order desires the person she desires to be would prefer to have, or what?

A second reason against the nonpaternalistic strategy is that social institutions shape not merely the environment and the options of the persons living under them – but also their values and aspirations, which cannot then provide an impartial standpoint from which alternative institutional schemes could be compared. We can have no determinate idea of how human persons define a good life for themselves apart from information about the social conditions under which they grew up. In response to this difficulty, one might propose that social institutions ought to meet the values and aspirations of existing persons and/or the values and aspirations that persons raised under those same institutions would develop.[50] But these proposals by themselves cannot deliver an adequate criterion of justice. Otherwise a highly oppressive institutional order would be rendered just by the fact that the oppressed are raised so as to accept their abysmal status, and a dictatorship by the fact that those living under it are brainwashed into adoring the leader.

The failure of the nonpaternalistic strategy to deliver a determinate criterion of justice should not be surprising. It reflects our predicament. We will unavoidably bequeath a social world to those who come after us – a social world into which they will be born without choice and one that will ineluctably shape their values and their sense of justice in terms of which they will then assess the social world we left them with. Facing up to this daunting responsibility requires that we develop, within our conception of the justice of social institutions, a substantive conception of human flourishing.

Shaping social institutions with such a conception in mind inevitably involves a dose of paternalism, which can, however, be made more palatable by honoring the following four desiderata:

1 The sought universal criterion of justice ought to work with a thin conception of human flourishing, which might be formulated largely in terms of unspecific means to, rather than components of, human flourishing. Though disagreements about what human flourishing consists in may prove intractable, it may well be possible to bypass them by agreeing that nutrition, clothing, shelter, certain basic freedoms, as well as social interaction, education, and participation are important means to it, which just social institutions must secure for all. Such a thin conception would express some respect of the autonomy of diverse cultures, favoring social institutions acceptable to persons from different (religious, social, ethnic, etc.) backgrounds representing a wide range of diverse more specific conceptions of human flourishing.
2 The sought universal criterion ought to be modest. Rather than define justice as the highest attainable point on an open-ended scale, it should define justice as a solid threshold compatible with an international diversity of institutional schemes that are merely required to treat the persons affected by them in a minimally decent and equitable way.

3 The requirements of the universal criterion should not be understood as exhaustive. They should, for instance, leave the various societies free to impose their own more demanding criteria of justice upon their own national institutions and even to judge foreign or global institutions by the lights of such more ambitious criteria.[51]
4 The supplementary considerations introduced by such more ambitious criteria of justice must not, however, undermine the universality of the modest criterion and therefore must not be allowed to outweigh the latter in situations of conflict or competition (e.g. over scarce resources). The requirements of the universal criterion should therefore be understood as preeminent within any more ambitious national criterion.

Taking all four desiderata together, the envisioned universal criterion should be able to function as a *core* in a dual sense – as the core in which a plurality of more specific conceptions of human flourishing and of more ambitious criteria of justice can overlap (thinness and modesty); and as the core of each of these criteria, containing all and only its most important elements (preeminence without exhaustiveness).[52] The task is, then, to formulate a criterion of basic justice that is morally plausible and internationally widely acceptable as the universal core of all criteria of justice.

1.3 Justice in first approximation

On the basis of the reflections introduced thus far, our task has taken on the following form: we are seeking a widely acceptable core criterion of basic justice that assesses social institutions by how they treat persons. Such a criterion presupposes interpersonal comparability,[53] but it should also respect the autonomy of the various persons and cultures. This suggests formulating the sought criterion in terms of certain basic goods, broadly and abstractly conceived – in particular, in terms of the extent to which the persons affected by an institutional order have the goods they need to develop and realize a conception of a personally and ethically worthwhile life. In the last few decades many theorists have indeed developed criteria of justice along these lines. Those following this general approach must answer three questions in order to specify an operational criterion of justice.

Question 1 How should these basic goods be defined? Here one might work with something like Rawls's social primary goods or Dworkin's resources adding perhaps freedom from pain as a further component, as Scanlon suggests.[54] An important alternative to this answer is Sen's account of capabilities.[55] Insofar as the quest is for a modest criterion of basic justice, one that marks only a solid threshold, the demand for basic goods should be severely limited, in four respects: (a) Only really essential goods, ones that are truly needed for developing or realizing a conception of a worthwhile life, should be placed on the list of basic goods. (b) The demand for the basic goods listed should be limited both quantitatively and qualitatively to what I call a *minimally adequate* share. Food and freedom of association are necessary for a worthwhile life, but we need these only in limited amounts and can get by entirely without delicacies and without meetings at certain times or places. (c) Persons truly need *access to* the basic goods, rather than these goods themselves. It is no intolerable flaw in a social order that some persons living under it choose to fast for long periods, to participate in boxing matches, to live as hermits cut off from human interaction, or even to obtain help in committing suicide – provided they could gain the basic goods they are renouncing without thereby incurring a serious lack in other basic goods. (d) Basic goods should also be limited *probabilistically*. Social institutions cannot be so designed that everyone affected by them has absolutely secure access to all goods that he needs. US society, for example, cannot be so structured that your physical integrity is guaranteed 100 percent. It cannot be completely ruled out that some punks or even police officers will attack you without provocation. Even when this can, or even does, happen, we should nonetheless say that you have here secure access to the basic good of physical integrity so long as the probability of such an attack does not exceed certain limits. What sounds paradoxical is nevertheless plausible: it is possible that your physical integrity but not that of your African-American colleague is sufficiently well protected in the US even though only you do in fact suffer an assault during your lifetime.

When social institutions work so that each person affected by them has secure access – understood always as reasonably rather than absolutely secure access – to minimally adequate shares of all basic goods then they are, according to my proposed core criterion of basic justice, fully just. But a criterion of justice should also facilitate comparisons of institutional schemes that are not fully just. We therefore need answers to two further questions that have to do with aggregation.

Question 2 How should the chosen basic goods be integrated into *one* measure of a person's standard of living? How should relevant shortfalls – in nutrition, freedom of movement and liberty of conscience, say – be weighted vis-à-vis one another so that it can be ascertained how far any affected person or group falls below the minimum standard of living required by our core criterion of basic justice? Here one might ascribe a standard of living, 1, to all affected persons who reach the threshold in regard to all basic goods and then ascribe lower numbers $0 \leq x < 1$ to all those who fall below the threshold with regard to one or more basic goods.[56] My use of the new expression "standard of living" is not merely meant to flag that we are dealing here with a thin core notion of human flourishing which, to be appropriate to the global plane and in contrast to the thicker notions that particular countries or groups might employ, is severely limited in the four ways (a)–(d) described above. It is especially also meant to flag the further point that the construction of a standard of living, and of a criterion of justice more generally, is also a pragmatic task. The constructed standard should be a good proxy for the appropriately thin core notion of human flourishing, of course, but it should also, when used within a public criterion of justice, promote human flourishing so conceived through its compelling unity, clarity, simplicity, and easy applicability. It is such pragmatic reasons that justify constructing the international standard of living as a numerical measure with a threshold. And one can therefore support this standard even if one does not believe that human flourishing itself is either discontinuous (so that gains and losses above some threshold are much less significant than gains and losses below it) or quantifiable.

Question 3 How should the measurements of the standard of living of the various affected persons (or groups) be integrated into *one* overall measure for the justice of social institutions? Here one might work with the arithmetic or geometric mean, for example, or else choose sum-ranking, maximin, or some indicator of inequality as an interpersonal aggregation function.[57] One might also want to give differential weights to persons depending on whether they are insiders or outsiders, and living in the past, present, or future.

1.4 Essential refinements

Before thinking further about these questions, we must take account of another complication which has been neglected in recent writings about justice. It is relevant for assessing the justice of social institutions *how* such institutions affect the flourishing of individuals. Let me introduce the point through a quick example. Imagine a hypothetical scenario in which every year some 10,000 US residents (27 per day) are killed by the police. US residents would then, on average, face an approximately 0.25 percent probability of dying through police violence.[58] If this were really the case, we would surely want to dispute that the physical integrity of US residents is here secure. We would want to say that the social institutions of the US are unjust in this regard and ought to be reformed toward reducing the number of police killings. This might be done through better police training, for instance, or through more effective and more severe punishments of unjustified police violence.

Persons are actually killed in motor vehicle accidents in the US at a rate that is over four times higher than the imaginary rate in the preceding story: over 43,000 in 1995, 1996, and 1997, or about 119 per day.[59] At this rate, the average US resident has a better than 1 percent chance of dying in a motor vehicle accident.[60] In this case, too, institutional reforms might bring relief. One might allow only cars with a built-in maximum speed of 50 miles per hour, for example. Or one might greatly increase punishments for drunk driving, which plays a role in some 38 percent of the fatalities in question.[61]

The juxtaposition of these two cases makes evident that we assign very different moral weights to different institutional influences on our risk of premature death. We view a significant and avoidable risk of premature death through police violence as a much greater injury to the justice of a society than an otherwise equal, or even a considerably greater risk of premature death through traffic accidents – and we do this even on the assumption that all other things (such as citizens' acceptance of these risks, possibility and social cost of reducing them) are equal in the two cases.

If we did not think in this way, if we assigned equal moral weight to such different kinds of institutionally reducible risks of premature death, then we would have strong reason to support the death penalty for the most dangerous drunk drivers. An institutional "reform" that causes some 100 of the worst offenders to be executed in the US each year – roughly doubling the current number of executions – would presumably have a very considerable deterrent effect, thus resulting in a significant reduction in the incidence of drunk driving. If it could reduce the total number of alcohol-related traffic fatalities by merely 5 percent (ca. 860 deaths annually), then some 760 fewer persons would die prematurely each year and all US residents would face a lower risk of premature death.[62]

If we want to avoid embracing this proposal as an easy and obvious step toward a more just society, then we need to make moral distinctions. We must not assess social institutions from the perspective of rational prospective participants, as modern hypothetical-contract theories have been doing starting with Rawls. For such prospective participants would prudently favor the imagined execution scheme over the status quo, so long as it really does entail an overall reduction in citizens' risk of premature death. This is so, because they are conceived as ranking feasible institutional arrangements solely in terms of the quality of life they could expect under each and thus as not caring *how* one institutional order produces a higher expected quality of life than another.

The dubious implications of consequentialist and hypothetical-contract theories are due to the fact that they assess social institutions *solely* on the basis of the quality of life they afford to their prospective participants. To avoid such implications, we must distinguish different ways in which social institutions affect the lives of individuals and then incorporate this distinction into our criteria of justice, including the universal core criterion sketched in sections 1.2 and 1.3. This core criterion must not define basic-good shortfalls simply as institutionally avoidable shortfalls from secure access to minimally adequate shares of basic goods, but must also take into account how social institutions relate to such shortfalls.[63]

Let me illustrate this thought by distinguishing tentatively six basic ways in which social institutions may relate to human flourishing. Because of our specific focus here, I formulate this sixfold distinction in terms of institutionally avoidable basic-good shortfalls – without assuming, however, that the universal core criterion we seek ought to be sensitive to shortfalls of all six kinds (classes 5 and 6, in particular, may well fall outside the core). For illustration, I use six different scenarios in which, owing to the arrangement of social institutions, a certain group of innocent persons is avoidably deprived of some vital nutrients V – the vitamins contained in fresh fruit, say, which are essential to good health. The six scenarios are arranged in order of their injustice, according to my preliminary intuitive judgment. In scenario 1, the shortfall is *officially mandated*, paradigmatically by the law: legal restrictions bar certain persons from buying foodstuffs containing V. In scenario 2, the shortfall results from *legally authorized* conduct of private subjects: sellers of foodstuffs containing V lawfully refuse to sell to certain persons. In scenario 3, social institutions *foreseeably and avoidably engender* (but do not specifically require or authorize) the shortfall through the conduct they stimulate: certain persons, suffering severe poverty within an ill-conceived economic order, cannot afford to buy foodstuffs containing V. In scenario 4, the shortfall arises from private conduct that is *legally prohibited but barely deterred*: sellers of foodstuffs containing V illegally refuse to sell to certain persons, but enforcement is lax and penalties are mild. In scenario 5, the shortfall arises from social institutions *avoidably leaving unmitigated the effects of a natural defect*: certain persons are unable to metabolize V owing to a treatable genetic defect, but they avoidably lack access to the treatment that would correct their handicap. In scenario 6, finally, the shortfall arises from social institutions *avoidably leaving unmitigated the effects of a self-caused defect*: certain persons are unable to metabolize V owing to a treatable self-caused disease – brought on, perhaps, by their maintaining a long-term smoking habit in full knowledge of the medical dangers associated therewith – and avoidably lack access to the treatment that would correct their ailment.

This differentiation of six ways in which social institutions may be related to human flourishing is preliminary in that it fails to isolate the morally significant factors that account for the descending moral significance of the shortfalls in question. Since trying to do this here would lead us too far afield, let me just venture the hypothesis that what matters is not merely the *causal* role of social institutions, how they figure in a complete causal explanation of the shortfall in question, but also (what one might call) the implicit *attitude* of social institutions to the shortfall in question.[64] Thus a high incidence of domestic violence (a shortfall in women's secure access to physical integrity) may show a society's legal order to be unjust if it could be substantially reduced through more vigorous enforcement of, and more severe punishments under, existing laws. But the same abuse of the same women would indicate an even greater injustice if it were not illegal at all – if spouses were legally free to beat each other or, worse, if men were legally authorized to beat the women in their households.

My preliminary classification is surely still too simple. In some cases one will have to take account of other, perhaps underlying causes; and one may also need to recognize interdependencies among causal influences and fluid transitions between the classes.[65] It is to be hoped that the formulation of a universal core criterion of basic justice, which is to be internationally acceptable, can bypass most of these complications by focusing narrowly on the morally most important institutionally avoidable basic-good shortfalls. In any case, I bypass these complications here, merely emphasizing once more the decisive point missed by the usual theories of justice: to be morally plausible, a criterion of justice must take account of the particular relation between social institutions and human flourishing. In the special case of a core criterion of basic justice, this relation may affect whether some institutionally avoidable basic-good shortfall counts as a basic-good deficit (a core injustice[66]) at all and, if so, how morally significant this deficit is (how great a core injustice it indicates).[67]

We have now seen, at least in outline, that a morally plausible criterion of justice must consider institutionally avoidable basic-good shortfalls not merely in regard to their magnitude and frequency, but also in regard to how social institutions are related to them. The identification of this new weighting dimension suggests the question whether there might be additional weighting dimensions that the usual theories of justice have overlooked. I believe there are two such, which I can only mention here. One further weighting dimension concerns the social costs that would arise from the institutional avoidance of a morally significant basic-good shortfall. Whether and how urgently justice demands reforms toward reducing the traffic-related risk of premature death may depend on the cost of such reforms. In order to save the lives of 2,000 pedestrians annually, would we merely have to lower the speed limit within residential areas from 30 to 25 miles per hour or would we have to invest billions into construction of tunnels and overpasses? To avoid 20,000 cases of child abuse annually, would we merely need to modify the training of schoolteachers or would we have to spy on millions of private homes with video equipment? Such questions are surely relevant to deciding whether given basic-good shortfalls are unjust at all and, if so, how much they detract from the overall justice of the relevant social institutions.

A third and final plausible weighting dimension concerns the distribution of basic-good shortfalls. Many of the usual theories of justice are, of course, distribution sensitive through their aggregation function (using maximin, the geometric mean, or some measure of inequality in this role). But these theories also tend to accept what economists call the anonymity condition. On the face of it, this condition looks harmless enough: it requires merely that permutations of persons over social positions should make no difference to judgments of justice. Thus, the injustice of certain basic-good deficits is exactly the same regardless of who is suffering these shortfalls. This requirement seems to express the very essence of justice. Surely, one wants to say, our moral assessment of an institutionally avoidable hardship ought not to be affected by whether this hardship is suffered by me or by you, by someone like us or unlike us, by someone we like, dislike, or don't even know – every person matters equally. But the anonymity condition becomes problematic in reference to certain groups. It may indeed not matter whether a particular hardship is suffered by a man or a woman, by a white or a black, by a Mormon or a Jew – but what if women or blacks or Jews are greatly overrepresented among those suffering the hardship? Is this still to be considered morally irrelevant, as the anonymity condition requires?[68] It would seem that a morally plausible criterion would have to take account of some such correlations. Whether such a correlation is unjust and, if so, how unjust it is, may well depend on how large a role social factors play in its genesis and on how salient the disadvantaged group is. For illustration, consider severe and avoidable poverty suffered by a certain fraction of a population. The injustice indicated by this poverty would not be much affected by the fact that some non-salient group (e.g. those with blood-type B) is, owing to statistically inferior genetic endowments, overrepresented among the very poor. The injustice might be seen as greater, if women (a salient group) were overrepresented owing to statistically inferior genetic endowments. And it would be seen as greater still, if women were overrepresented among the very poor owing to sexist cultural practices under which they do most of the housework and have fewer educational opportunities.[69]

In this section I have, at least in broad outlines, displayed the general structure of a morally plausible criterion of justice – and, in particular, the various parameters in regard to which alternative specifications of such a criterion would differ from one another. This structure is unfortunately rather complicated. The criteria of justice currently on offer tend to be simpler. Rawls's perspective of the original position ignores the first and third new dimensions entirely and the second for the most part, because the parties are conceived as interested solely in the quality of life of prospective citizens, irrespective of the institutional mechanisms that may condition such quality of life.[70] As I could here show only generally and in outline, these simpler theories of justice imply various demands that are either morally dubious or unable to cope with the actual complexities of contemporary social systems.[71]

1.5 Human rights

A complex and internationally acceptable core criterion of basic justice might best be formulated, I believe, in the language of human rights, at least if we are prepared to understand it in a special way. We should conceive human rights primarily as claims on coercive social institutions and secondarily as claims against those who uphold such institutions. Such an *institutional* understanding contrasts with an *interactional* one, which presents human rights as placing the treatment of human beings under certain constraints that do not presuppose the existence of social institutions.

The institutional understanding I have in mind diverges from a familiar one that conceives a human right to X as a kind of meta-right: a moral right to an effective legal right to X. So understood, human rights require their own juridification. Each society's government and citizens ought to ensure that all human rights are incorporated into its fundamental legal texts and are, within its jurisdiction, observed and enforced through an effective judicial system.[72]

This familiar institutional understanding leads to demands that are, in my view, both too strong and too weak. They are too strong, because a society may be so situated and organized that its members enjoy secure access to X, even without a legal right thereto. Having corresponding legal rights in addition is good, to be sure, but not so important that this additional demand would need to be incorporated into the concept of a human right. One's human right to adequate nutrition, say, should count as fulfilled when one has secure access to adequate nutrition, even when such access is not legally guaranteed. A human right requires its own juridification only when it is empirically true – as it may be for some civil and political rights – that secure access to its object presupposes the inclusion of a corresponding legal right in the law or constitution.

The demands entailed by this familiar institutional understanding are also too weak, because legal and even constitutional rights, however conscientiously enforced, often do not suffice to ensure secure access. Here I am not merely thinking of showcase constitutions that list many important rights but are widely ignored in governmental practice. It is likely that the proponents of the familiar institutional understanding would not rest content with such "rights" either. I am mainly thinking of cases where, though legal rights are effectively enforced, poor and uneducated persons are nonetheless incapable of insisting on their rights, because they do not know what their legal rights are or lack the knowledge or minimal economic independence necessary to pursue the enforcement of their rights through the proper legal channels. Even if there exists in India a legal path that would allow domestic servants to defend themselves against abuse by their employers, their human right to freedom from inhuman and degrading treatment (*UDHR*, Article 5) nonetheless remains unfulfilled for most of them.

In contrast to the ways in which human rights are currently understood, I thus propose to explain this concept as follows: the postulate of a human right to X is tantamount to the demand that, insofar as reasonably possible, any coercive social institutions be so designed that all human beings affected by them have secure access to X.[73] A human right is a moral claim *on* any coercive social institutions imposed upon oneself and therefore a moral claim *against* anyone involved in their imposition.

With this explication, one can clear away from the start the suspicion, common among communitarians and in communal cultures (e.g. in Southeast Asia), that human rights promote individualism or even egoism, and lead persons to view themselves as Westerners – as atomized, autonomous, secular, and self-interested individuals ready to insist on their rights no matter what the cost may be to others or the society at large.[74] This critique has some plausibility when human rights are understood as demanding their own juridification. But it has much less force when, as I propose, we avoid any conceptual connection of human rights with legal rights. We are then open to the idea that, in different economic and cultural contexts, secure access to the objects of human rights may be established in diverse ways.

Those hostile to a legal-rights culture can, and often do, share this norm: that any coercive institutional order must, insofar as reasonably possible, afford all those whose freedom it restricts secure access to certain basic goods. Even if we feel strongly that, in our own culture, human rights ought to be realized through matching individual legal rights, we should allow that human rights can be realized in other ways, that secure access to their objects is what really matters. This agreement can then be juridified in *international* law, committing states and cultures to designing all national and international social institutions so as to afford all those whom they constrain secure access to the objects of their human rights. There is no good reason to insist that such secure access must be maintained in the same way everywhere on earth.

Two things must be said to soften this point. First, it is clear that legal rights can be, and often are, an effective means for realizing human rights. Such legal rights need not, however, have the same content as the human right they help realize. Depending on the context, the best way of realizing a human right to minimally adequate nutrition may not be legal rights to food when needed, but rather some other legal mechanisms that keep land ownership widely dispersed, ban usury or speculative hoarding of basic staples, or provide childcare, education, retraining subsidies, unemployment benefits, or start-up loans. And non-legal practices – such as a culture of solidarity among friends, relatives, neighbors, compatriots – may also play an important role.

Second, it is at least theoretically possible to include certain legal rights in the object of a human right. An example would be a human right to constitutionally protected freedom of religion. I worry, however, that the inclusion of such demands would render the resulting conception of human rights too demanding for its intended role as a core criterion of basic justice. A society whose citizens know that their enjoyment of religious liberty is secure – perhaps because religious tolerance is an unquestioned way of life in that society – does not deserve the charge that it fails to realize human rights merely because there is no legal statute that explicitly guarantees freedom of religion.

The concept of human rights is especially well suited to take account of the necessary differentiations according to how social institutions relate to basic-good shortfalls. Such differentiations are already being made in regard to some constitutional rights. The German constitution, for instance, postulates: "Everyone shall have the right to life and to inviolability of his person."[75] According to the developed judicial understanding of this right, it is not the case that every avoidable death constitutes a violation of this right to life – let alone an exactly equally serious violation. Death during a violent police interrogation would certainly count as a serious violation of the basic right in question. Death due to unofficial violence condoned by state officials would count as a less serious violation. And a death that could have been prevented by expensive medical treatment that the patient was unable and the state unwilling to pay for would not count as a violation of the right to life at all. The concept of human rights I am proposing involves similar differentiations – though with the difference that human rights are not addressed to a government and its agents, but to the institutional structure of a society (or other comprehensive social system). Human rights are not supposed to regulate what government officials must do or refrain from doing, but are to govern how all of us together ought to design the basic rules of our common life. This suggests the probabilistic *ex-ante* perspective sketched above: a valid complaint against our social institutions can be presented by all those whose physical integrity is not sufficiently secure, not by all those who happen to suffer an assault. This is why it makes more sense, on my institutional understanding, to speak of non-fulfillment or underfulfillment rather than violation of human rights. A human right to life and physical integrity is fulfilled for specific persons if and only if their security against certain threats does not fall below certain thresholds. These thresholds will vary for different human rights and for different sources of threats to one human right; and they will also be related to the social cost of reducing the various threats and to the distribution of these threats over various salient segments of the population. These differentiations have to be incorporated into the specification of human rights.

1.6 Specification of human rights and responsibilities for their realization

The proposed path toward the formulation of an internationally acceptable core criterion of basic justice is now open to view. We start from the personal and ethical value of human life – not to ascertain wherein this value lies, but to determine the social context and means that persons normally need, according to some broad range of plausible conceptions of what human flourishing consists in, to lead a minimally worthwhile life. This goal expresses respect of human autonomy, especially insofar as the criterion we seek is to be based on very weak assumptions about the components of ethical value. The main assumption here is merely existential: it is a historically and geographically universal fact that almost all human persons feel a deep need for an ethical world view by reference to which they can judge whether their own life, and also the lives of others they may care about, is good – not merely for themselves, personally, but also in a larger sense, ethically.

Beyond this, one can perhaps make one further general statement: in today's highly interdependent and closely interconnected world there exists in every culture an insuppressible plurality of ethical world views and of opinions about the objectivity and universality of such world views as well as about the relative importance of ethical as against personal quality of life. Even a modest criterion of basic justice should therefore demand that social institutions be designed so that the persons affected by them can develop, deepen, and realize an ethical world view of their own. The essential presuppositions for this capacity can be presented under two headings. First, liberty of conscience, the freedom to develop and to live in accordance with one's own ethical world view so long as this is possible without excessive costs for others. This freedom must include various other liberties, such as freedom of access to informational media (such as books and broadcasts) and the freedom to associate with persons holding similar or different ethical views. And second, political participation: the freedom to take part in structuring and directing any comprehensive social systems to which one belongs. This includes the freedom publicly to express ethical criticisms of political institutions and decisions, freedom of assembly, and freedom to participate on equal terms in the competition for political offices and in the struggle over political decisions.

Other, more elementary basic goods are important for both the ethical and the personal value of human life. Among these are physical integrity, subsistence supplies (of food and drink, clothing, shelter, and basic health care), freedom of movement and action, as well as basic education, and economic participation. All of these basic goods should be recognized as the objects of human rights – but only up to certain quantitative, qualitative, and probabilistic limits: what human beings truly need is secure access to a minimally adequate share of all of these goods.

It is well known that many human beings today lack secure access to minimally adequate shares of these goods, that the realization of human rights has been only very partially achieved. This poses the question of how responsibility for the underfulfillment of human rights can be ascribed to particular social institutions, and thereby also to particular persons involved in designing and upholding these institutions. This question involves special difficulties in this era of global interdependence when social institutions influence one another and their effects intermingle. It is convenient for us citizens of wealthy countries, and therefore common, to ignore such interdependencies – to explain the severe underfulfillment of human rights in so many countries by reference to local factors domestic to the country in which it occurs. This *explanatory nationalism*, further discussed in later chapters,[76] diverts attention from the question of how we ourselves might be involved, causally and morally, in this sad phenomenon.

If we did pay attention to this question, we would better understand how global institutional factors play an important role in the reproduction of human misery and how plausible reforms of such factors could greatly advance the realization of human rights.[77] Such an understanding would lead us to take the underfulfillment of human rights abroad more seriously – provided we accept that persons involved in upholding coercive social institutions have a shared moral responsibility to ensure that these institutions satisfy at least the universal core criterion of basic justice by fulfilling, insofar as reasonably possible, the human rights of the persons whose conduct they regulate. If a particular underfulfillment of human rights – hunger in Brazil, say – comes about through the interplay of global and national factors and could be remedied through global as well as through national institutional reforms, then the responsibility for this underfulfillment lies with both institutional schemes and therefore also with both groups of persons: with all those involved in upholding the global or the Brazilian basic structure.

Those who have such a responsibility should either discontinue their involvement – often not a realistic option – or else compensate for it by working for the reform of institutions or for the protection of their victims. The word "compensate" is meant to indicate that how much one should be willing to contribute toward reforming unjust institutions and toward mitigating the harms they cause depends on how much one is contributing to, and benefiting from, their maintenance. Obviously, these matters deserve a far more elaborate treatment than I can give them here.[78]

1.7 Conclusion

This chapter is about what measure of, or proxy for, human flourishing is needed for purposes of assessing the justice of social institutions and what role this measure should play within such assessments. We have seen that measures of human flourishing differ in specificity. An internationally acceptable core criterion of basic justice requires a measure of low specificity. In this role a conception of human rights is far more suitable than all the theoretical constructs currently discussed by academics – or so I have argued. Such a conception is, on the one hand, substantial enough to support a severe and constructive critique of the status quo. And it also respects, on the other hand, the autonomy of the diverse cultures of this world – provided we are prepared to accept the institutional understanding I have sketched. A conception of human rights demands then that all social institutions be designed so that all human beings, insofar as reasonably possible, have secure access to the objects of their human rights.

Acceptance of such a universal core criterion of basic justice does not preclude particular societies from subjecting their national institutions to a stronger criterion of justice that involves a more specific measure of human flourishing. Such a national measure might, for instance, ascribe to citizens additional basic needs, such as: to have certain legal (constitutional) rights, not to be too severely disadvantaged through social inequalities, to be adequately compensated for genetic handicaps and bad luck, or to receive a subsidy for the discharge of important religious duties.[79] But such additional basic needs would everywhere be understood as secondary to the universal human needs recognized by the globally shared conception of human rights. The preeminent requirement on all coercive institutional schemes is that they afford each human being secure access to minimally adequate shares of basic freedoms and participation, of food, drink, clothing, shelter, education, and health care. Achieving the formulation, global acceptance, and realization of this requirement is the preeminent moral task of our age.

2

How Should Human Rights be Conceived?

2.0 Introduction

Supranational, national, and subnational systems of law contain various human rights. The content of these rights and of any corresponding legal obligations and burdens depends on the legislative, judicial, and executive bodies that maintain and interpret the laws in question. In the aftermath of World War II, it has come to be widely acknowledged that there are also moral human rights, whose validity is independent of any and all governmental bodies. In their case, in fact, the dependence is thought to run the other way: only if they respect moral human rights do any governmental bodies have legitimacy, that is, the capacity to create moral obligations to comply with, and the moral authority to enforce, their laws and orders.

This essay first appeared in *Jahrbuch für Recht und Ethik* 3 (1995): 103–20. Work on it was supported by a 1993–4 Laurance S. Rockefeller Fellowship at the Princeton University Center for Human Values. I am greatly indebted to my colleagues there, and very specially to Amy Gutmann, for a most productive discussion of an earlier version. I also wish to thank my fellow participants at the Law and Ethics Conference for their valuable comments, and Eric Goldstein for extensive and very helpful written criticisms. The last third of the essay has been significantly revised.

Human rights of both kinds can coexist in harmony. Whoever cares about moral human rights will grant that laws can greatly facilitate their realization. And human-rights lawyers can acknowledge that the legal rights and obligations they draft and interpret are meant to give effect to preexisting moral rights. In fact, this acknowledgment seems implicit in the common phrase "internationally recognized human rights." It is clearly expressed in the Preamble of the *UDHR*, which presents this *Declaration* as stating moral human rights that exist independently of itself. This acknowledgment bears stressing because the distinction between moral and legal human rights is rarely drawn clearly. Many are therefore inclined to believe that our human rights are whatever governments agree them to be. This is true of legal human rights. But it is false, as these governments have themselves acknowledged, of moral human rights. Governments may have views on what moral human rights there are – their (not legally binding) endorsement of the *UDHR* expresses such a view – but even all of them together cannot legislate such rights out of existence.

My aim here is to explicate the moral notion of human rights. I define this task narrowly. I do not address the ontological status of human rights – the sense in which they may be said to exist and the way in which their existence (in this sense) might be known and justified. Nor do I discuss the work of selection, specification, and justification that goes into formulating a full list or conception of human rights. Instead, I focus on an issue that is best examined before the others. How should human rights be conceived? What does the assertion of a human right assert, especially in regard to correlative responsibilities?

Beginning with this issue makes sense. An explication of what human rights are does not presuppose more than a rough idea about what goods are widely recognized as worthy of inclusion. But such an explication is presupposed in the selection and justification of particular human rights – even though it cannot by itself settle what human rights there are or even whether there are any human rights at all. The fact that some formulated right has all the conceptual features of a human right does not entail that it exists (can be justified as such) any more than the fact that King Arthur as described has all the conceptual features of a human being entails that there was such a person. Settling what human rights there are requires not merely conceptual explication, but also substantive moral arguments pro and con. Such arguments must be informed by an understanding of what human rights are.

2.1 From natural law to rights

The moral notion of human rights has evolved from earlier notions of natural law and natural rights. We can begin to understand and analyze it by examining the continuities and discontinuities in this evolution. I do this by focusing on the shifting constraints imposed, ideas suggested, and possibilities opened and closed by the three concepts rather than on the particular conceptions of them that have actually been worked out.[80]

All three concepts have in common that they were used to express a special class of *moral concerns*, namely ones that are among the most *weighty* of all as well as *unrestricted* and *broadly sharable*. These four common features of the three concepts constrain not the content of the select concerns, but their potential status and role. Regarding the first feature, it should be said that the natural-law and natural-rights idioms were also used to express the agent's liberty to pursue his own self-preservation and self-interest – as in Hobbes's famous claim that "every man has a Right to every thing; even to one another's body."[81] Since the concept of human rights, which is at issue here, has not been used in this vein, I leave such uses aside and focus on uses that present natural law, or the natural rights of others, as making moral demands on human conduct, practices, and institutions.

Conceiving the natural law, natural rights, or human rights as making weighty moral demands suggests that these demands ought to play an important role in our thinking and discourse about, and ought to be reflected and respected in, our social institutions and conduct. They should normally trump or outweigh other moral and nonmoral concerns and considerations.

In conceiving of moral demands as unrestricted, we believe that whether persons ought to respect them does not depend on their particular epoch, culture, religion, moral tradition, or philosophy.[82] Unrestricted moral demands need not assign obligations to everyone. The moral demand that rulers are to govern in the interest of the governed, for example, may be unrestricted even while it assigns obligations only to those in power. But, not being spatially or temporally confined, unrestricted moral demands are still, at least potentially, relevant to persons of all times and places and therefore should be understood and appreciated by all.

This suggests the fourth feature. In conceiving of moral demands as broadly sharable, one thinks of them as capable of being understood and appreciated by persons from different epochs and cultures as well as by adherents of a variety of different religions, moral traditions, and philosophies. They need not be (and perhaps no moral demands could be) accessible in this way to all human persons, irrespective of when and where they live(d) and irrespective of their particular culture, religion, moral tradition, and philosophy (or lack thereof). But they would not be broadly sharable if they were not detached, or at least detachable, from any particular epoch, culture, religion, moral tradition, and philosophy,[83] or if understanding and appreciating them required mental faculties that a significant proportion of humankind does not have and cannot develop. The sharability of a moral demand is, then, a function of how widely it can be shared across persons and cultures and of how accessible it is to each of them. The notions of being unrestricted and being broadly sharable are related in that we tend to feel more confident about conceiving of a moral demand as unrestricted when this demand is not parochial to some particular epoch, culture, religion, moral tradition, or philosophy.

Let us turn from the continuities in the conceptual evolution – from natural law to natural rights to human rights – to its discontinuities, which reveal what shift in the content of unrestricted and broadly sharable moral demands is associated with the shift in terminology. Expressing moral demands in the natural-rights rather than the natural-law idiom involves a significant narrowing of content possibilities by introducing the idea that the relevant moral demands are based on moral concern for certain subjects: rightholders. By violating a natural right, one wrongs the subject whose right it is. These subjects of natural rights are viewed as sources of moral claims and thereby recognized as having a certain moral standing and value. The natural-law idiom contains no such idea: it need not involve demands on one's conduct toward other subjects at all and, even if it does, need not involve the idea that by violating such demands one has wronged these subjects – one may rather have wronged God, for example, or have disturbed the harmonious order of the cosmos. In ruling out these formerly prominent alternative ideas, the shift from natural-law to natural-rights language constitutes a secularization which facilitates the presentation of a select set of moral demands as broadly sharable in a world that has become much larger and more heterogeneous. This secularization centers on a specific view about the point of the moral demands (duties) singled out as natural. The point of respecting them is the protection of others; one's concern to honor one's moral duties is motivated by a deeper and prior moral concern for the interests of others.[84]

This specification of the point of moral demands entails a narrowing of content possibilities. The natural-law idiom lends itself to expressing any moral demands that might apply to human persons; but not all of these demands can be expressed equally well in the language of natural rights. Three historically prominent categories of moral demands are endangered by the shift in terminology: religious duties, duties toward oneself, and moral demands upon our conduct toward animals. Ascribing rights to God seems awkward, because we do not think of him as having vital interests that are vulnerable to human encroachment. Speaking of rights against oneself or of animal rights is problematic because of the connection between having rights and being entitled to claim and to defend one's rights as well as to protest and sometimes to punish the infringement of these rights.[85] We do not engage in such claiming, defending, protesting, and punishing activities against ourselves; and animals seem unable to engage in them at all. In accepting this connection one need not endorse the stronger position, taken by Hart, that having a right presupposes the simultaneous ability to claim it.[86] One may instead, following Gewirth, find nothing odd in saying that a man who is now dead or in an irreversible coma has his rights violated when his will is overturned or when his body is kept alive against his express prior instructions. Here we can remember the man making claims before, and can imagine how he would have protested had he known about what is being done now. Similarly, one can say that maiming or killing an infant constitutes a violation of her rights, because we can once again imagine how she will protest the harms done to her, or would have done so in the future had she survived.[87] This contrasts with the case of nonhuman animals, which have no past or potential future ability to make claims: here the language of rights can seem out of place.[88]

2.2 From natural rights to human rights

The language of human rights partakes in the specification we have found to be involved in the shift from natural law to natural rights. Beyond that, it would seem to have a fourfold significance. First, it manifestly detaches the idea of moral rights from its historical antecedents in the medieval Christian tradition, thereby underscoring the secularization implicit in the first shift from the language of laws (commandments, duties) to that of rights. This serves the continued maintenance of broad sharability and makes fully explicit the connection between a special class of moral demands and the status of certain beings, rightholders, as subjects of moral value.

In the same vein, the shift also indicates a reorientation of the sort for which Rawls has coined the phrase "political not metaphysical."[89] The adjective "human" – unlike "natural" – does not suggest an ontological status independent of any and all human efforts, decisions, (re)cognition. It does not rule out such a status either. Rather, it avoids these metaphysical and metaethical issues by implying nothing about them one way or the other. The potential appeal of the select moral demands is thereby further broadened in that these demands are made accessible also to those who reject all variants of moral realism – who believe, for instance, that the special moral status of all human beings rests on nothing more than our own profound moral commitment and determination that human beings ought to have this status.

Third, and most obvious, the shift strongly confirms that it is all and only human beings who give rise to the relevant moral demands: all and only human persons have human rights and the special moral status associated therewith. The expression also suggests that human beings are equal in this regard. This view can be analyzed into two components. First, all human beings have exactly the same human rights. Second, the moral significance of human rights and human-rights violations does not vary with whose human rights are at stake; as far as human rights are concerned, all human beings matter equally.[90] Though the second component is only weakly suggested by the expression, it is, I believe, a fixed part of our current concept of human rights.

The fourth way in which the shift from natural to human rights has been significant is not suggested by the change in terminology, but seems to have contingently accompanied this change. One can approach the point through Article 17.2 of the *UDHR*: "No one shall be arbitrarily deprived of his property." If a car is stolen, its owner has certainly been deprived of her property, and arbitrarily so. Still, we are unlikely to call this a violation of Article 17.2 or a human-rights violation. Why? Because it is only a car? I do not think so: the car may be its owner's most important asset; and the theft of food would not be considered a human-rights violation either, even if it were her entire reserve for the winter. An arbitrary confiscation of her car by the government, on the other hand, does strike us as a human-rights violation, even if she has several other cars left. This suggests that human-rights violations, to count as such, must be in some sense official, and that human rights thus protect persons only against violations from certain sources. Human rights can be violated by governments, certainly, and by government agencies and officials, by the general staff of an army at war, and probably also by the leaders of a guerrilla movement or of a large corporation – but not by a petty criminal or by a violent husband. We can capture this idea by conceiving it to be implicit in the concept of human rights that human-rights postulates are addressed, in the first instance at least, to those who occupy positions of authority within a society (or other comparable social system).

We see here that the language of human rights involves a further narrowing of content possibilities – not on the side of the agent this time, but on the side of the recipient. Through the language of natural rights, one can demand protection of persons against any threats to their well-being and agency; through the language of human rights, one demands protection only against certain "official" threats. This narrowing is not, however, as severe as it may seem at first. As we shall see, the language of human rights involves a demand for protection not only against official violations but, more broadly, against official disrespect, and it addresses this demand not only to officials, those whose violations of a relevant right would count as human-rights violations, but also to those in whose name such officials are acting.

Before discussing these matters further in section 2.3, let me sum up my explication of the concept of human rights thus far. A commitment to human rights involves one in recognizing that human persons with a past or potential future ability to engage in moral conversation and practice have certain basic needs, and that these needs give rise to weighty moral demands.[91] The object of each of these basic human needs is the object of a human right.[92] Recognizing these basic needs as giving rise to human rights involves a commitment to oppose official disrespect of these needs on the part of one's own society (and other comparable social systems in which one is a participant).[93]

Let me now try to clarify further the modern concept of human rights by explicating the notion of official disrespect embedded in it. This explication is normative to some extent. Those who speak (outside legal contexts) of human rights often do not have a clear sense of what they take human rights to be. I want to be clearer here. And my account should then be tested not against what people actually say about human rights, but against what they would or should affirm upon reflection. Though my account is normative to this extent, its objective is still to reconstruct the meaning of a widely used expression. I am asking what we mean, or ought to mean, when we speak of a human right to X. I am not here asking the more significantly normative question as to which candidate human rights, if any, we should recognize. My examples from the *UDHR* should be taken in this spirit. I am not presupposing that the human rights I discuss exist or ought to be recognized. I am merely asking what the assertion of a particular human right should reasonably be taken to mean.

2.3 Official disrespect

In our world, official agents are paradigmatically exemplified by goverments and their agents and agencies. A paradigmatic instance of official disrespect of human rights is, then, their violation by a government. Governments may do so by issuing or maintaining unjust laws or orders that authorize or require human-rights violations or they may do so "under color of law," that is, by perversely construing existing legislation as licensing human-rights violating policies.

These paradigm cases of official disrespect bring out most clearly why, as is widely felt, there is something especially hideous, outrageous, and intolerable about official disrespect, why official moral wrongs are worse than otherwise similar "private" moral wrongs, quite apart from the fact that they often harm more severely, and harm and frighten more people, than private wrongs. Official moral wrongs masquerade under the name of law and justice and they are generally committed quite openly for all to see: laid down in statutes and regulations, called for by orders and verdicts, and adorned with official seals, stamps, and signatures. Such wrongs do not merely deprive their victims of the objects of their rights but attack those very rights themselves; they do not merely subvert what is right, but the very idea of right and justice. This conjecture explains, I think, why so many people feel more personally affronted by human-rights violations than by equivalent ordinary crimes, and also feel personally responsible in regard to them – why they see human rights as everyone's concern and feel implicated in, and experience shame on account of, what their government and its officials do in their name.

With these thoughts in mind, let us consider other candidate instances of official disrespect. One obvious way of expanding beyond the paradigm is by broadening the definition of "government" so as to include not merely the highest officials in its three branches, but also the lower echelons of authority, including all the various functional and regional subunits of the three branches down to the smallest and lowest agencies and officials. Here it emerges that moral wrongs committed by an official fit the better under the label of "human-rights violation" the more closely they are related to his job and the more tolerated or encouraged they are throughout officialdom. A murder committed by a mailman, even if on duty, would hardly count as a human-rights violation, but torture administered by a policeman to a suspect would count, unless, perhaps, it is a truly isolated incident of conduct that is strongly discouraged within the police force and severely punished when discovered.

More interesting cases are the following. A government may, for the time being, refrain from ordering or authorizing human-rights violations, and effectively prevent violations on the part of its various agencies and officials, but reserve for itself the legal power to order or authorize such violations at any time at its sole discretion. Conversely, a government may legally bind itself never to violate human rights and yet do nothing or very little to ensure that its various agencies and officers abide by this official prohibition. The government may also – while legally committing itself not to violate human rights and effectively enforcing this commitment against its agencies and officials – fail to make such violations illegal for some or all of the persons and associations under its jurisdiction. Or it may pass or maintain the appropriate legislation but then do little or nothing to enforce it. In view of this plurality of cases, how shall we explicate the idea of official disrespect of human rights?

To make these issues more concrete, let us focus on Article 19 of the *UDHR*: "Everyone has the right to freedom of opinion and expression; this right includes freedom to hold opinions without interference and to seek, receive and impart information and ideas through any media and regardless of frontiers." We may suppose that we know precisely what the right here postulated is a right to: what sorts of conduct it protects in what particular contexts and circumstances. Let us also suppose that we know precisely what does and does not constitute interference with such protected conduct and hence a violation of the postulated right on the part of individual and collective agents. How do we get from this knowledge to a measure for official disrespect: to a way of assessing a society's human-rights record in regard to Article 19? The answer to this question, as we have seen, cannot be that we must simply count violations (weighted for severity, perhaps), as this would gloss over the important issue of the more or less official character of these violations.

Making the law alone the decisive yardstick for a society's human-rights record is implausible. Societies may be officially committed to Article 19, may even incorporate an appropriate right to freedom of expression into their constitutions, and their officials may nonetheless violate this legal right frequently and with impunity – a possibility sadly illustrated by all too many showcase constitutions around the world. We can hardly celebrate such societies for their respect of human rights.

A more plausible explication of "official disrespect" would have us focus on the extent to which the government, including its various agencies and officials, is actually interfering with protected conduct. But this proposal leaves out officially tolerated private violence as exemplified by "outraged citizens" in former and present communist societies, death squads in various authoritarian societies of Latin America, militias in Indonesia, and "war veterans" in Zimbabwe. We should not settle for an understanding of official disrespect that provides an incentive to governments to let their opponents be killed by private government supporters rather than by the police. To make the proposal plausible, we must then go beyond the idea of "the government actually interfering." If protected conduct is suppressed with impunity by persons organized or encouraged by the government, then these interferences must be included under the notion of official disrespect.

This modification may not go far enough. Death squads may engage in their bloody activities even without open or tacit government encouragement. Rich landowners may organize bands of thugs, for example, who prevent – through disruption, intimidation, and violence – the expression of any political views that champion the interests of poor peasants or migrant workers. Veterans of the revolution may organize in similar ways to suppress anti-communist opinions. The government need not organize or encourage such activities – it merely stands idly by: fails to enact laws that proscribe such conduct or, if such laws are on the books, fails to enforce them effectively. (In such a scenario, government officials may even regret the activities and feel embarrassed by them. They nevertheless do not act because they fear that strong measures to protect the rights of an unpopular group – foreign residents with southern facial features in Germany, for instance – would diminish their own popularity.) We should consider such cases, as well, to exemplify official disrespect: some persons suffer restrictions of their freedom of expression and there is no official response, or at most a token response, to the deprivations.

Even this account is still not quite broad enough. A nearly complete absence of interferences with protected conduct in some society may be due to the fact that people know only too well what sorts of opinions cannot be publicly expressed without serious risk of violent interference or punitive measures against oneself or one's family. They know what could happen to them if they speak up, and they also know that their "protected" conduct would not be effectively protected in fact. Formerly defiant, they are now intimidated and demoralized. This change goes along with a dramatic decline in the frequency of actual interferences – yet surely we cannot say that the society's human-rights record has dramatically improved. This scenario, too, exemplifies official disrespect of the human right, even if this right is (in the unrealistic limiting case) never violated. It thereby presents in a most clear-cut way the need to detach the notion of official disrespect from that of violations. What is relevant to a society's record in regard to, or to its degree of official disrespect of, a given human right is, then, (a) a proper subset of the occurring violations of this right, namely the "official" or "human-rights" violations, and (b) various facts about the government's and also the people's attitude (commitment and disposition) toward the right and all its occurring violations. Unofficial violations of a right that is on the list of human rights do not constitute human-rights violations; but official indifference toward such private violations does constitute official disrespect.[94]

If official disrespect of this last kind is to be avoided, a society must ensure that persons are, and feel, secure in regard to the objects of their human rights. In considering what this entails, we tend to look, once again, to the government first and foremost: to how the concern for these objects is incorporated into the law and constitution,[95] and to the extent to which the government is disposed to suppress and punish (official and private) violations and makes this disposition known through word and deed.

But it makes sense to think more broadly here. What is needed to make the object of a right truly secure is a vigilant citizenry that is deeply committed to this right and disposed to work for its political realization. (This does not mean that every last citizen must have this commitment and disposition – a minority may suffice, so long as it is clearly preponderant among citizens actively engaged in the political life of their society.) More reliable than a commitment by the government, which may undergo a radical change in personnel from one day to the next, is a commitment by the citizenry. This latter commitment tends to foster the former – especially in democratic societies which tend to produce the strongest incentives for government officials to be responsive to the people. And it also tends to preclude cases where impotence, not indifference, makes a government stand idly by when organized groups of its citizens violate the rights of others. Such cases, too, exemplify official disrespect when the people, who bear the ultimate responsibility for what happens on their society's territory, do not care enough about the objects of human rights to enable, encourage, and (if need be) replace or reorganize their government so as to safeguard secure access to these objects for all.

While the government may, then, be the primary guardian of human rights and the prime measure of official disrespect, the people are their ultimate guardian on whom their realization crucially depends. Enduring respect of human rights is, then, sustained not just by the country's constitution, its legal and political system, and the attitudes of its politicians, judges, and police. It is sustained more deeply by the attitudes of its people, as shaped also by the education system and the economic distribution.

Such socioeconomic factors are important to the realization of human rights also in another way. Consider Article 5 of the *UDHR*: "No one shall be subjected to torture or to cruel, inhuman or degrading treatment or punishment." In many countries, domestic servants, some indentured or virtual slaves, do not enjoy the object of this human right. In some of these societies, inhuman or degrading treatment of domestic servants by their employers is perfectly legal. In others, certain legal prohibitions are in place but ineffective: most of the servants, often illiterate, are ignorant of their legal rights, convictions for mistreatment are difficult if not impossible to obtain, punishments are negligible. Moreover, servants are also often forced to endure illegal conduct on account of economic necessity: they do not dare file complaints against their employers for fear of being fired. This fear is both justified and substantial. They often have only minimal financial reserves and no other place to spend the night, there may be a general oversupply of servants, and they may have reason to believe that their present employer would refuse to issue them the favorable reference they need to find new employment.

When servants live in such conditions, their human right to be free from cruel, inhuman, or degrading treatment is not fulfilled. This flaw can perhaps be corrected through severe penal laws with aggressive enforcement. But it may also be tackled, probably more effectively, through other measures expanding literacy, knowledge of existing legislation, shelters for dismissed servants, educational and employment opportunities and unemployment benefits for the poor, and efforts to build a culture of civic solidarity and equal citizenship.

The arguments of the last four paragraphs may be accused of abusing the plausible, mostly civil rights of the *UDHR* to support their opposites: social and economic pseudo-rights. (Yet another social democrat dressed in liberal's clothing!) It is true that my view undercuts the sharp distinction between different kinds of rights to some extent. To see whether this makes sense, let us proceed, with the libertarian reservations about social and economic human rights in mind, to a more straightforward explication of my institutional understanding of human rights.[96]

2.4 The libertarian critique of social and economic rights

The concept of rights suggests an interactional understanding, matching each right with certain directly corresponding duties.[97] This understanding sustains a familiar dispute about what duties human rights entail. On one side are libertarians who require these to be exclusively negative duties (to refrain from violating the right in question). Such a minimalist account disqualifies the "human rights" to social security, work, rest and leisure, an adequate standard of living, education, or culture postulated in Articles 22–7 of the *UDHR* on the ground that they essentially entail positive duties. On the other side are maximalist accounts according to which all human rights entail both negative duties (to avoid depriving) and positive duties (to protect and to help). For the minimalist, human rights require only self-restraint. For the maximalist, they require efforts to fulfill everyone's human rights anywhere on earth: "A human right, then, will be a right whose beneficiaries are all humans and whose obligors are all humans in a position to effect the right."[98]

The institutional understanding of human rights I propose allows us to transcend the terms of this debate. By postulating a human right to X, one is asserting that any society or other social system, insofar as this is reasonably possible, ought to be so (re)organized that all its members have secure access to X, with "security" always understood as especially sensitive to persons' risk of being denied X or deprived of X officially: by the government or its agents or officials.[99] Avoidable insecurity of access, beyond certain plausibly attainable thresholds, constitutes official disrespect and stains the society's human-rights record. Human rights are, then, moral claims on the organization of one's society. However, since citizens are collectively responsible for their society's organization and its resulting human-rights record, human rights ultimately make demands upon (especially the more influential) citizens. Persons share responsibility for official disrespect of human rights within any coercive institutional order they are involved in upholding.

This institutional understanding can draw support from Article 28 of the *UDHR*: "Everyone is entitled to a social and international order in which the rights and freedoms set forth in this Declaration can be fully realized." As the reference to "the rights and freedoms set forth in this Declaration" indicates, this article does not add a further right to the list, but makes a statement about the concept of a human right, about what human rights mean or require. This statement might be unpacked in four steps:

1 How fully human rights *can* be realized in some institutional order is measured by how fully these human rights generally are, or (in the case of a hypothetical institutional order) generally would be, realized in it.
2 Any institutional order should be designed so that human rights are realized in it as fully as reasonably possible.
3 A human right is *realized* in some institutional order insofar as, and fully if and only if, this human right is fulfilled for all those whose conduct this order constrains.
4 A human right is *fulfilled* for some person insofar as she enjoys secure access to its object.

On the interactional understanding of human rights, governments and individuals have a responsibility not to violate human rights. On my institutional understanding, by contrast, their responsibility is to work for an institutional order and public culture that ensure that all members of society have secure access to the objects of their human rights. Thus linking rights fulfillment with insecurity rather than violation can make a difference in cases of two kinds. A person may fully enjoy X even while her access to X is insecure (as when persons relevantly like her, say blacks or vocal government opponents, are beaten or threatened). Conversely, a person may be temporarily deprived of X, through a crime by a rogue government official perhaps, in a society that is very effective in preventing crimes of the relevant type. Opposite to the interactional understanding, my institutional one regards only the first case as a human-rights problem.

In proposing this institutional understanding, I reject its interactional alternatives: I deny, for instance, that postulating that persons have a human right to X is tantamount to asserting that some or all individual and collective human agents have a moral duty – in addition to any legal duties they may have in their society – not to deny X to others or to deprive them of X. In rejecting this alternative account, I am not denying that the postulate of a human right to X suggests or even implies this assertion. It is hard to see how one can, on the one hand, be committed to the claim that societies, for the sake of the persons living in them, ought to be organized so that these persons need not endure inhuman or degrading treatment and yet, on the other hand, not consider it morally wrong for persons to treat others in inhuman or degrading ways. A commitment to human rights goes along with interactional moral commitments; but this is no reason to identify the former with the latter.

On my understanding, too, human rights (conceptually) entail moral duties – but these are not corresponding duties in any simple way: The human right not to be subjected to cruel or degrading treatment gives me a duty to help ensure that those living in my society need not endure such treatment. Depending on context, this duty may, as we have seen, generate obligations to advocate and support programs to improve literacy and unemployment benefits when such programs are necessary to secure the object of this human right for a class of my compatriots (domestic servants).

By reconceiving human rights in this way, the familiar dispute is transformed. Responsibility for a person's human rights falls on all and only those who participate with this person in the same social system. It is their responsibility, collectively, to structure this system so that all its participants have secure access to the objects of their human rights. In our world, national societies are the paradigmatic example of relevant social systems, and the responsibility for the fulfillment of your human rights falls then upon your government and your fellow citizens.[100] The institutional understanding thus occupies an appealing middle ground: it goes beyond (minimalist interactional) libertarianism, which disconnects us from any deprivations we do not directly bring about, without falling into a (maximalist interactional) utilitarianism of rights, which holds each of us responsible for all deprivations whatever, regardless of the nature of our causal relation to them.[101]

But this is not all. The most remarkable feature of this institutional understanding is that it can go well beyond minimalist libertarianism without denying its central tenet: that human rights entail only negative duties. The normative force of others' human rights for me is that I must not help uphold and impose upon them coercive social institutions under which they do not have secure access to the objects of their human rights. I would be violating this duty if, through my participation, I helped sustain a social order in which such access is not secure, in which blacks are enslaved, women disenfranchised, or servants mistreated, for example. Even if I owned no slaves or employed no servants myself, I would still share responsibility: by contributing my labor to the society's economy, my taxes to its governments, and so forth. I might honor my negative duty, perhaps, through becoming a hermit or an emigrant, but I could honor it more plausibly by working with others toward shielding the victims of injustice from the harms I help produce or, if this is possible, toward establishing secure access through institutional reform.

Libertarians insist on a minimalist constraint on what duties human rights can impose: human rights require that we not harm others in certain ways – not that we protect, rescue, feed, clothe, and house them. My institutional understanding can accept this constraint without disqualifying social and economic human rights. Given the minimalist constraint, such human rights give you claims not against all other human beings, but specifically against those who impose a coercive institutional order upon you. Such a coercive order must not avoidably restrict the freedom of some so as to render their access to basic necessities insecure – especially through official denial or deprivation. If it does, then all human agents have a negative duty, correlative to the postulated social and economic human rights, not to cooperate in upholding it unless they compensate for their cooperation by protecting its victims or by working for its reform. Those violating this duty share responsibility for the harms (insecure access to basic necessities) produced by the unjust institutional order in question.[102]

A human right to basic necessities, as postulated, for instance, in Article 25 of the *UDHR*, becomes more plausible when construed along these lines. On my institutional understanding, it involves no duty on everyone to help supply such necessities to those who would otherwise be without them. It rather involves a duty on citizens to ensure that any coercive social order they collectively impose upon each of themselves is one under which, insofar as reasonably possible, each has secure access to these necessities. Surprisingly perhaps, this duty was well expressed by Charles Darwin more than a century ago: "If the misery of our poor be caused not by laws of nature, but by our own institutions, great is our sin."[103]

2.5 The critique of social and economic rights as "manifesto rights"

Social and economic rights are often dismissed on the ground that, unlike the favored civil and political rights, they are in many actual social contexts fated to be mere "manifesto rights." There is no clear canonical explication of this polemical term. The basic charge is that such rights are somehow unrealistic or unclear about the duties they entail.

Sometimes the obduracy, even brutality, of those in power makes it unrealistic to expect the rights of their subjects to be fulfilled. But we do not want to say, I trust, that these rights are therefore manifesto rights. Doing so would belittle moral rights in just those cases where it is most urgent to assert them. The Nazis, at the peak of their power (1938–42), were not violating mere manifesto rights.

Perhaps the meaning of the expression is, then, best clarified as follows. A legal or postulated moral right is a manifesto right if and only if

(1) it is not now the case that all supposed rightholders have secure access to the object of this right; and
(2a) it is left unspecified who is supposed to do what in order to bring it about that all supposed rightholders have secure access to the object of the right; or
(2b) the agents upon whom specific demands are made cannot reasonably meet these demands to the extent necessary to bring it about that all supposed rightholders have secure access to the object of the right.[104]

Since the assertion of social and economic rights matters especially in contexts where these rights are not fulfilled, let us assume that (1) is satisfied. Rebutting the manifesto charge thus requires denying both (2a) and (2b).

Let us begin with (2b). A society cannot secure for all of its members a happy love life or a trip to the moon. Rights to such benefits would therefore be mere manifesto rights. This defect can be avoided by relativizing the objects of the relevant rights to a society's means. A society can work on removing restrictions and overcoming taboos and prejudices that make it harder for some of its members to enjoy a happy love life. The – now relativized – right not to be hampered in one's quest for a happy love life by nonessential restrictions or by avoidable taboos and prejudices is, then, not a manifesto right (which does not mean, of course, that it deserves inclusion on the list of human rights).

It can be demanded even of a very poor society that it reduce insecurity of access to basic necessities as far as reasonably possible toward a plausible security threshold. By understanding Article 25 as requiring this and nothing more – as not requiring that all must have enough to eat when enough food can simply not be produced – we rescue it from the charge that the right it postulates satisfies (2b) and hence is a mere manifesto right. And this understanding accords with common usage: a society's human-rights record is not stained merely because it is, under prevailing conditions, unable to secure minimally adequate nutrition for all. The human right does not, then, entitle one to food that would have to be withheld from others who also need it to survive. Some may starve to death without any official disrespect of Article 25.

An analogous point holds true of civil rights: a poor society may not have the resources effectively to protect the bodily integrity of all its citizens. This does not show that Article 3 postulates a manifesto right. The human right there postulated does not entitle one to protection that would have to be withheld from others who need it just as much. So rights of both kinds are here on a par.

It may seem at first that the two kinds of rights fare quite differently with regard to (2a). The civil rights postulated in the *UDHR* make clear and specific demands on governments, while the right postulated in Article 25 seems merely to assert that it would be a good thing if any society were so organized that all had enough to eat. But this contrast is deceptive if the realization of even the clearly civil human right not to be subjected to cruel, inhuman, or degrading treatment (Article 5) requires that such treatment by private agents, too, must be effectively discouraged and presupposes certain commitments and dispositions on the part of the citizenry. Understanding human rights in this way does not turn them into manifesto rights: each member of society, according to his or her means, is to help create and sustain a social and political order under which all have secure access to the objects of their civil rights. This demand, so abstractly put, is unspecific but, within any particular social context, quite specific. In a society where domestic servants must often suffer inhuman and degrading treatment from their employers, citizens have a human-rights-based obligation to help institute appropriate legal protections as well as perhaps a literacy program or unemployment benefits.

My understanding of the economic rights of Article 25 is closely parallel. Each member of society, according to his or her means, is to help bring about and sustain a social and economic order within which all have secure access to basic necessities. This unspecific demand may have quite specific implications in a given social context, such as a society whose poorest members lack secure access to minimally adequate nutrition. Rights of both kinds are, then, on a par in this respect. And if situational specificity is what matters, then rights of both kinds also escape clause (2a) and therefore cannot be dismissed as mere manifesto rights.

2.6 Disputes about kinds of human rights

This chapter develops a specific institutional understanding of what human rights are. It does not directly address the question of what human rights there are. In sections 2.4 and 2.5 I have tried to show, however, that my institutional understanding of human rights narrows the gap between those who, in line with some Western governments, emphasize civil and political rights and those who, in line with various socialist and developing states, emphasize social, economic, and cultural rights.

This institutional understanding narrows the philosophical gap because it does not sustain the thought that civil and political human rights require only restraint, while social and economic human rights also demand positive efforts and costs. Rather, it emphasizes negative duties across the board. Human agents are not to collaborate in upholding a coercive institutional order that avoidably restricts the freedom of some so as to render their access to basic necessities insecure without compensating for their collaboration by protecting its victims or by working for its reform.

This institutional understanding also undercuts any systematic correlation between categories of human rights and ways of fulfilling them. The latter may vary in time and place. Thus, in order to realize the classical civil right to freedom from inhuman and degrading treatment, a particular society may need to establish certain social and economic safeguards. And in order to realize a human right to adequate nutrition, perhaps all that is needed is an effective criminal statute against speculative hoarding of foodstuffs. In this way, the concrete demands different categories of human rights make on an institutional order may in fact turn out to be similar, and, if so, my institutional understanding would narrow also the practical-political gap between the two sides. Those who endorse only civil and political human rights will work for institutional reforms that reduce poverty and illiteracy where doing so is an effective strategy for reducing insecurity of access to the objects of civil and political human rights. And those who endorse only social and economic human rights will work for institutional reforms that grant the poor genuine political participation and ways of defending their legal rights in the courts where doing so enhances the capacity of the poor to fend for themselves and thus reduces insecurity of access to the objects of social and economic human rights.

All this is not to say that it makes no difference which rights we single out as human rights. But if my institutional understanding indeed reduces the philosophical and the practical-political importance of the actual controversies about this question, then this is another reason in its favor. Even if we continue to disagree about which goods should be included in a conception of human rights, we can then – provided we really care about the realization of human rights rather than about ideological propaganda victories – work together on the same institutional reforms instead of arguing over how much praise or blame is deserved by this state or that.

3

Loopholes in Moralities

3.0 Introduction

One can think of a morality as an abstract standpoint outside the world from which what occurs within it – actions, persons, institutions, states of affairs – is evaluated. One can also think of a morality as itself in the world, as a more or less unified set of moral beliefs, attitudes, and conduct dispositions characteristic of particular persons or groups. In this second sense, moralities have real effects; and these may themselves be made a subject of evaluation. Such a perspective upon conduct-guiding structures of values and norms – or *codes* – is familiar to economists and legislators, who take social effects into account in designing or evaluating a tax code, for example. My aim is to extend this perspective to both key domains of morality: to *ethics*, concerned with the moral evaluation of conduct and character, with the life one should lead and the person one should strive to be, and to *justice*, concerned with the moral evaluation of social

This chapter was first published in the *Journal of Philosophy* 89, 2 (February 1992): 79–98. It has greatly benefited from criticisms and suggestions by many persons, including Bruce Ackerman, Rogers Albritton, Christian Barry, Rüdiger Bittner, Alex George, Robert Guay, Amy Gutmann, Charles Larmore, David Luban, Sidney Morgenbesser, Warren Quinn, and Ling Tong. Note 115 is newly added.

institutions which regulate and structure human interactions. My general question is then: what role, if any, should an evaluation of the effects of moral codes play in our substantive moral reflection?[105]

Clearly, we should take account of such effects only if their connection to the relevant code is reasonably firm. It is not rational to worry about any fortuitous effects a morality (in the second sense) may have had in the past, if they tell us nothing about what effects it is likely to have in the future. Taking account of the differential effects of alternative moralities makes sense only insofar as we can estimate these effects in advance. My question concerns, then, effects of moral conceptions that are predictable at least in a rough, probabilistic way.

This may be reminiscent of Nietzsche's question: what is the value of our morality? Yet I am not judging a morality by some novel, alien measure of value, but by its own standards: have we organized our moral commitments in a way that reflects, and helps effectively achieve, what by their own lights matters? My goal is to uncover new kinds of considerations that, if relevant to our moral reflection and discourse, may help break the stalemate of conflicting appeals to moral intuitions and thereby make moral dialogue more fruitful, moral convergence more likely, and our moral values more effective.

This chapter is limited to one class of predictable effects of moral codes, namely to cases where a code is *counterproductive* by giving *incentives* toward conduct that is *regrettable* by the code's own lights.[106] In saying that a moral code can be counterproductive, I am assuming that it is understood as having some point, rationale, purposes, or objectives. This is the typical case in the modern world. But it is also possible, of course, to think of a moral code as the moral truth or God's law. We can then think of it as not being in the business of producing anything, and hence as incapable of being counterproductive. On this understanding, we would not have second thoughts about our morality even if our holding it predictably led to the extinction of the human species or the disappearance of this morality itself.

That a code gives someone an *incentive* to act in a certain way means only that it gives her a reason to act in this way. Such a reason for conduct need not affect conduct itself: a code can encourage conduct without triggering or influencing conduct.[107] I count both the incentives a code gives and any conduct these may elicit as effects of this code. My general question has thus become more specific. Can the fact that a morality gives incentives toward regrettable conduct constitute at least some reason to revise this morality?

I believe so. But let me attach three cautionary notes to this claim. First, the fact that a code gives an incentive toward conduct that in some instances is regrettable in some respect does not automatically render this code counterproductive *tout court*. The conduct in question may be, by the lights of the same code, valuable in other instances or in other respects and thus not be regrettable on the whole. Alternatively, the overall point, rationale, purposes, or objectives of the code may demand that it give the relevant incentive, or that it have certain features of which this incentive is an unavoidable byproduct, despite the fact that the incentive is also regrettable, even on the whole. The problems I want to examine are raised only when a code is counterproductive *all things considered*, that is, when its overall point, rationale, purposes, or objectives would be better fulfilled if this code were replaced by a somewhat different code. I therefore assume in my more abstract discussions, or seek to show in my more concrete examples, that there really are no redeeming virtues that would allow one to say that the moral code under discussion – though it gives regrettable incentives – is not counterproductive all things considered.

Second, the effects of a code that is prevalent in some society depend to some extent on the life context of this society, including its culture, technology, and natural environment. Likewise, the effects of a code held by an individual are shaped by the life context of that particular person.[108] It may, then, sometimes be possible to reduce or eliminate the regrettable effects of a moral code through deliberate modifications of the life context in which it is held. There are other cases, however, where such strategies are either unavailable or themselves very costly in moral terms.

Thus my claim specifically targets cases where a morality is counterproductive all things considered in virtue of giving regrettable incentives that are not reasonably avoidable. In such cases we have reason to revise our morality. But – and this is the third cautionary note – such a reason may not be decisive. I do not claim, by any means, that the effects of moralities are all that counts in moral reflection. Only that they are important, and decisive in some cases.

3.1 Types of incentives

It may seem that an incentive given by a code can be problematic only insofar as it actually elicits regrettable conduct. This view may indeed be plausible as regards *concrete incentives*, that is, reasons for conduct that a code gives to fully specific agents who actually do or will exist (or to statistical aggregates of such agents – such as the French taxpayer). But one can speak of incentives in another sense as well. *Ideal incentives* are encouragements or discouragements that a code, as it were, "wants" or "intends" to give (which does not mean that they must have been thought of, let alone intended, by some creator(s) of it). Less metaphorically: ideal incentives are reasons for conduct that a code would provide to persons in the given life context, if they were *ideal adherents*, that is, agents who are fully rational, who fully understand the code and interpret it correctly, who are fully committed to comply with any requirements of the code, and whose circumstances and remaining interests fall within the normal range. Insofar as a code provides ideal incentives, we can say that it *guides* persons toward certain conduct – or misguides them, if this conduct is regrettable on the whole.

Ideal incentives are of two kinds. With *compliance incentives*, ideal adherents are motivated solely by their commitment to do what the code requires or suggests. Incentives deriving from the code's requirements are always decisive for an ideal adherent (assuming the code is consistent), while incentives deriving from its suggestions need not be. With reward incentives, ideal adherents are motivated by other, code-independent interests of theirs insofar as these can be pursued without violating requirements of the code. Here a code encourages conduct by affecting the official pay-offs: eligibility for benefits or liability to burdens. Reward incentives need not be decisive.

Two examples. A tax code requiring that one pay taxes on interest income not deriving from municipal bonds provides a compliance incentive to pay taxes on such income, and a reward incentive to invest in municipal bonds. A morality that requires single young adults to volunteer for a stint in the military provides a compliance incentive to enlist and a reward incentive to get married early.[109]

By providing ideal incentives, a code guides (or misguides) agents. Like a traffic sign, it can do so without affecting their conduct. It is possible that agents differ from ideal adherents, so that the code's ideal incentives do not manifest themselves as concrete incentives to them. Neither the compliance incentives, nor the reward incentives in our two examples would manifest themselves as concrete incentives to persons who do not know the relevant parts of the codes or do not care whether they are in compliance or not. If ideal adherents of the code or persons sufficiently similar to them actually exist, ideal incentives manifest themselves in concrete incentives. Even then, they may fail to affect conduct. Concrete reward incentives and concrete compliance incentives deriving from the code's suggestions may be outweighed by other reasons for action; and any concrete incentives given by the code may merely reinforce how adherents are inclined to act independently of the code.

As a code may provide ideal incentives that do not manifest themselves as concrete incentives, it may also give concrete incentives that do not correspond to any ideal incentives it provides. Thus a tax law may incline certain persons to keep their fortune abroad, where it can more easily be hidden from the tax authorities. And our ethic may incline certain persons to pretend to be needy, in order fraudulently to exploit the ethical command to help the needy. In these cases, a code gives persons reasons to transgress a requirement of this code, which would not be reasons for them if they were ideal adherents of it.

This distinction between ideal and concrete incentives splits our more specific question into two.[110] One is the ideal question: may we have reason to revise our morality if, in the given life context, it provides ideal incentives that are regrettable by its own lights? The other is the concrete question: may we have reason to revise our morality if, in the given life context, it produces concrete incentives that are regrettable by its own lights? This chapter focuses exclusively on the former question.[111]

3.2 Loopholes

Even if they affect no one's conduct, regrettable ideal incentives can be problematic, by revealing a structural flaw in the code providing them. Suppose some tax code provides a compliance or reward incentive that would induce some taxpayers, if they were ideal adherents, to act in ways that directly undermine a central purpose of this code. The code may then be criticized for containing a loophole and thus being in a sense incoherent. And this critique can be sustained even if corresponding concrete incentives do not exist or are not noticed, so that the loophole does not actually elicit any regrettable conduct at all.

A *loophole* exists only if the connection between the code and the regrettability of the conduct it encourages is tight in two respects. First, the relevant incentive must be an ideal one, so that the code can be said to *guide* agents toward the regrettable conduct. Second, the conduct it encourages must be regrettable *in itself* rather than in virtue of any further effects it may bring about, however predictably. So, through loopholes agents are guided toward conduct that is in itself regrettable on the whole.

Conduct is regrettable in itself if and only if it goes against what the code requires, or essentially aims at outcomes that are, by the code's own lights, regrettable on the whole. By definition of "ideal adherent," a consistent code does not provide *ideal* incentives toward conduct that is in the first way regrettable in itself – it does not, that is, guide agents toward conduct that it also forbids. The topic of loopholes thus boils down to cases where a code guides agents toward conduct that essentially aims at outcomes that are regrettable on the whole. I call such ideal incentives *inherently regrettable*.

3.3 Social arrangements

To illustrate the problem, let me here concentrate on moral loopholes involving *social arrangements*, by which I mean relationships, associations, or social systems, such as marriages, lawyer–client relationships, families, firms, churches, and states. Social arrangements tie their members together through normative expectations that are based upon special ties, including moral ties, which define special rights and obligations, powers and responsibilities. Such special moral ties vary in formality – ranging from the justiciable and enforced explicit provisions of a legal code to the vague understandings that give rise to moral expectations and disappointments among friends or compatriots.

Consider the ethical view that as a member of a social arrangement one may sometimes – when acting in behalf of other members or of the entire group – deliberately harm outsiders in some specific way, even though one may not do so when one is acting on one's own. Such views are, I believe, widely held. In the business world, those who implement a corporate policy that is harmful to consumers, employees, or the general public often stress their status as managers and their obligations toward the firm's owners, whose financial interests they were hired to promote. How is this supposed to be ethically relevant? Such a manager is not trying to pass the buck by suggesting that the owners, too, must bear some of the responsibility for the offensive policy and that he therefore bears less. What he implies, rather, is this: thanks to the differentiation of roles between owners and manager, the policy in question can be implemented without wrongdoing – though this would not be the case, if he were managing his own firm so as to promote his own financial interests.[112]

Ethical views of this sort guide their adherents to form or join social arrangements in order to effect, through the special ties these involve, a unilateral reduction of responsibility toward those left out of these arrangements. Such guidance is inherently regrettable – not, of course, because additional social arrangements may be formed, but because harms that are straightforwardly morally precluded can be indirectly brought about after all. Let us consider two examples in some detail.

3.4 Case 1: the converted apartment building

Your father owns a large apartment complex. Renting the apartments as they are is profitable, but market conditions are such that it will soon become preferable to convert them into luxury accommodations while doubling the rents. Your father knows, however, that most of the apartments are occupied by elderly tenants who have lived there for decades. Few, if any, of them could afford to stay. The others would have a hard time finding new homes. More importantly, they would be scattered all over town and thus would lose the companionship they have found with one another – the greatest source of pleasure in their final years. Your father understands that it would be wrong of him to force the tenants out. But he also resents the idea of giving up the extra income. It occurs to him that many landlords like himself employ lawyers to manage their real estate in the owners' best interest. So your father hires a lawyer as well and instructs her to manage his real estate in a professional way. As was to be expected, the lawyer eventually initiates the conversion of the complex. Rents double and the old tenants are scattered all over town.

The assumptions I am making about the prevalent ethical code, E, are indicated in the top row of the table:

	Option A1	Option A2	Option B
(aggregate) moral status:	permitted	forbidden	permitted
aggregate nonmoral gain:	zero	very high	high

E forbids your father to initiate the conversion on his own (A2). As for the remaining two options, E does not require (though it may suggest) abandonment of the conversion (A1) in preference to the lawyer's initiation of the conversion in the owner's behalf (B). A landlord is not required to be personally involved in the management of his property. He may surely entrust his real estate to a lawyer. And such a lawyer is not required to refrain from the conversion. She has a professional responsibility to her client, and therefore may, or even should, administer property entrusted to her in the client's best interest. It is simply not her role to ponder whether her client is not rich enough as it is, and should not therefore forgo some gain in order to preserve the tenants' community and form of life.[113]

An ethic incorporating these beliefs provides an ideal incentive to hire the lawyer.[114] This incentive is inherently regrettable, provided the responsibility of the "solitary" landlord is conceived as, to some extent at least, a responsibility *toward his tenants*; and the wrong he would commit by converting the building (A2) as a wrong done *to them*. I assume here that one main rationale for E's forbidding such single-handed conversions is to protect the tenants' community against deliberate destruction for the sake of greater landlord profits. E itself suggests this rationale if, for example, its evaluation of the single-handed conversion varies with the extent to which it would foreseeably harm the tenants. Insofar as this rationale is present, the incentive in Case 1 indicates a loophole: E guides the landlord toward the profitable conversion by enabling him to render it free of wrongdoing. Yet, according to E's rationale, as implicitly suggested in E, this conversion is regrettable on the whole: the tenants' suffering is not outweighed by the landlord's gain. E's own rationale thus gives a reason for closing the loophole – for blocking the opportunity unilaterally to reduce aggregate responsibility.

This does not mean, of course, that an acceptable ethic must require a lawyer to give no more weight to her client's interests than to those of other persons. It is not objectionable that persons may form or join social arrangements whose members agree to owe one another much more than persons owe one another in general as a matter of common decency. So I have no quarrel with the idea that persons, by becoming members of a social arrangement, may *increase* what they owe the other members and may thus come to owe them more than they owe all outsiders. What I find problematic is the idea that persons, by so increasing what they owe certain others, may *reduce* what they minimally owe everyone else.[115]

I write "minimally," because an ethic may of course allow persons to reduce what they owe others; it may, for instance, allow one to get a divorce through which one reduces what one owes to the person one had married. So my point concerns only those basics that persons owe all others in the absence of any special ties and relations. However an ethic may fix these minimal general demands, it should not enable persons unilaterally to reduce or dilute them. Specifically, it should not allow them, by forming or joining a social arrangement, to subject themselves to new, countervailing obligations to its members that may outweigh, trump, or cancel their minimal obligations to everyone else. Forming or joining a social arrangement should not have that sort of moral efficacy, should not introduce that sort of moral change. It should not be among the legitimate benefits of forming or joining a social arrangement that one thereby weakens the minimal moral protections that those who are now outsiders enjoy against oneself.

Even this narrow demand is defeasible because an incentive – even though it depends on the opportunity unilaterally to sidestep aggregate responsibility for given harms – can be desirable in another respect and so not regrettable on the whole. About Case 1, for example, someone might object that I have underdescribed E's rationale. There is a point after all to the incentive E provides, namely the eminent moral importance of the hiring of lawyers. It matters more, morally, that landlords should hire lawyers than that they and their lawyers should not knowingly destroy their tenants' community for extra profit. This objection marks a weak spot in my entire approach, because, quite generally, the claim to have found a loophole can always be countered by claiming that the relevant ideal incentive is not in fact regrettable *on the whole*.

Still, I am not too worried about this weak spot, because what counts is not making a counterclaim but making it plausible. To see whether it is plausible, we must examine whether the code overall really reflects the suggested rationale for the questionable incentive. If it is part of E's rationale that additional hiring of lawyers is morally important, then this value should be surfacing throughout the code. If there are no other indications of such a value in the code, then the conjecture proposed by the objector is implausible.

Insofar as E is merely a creature of my own imagination, there is no point in conducting such an examination for Case 1. But insofar as E is meant to be a realistic code that may actually be held in our society, we can dismiss the counterclaim. For no one (except a few lawyers?) seriously believes it to be morally important that there be more hiring of lawyers.

I conclude that, if E prohibits self-initiated conversions at least partly on account of the damage they would do, for the sake of greater landlord profits, to the tenants' form of life, then any ideal incentive E provides toward such hiring of lawyers indicates a loophole. Such an incentive manifests a kind of incoherence: the point of forbidding a given deliberately imposed correlation of harms and benefits in one context is defeated, for no good reason, when this prohibition can be avoided by switching to another context in which the same deliberate imposition of the same correlation of harms and benefits is permitted.[116] To avoid this incoherence, E must not allow aggregate responsibility for the conversion, or aggregate wrongdoing involved in initiating the conversion, to be so significantly reduced by the hiring of a lawyer.[117]

3.5 Case 2: the homelands policy of white South Africa

The year is 2100. Like their ancestors, South Africa's whites are quite affluent thanks to an abundance of black workers available at subsistence wages, who now, however, are nationals of sovereign states. This change was instituted by an earlier generation of South African whites, who intended that their progeny should not only, like themselves, be economically advantaged but should also be free from any special responsibility for the fate of blacks in the region. The former white leaders (in the 1980s) keenly appreciated that the prevailing conception of justice, J, allows even its minimal constraints on economic relations to be undermined through the interposition of national borders. And so they made sure the blacks of the twenty-first century would be foreigners.

The incentive operative here is again a *moral* incentive, in that the creation of the homelands is motivated by a feature of J: by the weight J gives, in its assessment of economic relations, to the existence of states and of ties among compatriots. It corresponds to an *ideal* (compliance) incentive, because the reform instituted by the former white leaders really relieves the injustice (in terms of J) in the relations between whites and blacks in southern Africa, and thus would matter even to persons who are genuinely committed to J and aware of all relevant facts. Finally, insofar as J condemns the earlier pattern (prevailing in the 1970s) on account of the disadvantaged position of blacks, the incentive it provides is also *inherently regrettable*: through the encouraged "reform," those disadvantages get preserved, even entrenched, rather than eradicated.

A conception of justice providing this incentive would, I think, be incoherent in a sense. J strongly disapproves of the pattern that existed in the old South Africa (of the 1970s) as violating basic justice. Blacks are, by law or convention, barred from the more lucrative positions in their economy; they compete for the remaining positions at a great disadvantage due to grossly inferior schooling, discriminatory hiring and promotion practices, legal prohibitions against residing in certain areas, and so on. However, J then approves of the "reformed" pattern in which all the features and relations relevant to condemning the old pattern as grossly unjust continue unaltered, the only change being that the blacks are now nationals of sovereign states. And what is worse: J even encourages such "reform" by offering that attractive opportunity to reduce injustice without forgoing its benefits. Of course, J isn't strictly inconsistent. But it doesn't make sense to let the same inequalities continue in the context of a slightly changed pattern that can so easily be reached from the old pattern through a (by the lights of J) merely cosmetic reform, which leaves intact all advantages, disadvantages, and correlations between them.

For all I have said, an acceptable conception of justice may allow persons to form a state, to draw borders around it, and to exclude other persons from it. It may also allow that compatriots attempt – solely amongst themselves – to meet a standard of fair cooperation that is much more ambitious than whatever minimal constraints (of "basic justice") it may impose on cooperation in general. So, an acceptable conception of justice may allow the creation of states to lead to a higher standard and to discrepant standards. What it should not allow is that persons, by making others into foreigners, can dilute or evade even its minimal standard, which would otherwise govern relations between them.

I write "minimal," because I am not here worried about a conception of justice that allows a group to evade a higher standard, for instance by seceding from a state that is more egalitarian than this conception minimally requires. My point concerns only whatever minimal standard a conception of justice applies to *any* pattern of interaction – even in the absence of communal bonds, fellow feeling, a common history, shared projects, and so forth. However such a conception may fix this standard of basic justice, it should not allow groups unilaterally to circumvent or dilute it. Specifically, it should not allow such a group, by forming a social arrangement within the larger pattern of interaction, to bring a new moral standard into play that may outweigh, trump, or cancel the minimal protections justice requires for those left out of this arrangement.[118] The introduction of states should not have that sort of moral efficacy, should not produce that sort of moral change. A conception of justice should not guide persons toward, and reward them for, deliberately creating borders in order to "just-ify" a given correlation of harms and benefits, that is, in order to make it compatible with the requirements of basic justice without materially changing it.

Here it is, once again, possible to make a counterclaim. It is regrettable that the old white leaders, by instituting the homelands, are able morally to avoid a genuinely reformed regime under which blacks would have attained legal, political, and economic equality. But this is not regrettable *on the whole*, because J's rationale also includes the view that the multiplication of states has great moral value which here outweighs the value of nonexploitation. We can leave this counterclaim aside as implausible. No such rationale is reflected in the conceptions of justice that are seriously held in our society.

This concludes the illustration of my anti-loophole constraint: a code of ethics or justice must not without good reason encourage changes through which its own minimal standard of common decency or basic justice can be deliberately undermined through the creation of social arrangements and the special moral ties these involve.

3.6 An objection

There is a way of defending the belief in the moral efficacy of creating social arrangements. E and J do not generate the offending incentive, one might claim, so long as they forbid forming or joining social arrangements in such cases.[119] In this way one can preserve the judgments that the lawyer-initiated conversion of the apartment complex is not wrong, and that economic relations in southern Africa are not unjust once the homelands have been introduced. It was wrong to create the relevant social arrangements with the motives in question, but their creation nevertheless has the intended moral effect. E and J could then hold the creators of the social arrangements – those who hire lawyers or institute national borders in cases like 1 and 2 – fully responsible for the harms inflicted upon outsiders.

I consider this defense implausible on three counts. First, the proposed moral codes would provide no reasons to derail harms that are yet in the future. Thus, suppose your father dies before the conversion is initiated and you inherit the complex with the lawyer already in charge of it. Since what is wrong is only the hiring of the lawyer – spilt milk – and not her continued efforts in your behalf, neither you nor she have any moral reason to oppose the conversion – even though it will bring about serious harms in which you both are essentially involved. You and the lawyer are not just bystanders who are merely failing to prevent harms done by another: at least one of you, and no one else, is intending to increase the rental income, deciding that and how the conversion should take place, increasing the rent to its new level, evicting the tenants who cannot pay, and profiting from the conversion. An analogous point applies in Case 2.

Implausible is also, second, the idea of saddling the creators with open-ended posthumous responsibility. After all, the harms they are held responsible for (unlike future catastrophes caused by sloppy hazardous-waste disposal) do not arise from their conduct directly. Rather these harms are, in Case 1, consciously brought about by the lawyer who, in turn, serves at the pleasure of the current owner; and, in Case 2, arise in the context of a pattern that is deliberately perpetuated by later whites.

Third, and most importantly, it is unclear how it can be so wrong for your father to create the agent–client team, given that, as the objection contends, this team does nothing wrong. And similarly for the old white leaders who initiate a pattern of interaction that, by hypothesis, is not unjust. Here it even seems that, if anything, we should have to congratulate these leaders for having replaced the former unjust pattern by the "reformed" one – exactly as we would have congratulated them for creating a new, just pattern that does not disadvantage blacks.

For these three reasons, we should disqualify a revision of E that meets the anti-loophole constraint by allocating responsibility for the suffering of the tenants to the creator of the landlord–lawyer team while assigning no responsibility to this team itself. The team's aggregate wrongdoing in initiating the conversion must not be less – though it may of course be greater – than the solitary landlord's wrongdoing in initiating the same conversion single-handedly.[120] Similarly, we should disqualify a revision of J that meets my anti-loophole constraint by allocating responsibility for the suffering of blacks to those who internationalized the pattern while finding no fault with the "reformed" pattern itself, nor with those who maintain it in existence.

The general point is that, when matters of common decency or basic justice are at stake, a morality must not be sensitive to changes that are consciously instituted in order to secure a more favorable evaluation, but are, by the lights of this morality itself, merely cosmetic.

3.7 Strengthening

Let me proceed by sketching – again for the topic of social arrangements – a way of strengthening this initial thesis. Suppose, in a variation of Case 1, that we find new evidence about your late father's motivations. Though he might have hired the lawyer in order to enable you to reap the gains from the conversion without wrongdoing, he actually did this because he thought you would not cope well with the requisite paperwork. Would this finding make it permissible, or more permissible, for you and the lawyer to convert the complex? Or suppose, in a similar variation of Case 2, that we are ignorant of why the old white leaders (of the 1980s) instituted the homelands. Does such ignorance make it impossible to evaluate the justice of the economic relations that prevail in southern Africa more than a century later?

This would be quite strange. For the creators of the relevant social arrangements are not directly involved in the production of the harms that are currently inflicted upon tenants and blacks. Their motives thus seem irrelevant to the question of what moral protections these victims should enjoy against the landlord–lawyer team or against the present whites who are upholding the multinational economic regime in southern Africa of 2100.

This consideration shows that it is implausible to close the loopholes by the narrowest revision of E and J, which would cancel the moral efficacy of creating (or joining) a social arrangement if and *only if* this creation was actually motivated by the offending incentive. But if information about why a social arrangement was originally created or joined is irrelevant, then the loopholes we have analyzed show more than one might have thought at first. They indicate not merely that the moralities in question are overly sensitive to certain *changes* that are, and are meant to be, merely cosmetic; but, more generally, that these moralities are overly sensitive to certain merely cosmetic *differences*. The loopholes indicate that E and J overstate not merely the moral efficacy of creating social arrangements, but, more generally, the moral significance of such arrangements themselves.

To clarify this point, let me go through the strengthening move once more in a tax-code context. Suppose a tax code contains the provision that firms whose name begins with a "P" shall be exempt from a certain tax. Assuming that firms can choose to name or rename themselves as they please, and assuming also that no serious purpose is served by bringing the capital-P to social prominence, this exemption constitutes a straightforward loophole; it provides an inherently regrettable ideal reward incentive. This incentive can be eradicated by excluding from the scope of the exemption any firms that deliberately name or rename themselves in order to reduce their tax liability. But, on reflection, this revision seems implausibly narrow: Why should the tax treatment of Pacific Ice-cream (affecting its current owners) hinge on the motives of those who, perhaps quite some time ago, chose this name for the firm? Why should it hinge on any historical facts about its naming? Inherently regrettable ideal incentives may thus indicate the need for a broader revision of the relevant code – one that eradicates the code's sensitivity to the cosmetic *difference*, rather than only the opportunity to exploit this sensitivity through cosmetic *changes*.

Hence my hypothesis: a loophole in a morality supports the conclusion that this morality is sensitive to a merely cosmetic difference. In light of Case 1, we should thus question quite generally why the minimal moral concern tenants are owed should vary with whether their building is managed by a lawyer in the owner's behalf or by the owner himself. And Case 2 should lead us to question quite generally why national borders should make a difference to what standards an economic order must meet as a matter of basic justice.

We can test this hypothesis by examining two argumentative strategies that should work if this hypothesis is correct. In sections 3.8 and 3.9, I try to make plausible that these two strategies do indeed have some appeal, and thereby, I hope, reinforce my hypothesis.

3.8 Fictional histories

Arguments of the first strategy consist of two steps which correspond, respectively, to my initial thesis and the strengthening move. Imagine someone who believes there is nothing wrong with a lawyer's converting her client's apartment complex in his behalf, even though it would be wrong for the landlord to initiate this conversion on his own. The first step in challenging this belief consists in constructing a fictional history of the existing landlord–lawyer relationship which differs from the actual history by taking the creation of this relationship to have been motivated by the desire to exploit precisely the moral differential that our interlocutor is postulating. This fictional history may recount, for example, how the landlord's father had once hired the lawyer in order to make possible a conversion without wrongdoing. Through use of arguments from sections 3.5 and 3.7, we then try to get our interlocutor to concede that an acceptable morality must not encourage that fictional conduct, nor allow it to succeed. That is to say: in the fictional history the hiring of the lawyer fails to enable a conversion without wrongdoing.

To transform this conclusion about a fictional case into a conclusion about the actual case, we must draw upon the strengthening move. The second step consists, then, in challenging the moral relevance of the difference between the actual and the fictional history. Why should the fact that our landlord hired the lawyer from quite harmless motives (perhaps because he wanted to live in another town) entail that he is morally entitled to reap the extra profits at the tenants' expense which he would not be morally entitled to reap in the fictional scenario? And why should this same fact entail that the tenants are not morally entitled to the preservation of their community whereas they would be otherwise? Failing a convincing reply to these questions, we are bound to conclude that the conversion with its actual history is wrong if the conversion with the fictional history is so. Both steps together show that the existence of the lawyer in the actual conversion episode cannot have the moral significance that our interlocutor had ascribed to it.

Here is a parallel expansion of our international justice example. Many are initially inclined to approve of a regime in which each state's citizens are free to elect whatever leaders they prefer and these elected leaders are expected to safeguard and promote the interests of the citizenry and the state, even at quite some cost to foreigners. People tend not to be disturbed by existing extreme international inequalities in bargaining power that engender, and are reinforced by, radical inequalities in rights and powers, in income and wealth, and in access to education and health care. Yet they do find such inequalities unjust when they occur within a single state.

To challenge such a conception of justice, we first construct a fictional history of the present world order which differs from our actual history in that in it the creation of national borders was motivated by a desire to exploit precisely the moral differential that our interlocutors are postulating. About this fictional history we draw the same conclusion as we drew about the South Africa case: national borders so created lack the alleged moral significance. Economic interaction on the basis of extreme inequality is as unjust after their creation as before.

The second step of the challenge consists in the question of how the moral evaluation of the present economic relations between the so-called First and Third Worlds can depend on the motives of those who once transformed colonies into sovereign states. How can the way in which the actual history of our global economic arrangements differs from their fictional history make a moral difference to the claims that today's rich and poor have upon global economic institutions? Why should economic relations on the basis of radical inequality be any more acceptable in our world now than they would be in the hypothetical southern Africa of 2100? Failing convincing replies to these questions, we must conclude that terms of cooperation that, within any state, would count as violating basic justice are also unjust across national borders.

3.9 Puzzles of equivalence

I have suggested that we should avoid inherently regrettable ideal incentives toward creating or joining social arrangements by denying altogether the moral significance of social arrangements in matters of common decency and basic justice. A further test of this proposal is provided by an argumentative strategy that can challenge an approving moral judgment directly – without any reference to actual or fictional incentives. If someone condones a course of conduct or pattern of interaction involving social arrangements, we may challenge this judgment by constructing a parallel scenario that differs from the first only in that it lacks the relevant social arrangement(s). Such a challenge may show that the judgment in question implicitly relies upon the moral significance of a difference that, on reflection, turns out to be merely cosmetic. Through this strategy one can challenge the alleged moral significance of differences even in cases where it would not give rise to inherently regrettable incentives, that is, where it would not be practicable to exploit this significance.

Our landlord case can be recast so that it centers on the moral differential itself, rather than the incentives this differential may generate, by telling a story about two landlords, in similar circumstances, whose apartment complexes get converted at great cost to existing tenants. One of the landlords employs a lawyer, who initiates the conversion in the owner's behalf, while the other landlord is acting on her own. Why should the first conversion – no matter how the lawyer was originally hired – be any less wrong than the second?

Let me give two sample challenges in this vein to moral judgments that it would be virtually impossible to attack in the fictional history mode. Imagine someone who believes that it is ethically permissible, if not obligatory, for a lawyer defending a rapist, whose guilt is not in doubt, to use any and every legal means likely to reduce his client's sentence. Thus it is perfectly alright for him to try to divert the attention of the jury and the general public with various fabrications about the victim's sexual past and preferences which, even if true, would not have the slightest legal relevance. This judgment can be challenged by constructing a parallel scenario without attorneys, in which accuser and defendant present their cases in person. In this scenario, a man, after raping his victim, is now trying to divert the attention of the jury and the general public with various fabrications about the victim's sexual past and preferences which, even if true, would not have the slightest legal relevance. The challenge is: if it is unethical so to slander the victim for the sake of a lighter sentence in one's own behalf, then why should it not be unethical to do so in behalf of another? What is it about the existence of attorney–client teams that supposedly overcomes the ordinary moral claims of rape victims against groundless slander for the sake of a lighter sentence?

The second example concerns an aspect of international relations. Suppose someone believes that it is permissible for the elected President of the American people, acting in the best interests of his constituency, to bring about the deaths of many unarmed civilians in order to reduce dangers and losses to American soldiers. He may, for example, order the aerial bombardment of population centers so as to demoralize the government and armed forces of the enemy and thus to increase the chances for their surrender. This moral judgment can be challenged by constructing a parallel scenario without social arrangements – such as the following. Operating on their own in enemy territory, individual American soldiers cause the deaths of many unarmed civilians in order to reduce their own dangers and losses. For example, they indiscriminately throw hand grenades into civilian homes so as to protect themselves against the possibility of enemy snipers hiding inside.

When comparing these two scenarios, we must assume, of course, that other things are, as far as possible, the same. In particular, both cases are such that the following facts obtain, and are known to obtain by the relevant decision-makers. The US involvement in the war is justifiable. Victory or defeat, with any cosmic consequences either of these might entail, are not at stake. Interspersed among the civilians, there is a small proportion of enemy soldiers, the same in both cases, who get killed as well. Both scenarios produce the same predictable and rather high ratio of their civilians killed to our soldiers saved: there is the same unilaterally imposed correlation of benefits for us and harms deliberately inflicted upon noncombatants. The challenge is, then, to explain why the destruction of civilian targets as ordered by the President in behalf of his constituents should be ethically permissible while a similar destruction of civilian targets by individual soldiers is not. Why should whether Hiroshima civilians may be sacrificed for the sake of American soldiers hinge on whether or not the Americans make this decision individually or through an authorized representative?

3.10 Conclusion

Even if everything I have said thus far were convincing – a rather big "if" – it would compel no substantive moral conclusions. There is, as we have seen, vulnerability to counterclaims. A defender of the moral judgments I have challenged may be able to show that a change or difference I have diagnosed as "merely cosmetic" is morally relevant after all. She may be able to show, for instance, that her morality attributes intrinsic moral value to the creation of certain social arrangements, so that it is morally important after all that lawyers be hired, states be multiplied, and so forth.

Even if the defender can be forced to concede that the change or difference in question really is merely cosmetic, the revision of her morality might still go either way. My challenge may open her eyes to wrongs and injustices suffered by those excluded from the more powerful social arrangements that tie together the rich and mighty. But then it might, instead, also lead her to change her morality in ways that would make their suffering acceptable even in the absence of any social arrangements whatever. Thus she might cease to find wrong even the landlord's direct destruction of his tenants' community for the sake of extra profits. She might now condone apartheid even within a single state. She might come to endorse weaker ethical constraints even upon the investment of one's own money. She might now tolerate the deliberate killing of civilians in war even when this is done by individual soldiers acting on their own. And she might convert to a libertarian conception of economic justice that permits radical inequalities even among compatriots. I hope, of course, that no one will be attracted to such revisions. But I cannot rule them out. The examples show, then, that the incoherences we have diagnosed through the analysis of loopholes can be repaired through quite diverse revisions.

This problem highlights that I have been arguing for a *structural* constraint upon moral conceptions: I am trying to upset received moral convictions not by confronting them with a new set of substantive moral intuitions, but by trying to show how we sometimes structure and organize our moral convictions in a way that tends to obstruct and undermine their practical significance.

The character of such structural defects in a morality is likely to bear some relation to the position of those holding it. For people in the developed West, for example, it is comfortable to believe that – thanks to intervening borders – the moral demands on our relations with people in Latin America, say, are much weaker than even the minimal moral demands on relations with one's compatriots. If this is right, the present chapter may also make a contribution to the explanation of complacency: how can we live so easily with the enormous advantages we enjoy in our political and economic relations with Third World populations?

My main objective, however, was to sketch a way in which we might advance our ordinary and academic moral discourse. Even while there is a good deal of substantive disagreement, it may still be possible to establish some structural constraints that any acceptable (conception of) morality must satisfy. Agreement on such constraints would tend to narrow the existing spectrum of moral debate. It would thereby make a contribution toward moral convergence, which cannot but enhance the practical significance of moral values.

4

Moral Universalism and Global Economic Justice

4.0 Introduction

Socioeconomic rights, such as that "to a standard of living adequate for the health and well-being of oneself and one's family, including food, clothing, housing, and medical care" (*UDHR*, Article 25), are currently, and by far, the most frequently unfulfilled human rights. Their widespread underfulfillment also plays a major role in explaining global deficits in civil and political human rights demanding democracy, due process, and the rule of law. Extremely poor people – often physically and mentally stunted owing to malnutrition in infancy, illiterate owing to lack of schooling, and much preoccupied with their family's survival – can cause little harm or benefit to the politicians

This chapter originally appeared in *Politics, Philosophy, and Economics* 1, 1 (2002): 29–58, and is reproduced with permission by Sage Publications Ltd. It elaborates ideas first formulated in a lecture presented in German at the Catholic University of Eichstätt in February 2000 and published in Karl Graf Ballestrem, ed., *Internationale Gerechtigkeit* (Opladen: Leske und Budrich, 2001). I am very grateful to Dana Tulodziecki for her initial translation into English, to Paula Casal, Keith Horton, David Miller, Ling Tong, and Andrew Williams for extensive and very helpful written comments, and to the Program on Global Security and Sustainability of the John D. and Catherine T. MacArthur Foundation for a generous grant which has supported this work.

and bureaucrats who rule them. Such officials therefore pay much less attention to the interests of the poor than to the interests of agents more capable of reciprocation, including foreign governments, companies, and tourists.

It is not surprising, perhaps, that those who live in protected affluence manage to reconcile themselves, morally, to such severe poverty and oppression. Still, it is interesting to examine how, and how convincingly, they do so. In this regard, earlier generations of European civilization had two noteworthy advantages over ours. First, the advanced industrial societies were then much less affluent in absolute and relative terms.[121] Fifty years ago, the eradication of severe poverty worldwide would have required a major shift in the global income distribution, imposing substantial opportunity costs upon the advanced industrialized societies. Today, the required shift would be small and the opportunity cost for the developed countries barely noticeable.[122] Second, earlier generations of European civilization were not committed to moral universalism. Their rejection of this idea was forcefully expressed, for instance, when the Anglo-Saxon powers blocked Japan's proposal to include language endorsing racial equality in the Covenant of the League of Nations.[123] Today, by contrast, the equal moral status of all human beings is widely accepted in the developed West. These two historical changes make our acquiescence in severe poverty abroad harder to justify than it would have been in the past. Still, we are quite tolerant of the persistence of extensive and severe poverty abroad even though it would not cost us much to reduce it dramatically. How well does this tolerance really fit with our commitment to moral universalism?

4.1 Moral universalism

A moral conception, such as a conception of social justice, can be said to be universalistic if and only if

(A) it subjects all persons to the same system of fundamental moral principles;

(B) these principles assign the same fundamental moral benefits (e.g. claims, liberties, powers, and immunities) and burdens (e.g. duties and liabilities) to all; and

(C) these fundamental moral benefits and burdens are formulated in general terms so as not to privilege or disadvantage certain persons or groups arbitrarily.

I cannot fully explicate these three conditions here, but some brief comments are essential.

Condition A allows a universalistic moral conception to be compatible with moral rules that hold for some people and not for others. But such differences must be generated pursuant to fundamental principles that hold for all. Generated *special* moral benefits and burdens can arise in many ways: from contracts or promises, through election or appointment to an office, from country-specific legislation, from conventions prevalent in a certain culture or region, from committing or suffering a crime, from being especially rich or needy, from producing offspring, from practicing a certain occupation, from having an ill parent, from encountering a drowning child, and so on. Only *fundamental* moral principles, including those pursuant to which special moral benefits and burdens are generated, must be the same for all persons. This condition raises the difficult question of who is to count as a person in the relevant sense: what about the severely mentally disabled, infants, higher animals, artificial or extraterrestrial intelligences?

Condition B raises various problems about how a universalistic moral conception can respond to pragmatic pressures toward allowing the assignment of lesser fundamental moral benefits and burdens to children and to the mentally disabled and perhaps greater fundamental moral burdens to the specially gifted. It is possible that the development of a plausible universalistic moral conception requires that this condition be relaxed somewhat to allow certain departures from equality. Still, equality remains the default – the burden of proof weighs on those favoring specific departures. This suffices to disqualify traditional assignments of unequal fundamental moral benefits and burdens to persons of different sex, skin color, or ancestry.

Moral universalism is clearly incompatible with fundamental principles containing proper names or rigid descriptions of persons or groups. But fundamental principles may legitimately involve other discriminations, as when they enjoin us to respect our parents or to give support to the needy. This distinction between acceptable and unacceptable discriminations cannot be drawn on the basis of formal, grammatical criteria, because it is possible to design gimmicky general descriptions that favor particular persons or groups arbitrarily. Thus, principles meant to discriminate against the Dutch need not refer to them by name, but can refer instead to persons born at especially low elevations or something of this kind – and similarly in other cases. If moral universalism is not to be robbed of all content, we must understand condition C as including the demand that a moral conception must justify the discriminations enshrined in its fundamental principles. An injunction to show special concern for the well-being of the needy can be given a plausible rationale – for instance by reference to the fact that they need help more than others do or that such aid yields larger marginal benefits to its recipients. An injunction to be especially concerned with the well-being of lawyers, by contrast, lacks such a rationale. Why should lawyers, of all people, enjoy special care? Why not also public prosecutors, brokers, dentists?

From this reflection we can see that moral universalism cannot be defined formally. (This is why it makes sense to explicate it through an exemplary application: to the topic of economic justice.) All three conditions raise substantive questions. Who is to count as a person? Can persons differ from one another so much that somewhat different fundamental principles may hold for them? And when is a distinction made by a fundamental principle arbitrary? These are difficult questions that have more than one plausible answer. And even if we could agree on how to answer them, we still would not have achieved moral agreement. From the fact that the rule of helping the needy, for instance, cannot be disqualified as arbitrary, nothing follows about whether this rule is morally valid and, if so, what moral weight it has. Universalism is thus not a moral position with a clearly defined content, but merely an approach – a general schema that can be filled in to yield a variety of substantive moral positions. Universalism can at best provide necessary, not sufficient, conditions for the acceptability of a moral conception. These conditions amount to a call for systematic coherence in morality: the moral assessment of persons and their conduct, of social rules and states of affairs, must be based on fundamental principles that hold for all persons equally; and any discriminations built into such fundamental principles must be given a plausible rationale.

4.2 Our moral assessments of national and global economic orders

Consider two important questions about economic justice:

1 What fundamental moral claims do persons have on the global economic order and what fundamental responsibilities do these claims entail for those who impose it?
2 What fundamental moral claims do persons have on their national economic order and what fundamental responsibilities do these claims entail for those who impose it?

The prevailing opinion is that the correct answers to these questions are very different, that moral claims and burdens are far less substantial in the first case than in the second. But this discrepancy in moral assessment, much like preferential concern for the well-being of lawyers, looks arbitrary. Why should our moral duties, constraining what economic order we may impose upon one another, be so different in the two cases? Let us consider whether this discrepancy stands in need of justification, as moral universalism affirms, and whether such a justification is available.

In discussions of national economic justice it is commonly mentioned that national populations, like families, may understand themselves as solidaristic or fraternal communities bound together by special ties of fellow feeling. Such ties generate special moral claims and burdens, and our responsibilities toward fellow citizens and family members may then greatly exceed, and weaken, our responsibilities toward outsiders.[124] Conceding all this does not, however, invalidate the universalist challenge, but merely gives it a different form, involving more specific versions of our two questions:

1′ What moral constraints are there on the kinds of global economic order persons may impose on others even when they have no bond of solidarity with them and a strong bond of solidarity with a smaller group such as their own nation?
2′ What moral constraints are there on the kinds of national economic order persons may impose on others even when they have no bond of solidarity with them and a strong bond of solidarity with a smaller group such as their own family?

The latter question is not concerned with the more ambitious criteria to which specific societies might choose to subject their national economic order, but with the weaker criterion of justice to which we would subject *any* national economic order, regardless of how the society in question understands itself. This weaker criterion is still much stronger than the criterion we apply to the global economic order. There is, then, a discrepancy between the *minimal* criteria of economic justice we apply on the global and national levels. Moral universalism demands that this discrepancy be given a plausible rationale.

Let us first examine, however, whether such a discrepancy is really widely presumed, as I claim. My impression is that most people in the rich countries think of our global economic order as basically just – although this order does not meet two important minimal requirements we place on any national economic order.

The first minimal requirement is that, at least within the limits of what justice allows, social rules should be liable to peaceful change by any large majority of those on whom they are imposed. The global economic order, though it does stabilize a largely violence-free coordination of actors, nonetheless relies on latent violence in two ways. On the one hand, its stability – like that of any other realistically conceivable economic order – depends on the presence of substantial police forces that prevent and deter rule violations. On the other hand, the design of the global economic order – in contrast to that of a democratically governed state – is determined by a tiny minority of its participants whose oligarchic control of the rules ultimately also rests on a huge preponderance of military power. The crucial asymmetry concerns the latter point: we deem it unjust when a national economic order is coercively imposed by a powerful minority and demand that any large majority of its participants should be able to change its rules without the use of force. But few in the wealthy countries place the same moral requirement on the global economic order – most would dismiss it as ridiculous or absurd.

The second minimal requirement is that avoidable life-threatening poverty must be avoided. Insofar as is reasonably possible, an economic order must be shaped to produce an economic distribution such that its participants can meet their most basic standard needs. In regard to the global economic order, most citizens of the rich countries would reject this requirement as well. We know that billions abroad are exposed to life-threatening poverty. We think that we should perhaps help these people with sporadic donations, just as we should occasionally support the worse-off in our own country. But few of us believe that this extensive and severe poverty, even if avoidable, shows our global economic order to be unjust.

4.3 Some factual background about the global economic order

The moral assessment of an economic order must be responsive to information about three factors: the extent of absolute poverty, how severe and widespread it is; the extent of inequality, which is a rough measure of the avoidability of poverty and of the opportunity cost to the privileged of its avoidance; and the trend of the first two factors, that is, how poverty and inequality tend to develop over time. Let me summarize the state of our world in regard to these three factors.

4.3.1 The extent of world poverty

The World Bank estimates that 1,214 out of 5,820 million human beings were in 1998 living below the international poverty line, which it currently defines in terms of $32.74 PPP 1993 per month or $1.08 PPP 1993 per day.[125] "PPP" stands for "purchasing power parity." So the income per person per year of people at the international poverty line has as much purchasing power as $393 had in the US in 1993. According to the US consumer price index, $393 had as much purchasing power in 1993 as $483 has in 2001 (www.bls.gov/cpi/home.htm). The World Bank's $1/day poverty line corresponds, then, roughly to an income of $483 per person per year.[126] Those living below this poverty line fall, on average, 30 percent below it.[127] So they live on roughly $338 PPP 2001 per person per year on average. Now the $PPP incomes the World Bank ascribes to people in poor countries are on average at least four times higher than their actual incomes at market exchange rates.[128] Since virtually all the global poor live in such poor countries, we can then estimate that their annual *per capita* income of $338 PPP 2001 corresponds to at most $85 at market exchange rates. On average, the global poor can buy about as much per person per year as can be bought with $338 in a typical rich country or with $85 in a typical poor one.

These are the poorest of the poor. The World Bank provides data also for a less scanty poverty line that is twice as high: $786 PPP 1993 ($965 PPP or roughly $241 in the year 2001) per person per year. It counts 2,801 million people as living below this higher poverty line,[129] falling 44.4 percent below it on average.[130] This much larger group of people – nearly half of humankind – can, then, on average buy as much per person per year as can be bought with $537 in a typical rich country or with $134 in a typical poor one.

The consequences of such extreme poverty are foreseeable and extensively documented: 14 percent of the world's population (826 million) are undernourished, 16 percent (968 million) lack access to safe drinking water, 40 percent (2,400 million) lack access to basic sanitation, and 854 million adults are illiterate.[131] Of all human beings 15 percent (more than 880 million) lack access to health services,[132] 17 percent (approximately 1,000 million) have no adequate shelter, and 33 percent (2,000 million) no electricity.[133] "Two out of five children in the developing world are stunted, one in three is underweight and one in ten is wasted."[134] One-quarter of all 5- to 14-year-olds work outside their family for wages, often under harsh conditions, in mining, textile and carpet production, prostitution, factories, and agriculture.[135]

These statistics are depressing enough. Yet, they can plausibly be accused of making things look better than they are. By focusing on human beings *alive at any given time*, all these statistics give less weight to persons whose lives are short. Thus, if the poorest third of humankind live, on average, half as long as the rest (which is approximately true), then they account for fully half of all human lives. To give the same weight to each human life irrespective of its duration, all the above statistics would have to be similarly adjusted for differences in life expectancy. No such adjustment is needed for statistics about births and deaths, as they already give equal weight to every human life. One-third of all human deaths are due to poverty-related causes, such as starvation, diarrhea, pneumonia, tuberculosis, malaria, measles, and perinatal conditions, all of which could be prevented or cured cheaply through food, safe drinking water, vaccinations, rehydration packs, or medicines.[136] If the developed Western countries had their proportional shares of these deaths, severe poverty would kill some 3,500 Britons and 16,500 Americans per week. Each year, 15 times as many US citizens would die of poverty-related causes as were lost in the entire Vietnam War.

The extent of human suffering and premature deaths due to poverty-related causes is not well known in the West. As the media presented retrospectives on the twentieth century, they gave ample space to some of its human-made horrors: 11 million murdered in the German holocaust, 30 million starved to death in Mao's Great Leap Forward, 11 million wiped out by Stalin, 2 million killed by the Khmer Rouge, 800,000 hacked to death in Rwanda. The media also give considerable attention to natural disasters. When there are earthquakes, storms, and floods, we have them on the evening news, with footage of desperate parents grieving for their dead children. Not mentioned in the retrospectives and not shown on the evening news are the ordinary deaths from starvation and preventable diseases – some 250 million people, mostly children, in the 14 years since the end of the Cold War. The names of these people, if listed in the style of the Vietnam War Memorial, would cover a wall 350 miles long.[137]

4.3.2 The extent of global inequality

Severe poverty is nothing new. What is new is the extent of global inequality. Real wealth is no longer limited to a small elite. Hundreds of millions enjoy a high standard of living with plenty of spare time, travel, education, cars, domestic appliances, mobile phones, computers, stereos, and so on. The "high-income economies" (comprising 32 countries plus Hong Kong), with 14.9 percent of world population and 79.7 percent of aggregate global income, have annual *per capita* income of $27,510.[138] For the world as a whole, annual *per capita* income is $5,150.[139] With annual *per capita* income of about $85, the collective income of the bottom quintile is about $103 billion annually, or one-third of 1 percent of aggregate global income. This contrast gives us a sense of how cheaply severe poverty could be avoided: one-eightieth of our share is triple theirs[140] – which should give pause to those who conclude from the very large number of extremely poor people that eradicating world poverty would dramatically impoverish the developed countries.

Global inequality is even greater in regard to property and wealth. Affluent people typically have more wealth than annual income, while the poor normally own significantly less than one annual income. The enormous fortunes of the super-rich in developed societies were given special emphasis in recent *Human Development Reports*: "The world's 200 richest people more than doubled their net worth in the four years to 1998, to more than $1 trillion. The assets of the top three billionaires are more than the combined GNP of all least developed countries and their 600 million people."[141]

4.3.3 Trends in world poverty and inequality

The last 50 years give the impression of rapid progress, punctuated by a long series of human-rights declarations and treaties, new initiatives, summits, as well as detailed research into the quantification, causes, and effects of poverty. Such things are not unimportant. But they disguise the fact that real progress for the poor themselves is less impressive. Yes, life expectancy has risen markedly in many countries and infant mortality has fallen substantially owing to better disease control. But the number of people in poverty has not declined since 1987[142] – despite the fact that this period has seen exceptional technological and economic progress as well as a dramatic decline in defense expenditures.[143] Since 1996, when 186 governments made the very modest commitment to halve the number of undernourished people within 19 years, this number has barely changed – despite a 22 percent drop in the real wholesale prices of basic foodstuffs.[144] These trends are all the more disturbing as the ranks of the poor and undernourished are continuously thinned by some 50,000 premature deaths daily from poverty-related causes.

While poverty and malnutrition are stagnant, global inequality, and hence the avoidability of poverty, is escalating dramatically: "The income gap between the fifth of the world's people living in the richest countries and the fifth in the poorest was 74 to 1 in 1997, up from 60 to 1 in 1990 and 30 to 1 in 1960. [Earlier] the income gap between the top and bottom countries increased from 3 to 1 in 1820 to 7 to 1 in 1870 to 11 to 1 in 1913."[145] There is a long-established trend toward ever greater international income inequality – a trend that has certainly not decelerated since the end of the colonial era 40 years ago.[146]

So much by way of data about the world economy which is deemed tolerably just here in the developed countries.

4.4 Conceptions of national and global economic justice contrasted

Let us compare this case to that of a national society in which the various economic parameters we have considered resemble those of the world at large. No national society displays anything like the current degree of global income inequality, but because Brazil has one of the highest quintile income inequality ratios (24.4),[147] and because its PPP gross national income *per capita* is close to that of the world at large,[148] we might call our fictional country Subbrazil. The point of the contrast is to pose this challenge: if we consider Subbrazil's economic order unjust, how can we find the global economic order morally acceptable?

One may object here that the economic order of Subbrazil is not really unjust. It appears unjust to us because we imagine that most of its citizens, like most citizens of European countries, conceive of their society as being, at least in some weak sense, a solidaristic community. Subbrazil's failure to meet even weak solidaristic standards constitutes no injustice, however, because most Subbrazilians do not want their national economic order to meet such a standard. If they desired otherwise, a majority of Subbrazilians could reform their economic order through the ballot box.

This objection could be contested by asserting that we do not accept as just a national economic order that avoidably produces life-threatening poverty for a sizable minority merely because this economic order is approved by the majority. But even if we accept the objection despite this worry, the challenge is not yet dissolved. The objection assumes that the Subbrazilian economy meets at least the first minimal requirement. It assumes that, if some large majority of

Subbrazilians wanted to reform their national economic order so as to reduce life-threatening poverty, they could bring about such reforms. I can thus circumvent the objection by weakening my claim. Instead of claiming that we would condemn as unjust any national economic order that does not meet *both* minimal requirements, I claim instead that we would condemn as unjust any national economic order that does not meet at least *one* of them.

Let us imagine, then, a fictive Sub-Subbrazil: a society whose economic order avoidably produces life-threatening poverty for a sizable minority and is also not subject to peaceful change from below, even by a large majority.[149] Such an economic order would be condemned as unjust by most people in the developed countries. (What is to count as an unjust national economic order, if not this?) And we arrive then at this reformulated challenge: if we condemn as unjust the imposition of the national economic order of Sub-Subbrazil, how can we condone the imposition, by governments acting in our name, of the existing global economic order? The latter order is, after all, like the former in the extent of poverty and inequality it produces and also in that even a large majority of those on whom it is imposed – the poorest four-fifths of humankind, for instance – cannot reform it by peaceful means. How can the flagrant discrepancy between our minimal criteria of national and global economic justice be justified?

As here explicated, moral universalism demands such a justification. In the face of this demand, we have three options. First, we can evade the demand by surrendering the discrepancy: by strengthening the minimal criterion we apply to the global economic order and/or by weakening the minimal criterion we apply to any national economic order (perhaps even reversing our opinion that Sub-Subbrazil's economic order is unjust). Second, we can try to meet the demand by defending a discrepancy of minimal criteria – by justifying the view that our global economic order may not be unjust even if it fails to meet the minimal criterion of justice we apply to any national economic order. Third, we can insist on a discrepancy of minimal criteria while rejecting the universalist demand to justify this discrepancy.

Responses of the first two kinds accept the universalist challenge and are willing to engage in the debate about minimal criteria of national and global economic justice. The third response declines to join this debate with the tripartite claim that national economic regimes are subject to some minimal criterion of justice, that the global economic order is not subject to this criterion, and that no justification can or need be given for this discrepancy. Section 4.5 focuses on this third, most antagonistic response.

4.5 Moral universalism and David Miller's contextualism

The third response can point to existing moral intuitions or convictions. Our discrepant criteria of national and global economic justice are fixed points that any philosophical account of our morality must reaffirm. An account that does not vindicate our deepest convictions must be rejected for this reason alone. We are deeply convinced that we do not share responsibility for starvation abroad. This conviction, which we are more sure of than we could ever be of the merits of any complex philosophical argument, refutes any moral conception that concludes otherwise. To be sure, our discrepant standards of economic justice may seem incoherent. But the moral data (our intuitions or deepest convictions) are what they are, and coherence, in any case, is in the eye of the beholder.

In this simple version, the third response is hard to swallow. The view that moral reflection exhausts itself in compiling our favorite convictions, that what we firmly enough believe to be right is right, trivializes the ambition of leading a moral life. But perhaps the third response can be made more palatable by presenting it as including a justification for its rejection of the universalist demand for justification. David Miller may appear to develop such a more sophisticated position, arguing for the anti-universalist claim that we should allow diverse moral principles to hold in different contexts without demanding any justification for such diversity.[150] I try to show that this appearance is misleading, that Miller's contextualism overlaps with moral universalism, and that moral conceptions within this overlap seem more promising than moral conceptions exemplifying more extreme variants of either universalism or contextualism. Let me add that I am here setting aside Miller's interesting and important work on national and international justice,[151] attending solely to his more general account of contextualism.

Miller may appear to embrace the general statement of the anti-universalist response when he associates the contextualism he favors – "a species of intuitionism in Rawls's sense"[152] – with bald, conversation-stopping pronouncements of the form "equality is simply the appropriate principle to use in circumstances C."[153] He also argues against the demand for justification: attempts to construct a unified account of all of morality cannot achieve "a reasonably close fit between the theory and our pre-theoretical considered judgements."[154] Such attempts, he believes, lead to the proliferation of neat but implausible moral theories whose disagreements raise questions we cannot convincingly resolve and therefore foster a skeptical attitude toward morality which sets back efforts toward achieving moral progress on concrete and urgent practical problems.

I respect and share these concerns. But it is not clear that anti-universalism can do any better. Those who walk out of specific moral discussions with an emphatic declaration that C_1 and C_2 simply *are* different contexts to which different principles P_1 and P_2 are appropriate will fail to convince, and quite possibly seem offensive to, those who believe otherwise – even if they also argue in general terms that morality is too heterogeneous to yield to the universalist demand for justifications. (Think of those who, in accord with the convictions of their time, emphatically declared that moral principles appropriate to one social class simply *are* inappropriate to another.) By declining to give any specific reasons for delimiting the various contexts, and for assigning the various moral principles to them, in the way they do, such people will moreover foster a cynical attitude toward moral theorizing as the bare assertion of favorite convictions, invariably distorted by the asserter's interests, social position, and prejudices.

Miller is sensitive to these countervailing concerns when – setting his contextualism apart from conventionalism – he writes: "Contextualism . . . recognizes that we are likely to find different principles of justice being used at different times and in different places, but it argues that this variation itself has an underlying logic that we can both grasp and use as a critical tool when assessing the prevailing conceptions of justice at any particular moment."[155] This remark shows, I believe, that Miller rejects the third response by recognizing that morality is subject to an underlying transcontextual logic which may, on the one hand, provide a rationale for applying different moral principles in different contexts (e.g. under different natural, historical, cultural, technological, economic, or demographic conditions) and may also, on the other hand, serve as a basis for criticizing prevailing moral conceptions. Once we can, by appeal to such an underlying logic, formulate justifying reasons for or against the application of different moral standards to persons from different social classes, and for or against the differential assessment of national and global economic regimes, we have moved beyond *dogmatic* contextualism and the unsupported endorsements or rejections it takes to be appropriate responses to moral disagreement.

Insofar as contextualism endorses a justificatory discourse about the delimitation of contexts and the variation of principles across them – and other work by Miller (see n. 151) contains plenty of argument in this vein – it overlaps with moral universalism. As explicated here, universalism does not require that, if moral principles P_1,

P_2, P_3 are to apply in contexts C_1, C_2, C_3, respectively, then there must be one supreme "transcendent" principle or set of principles of which P_1, P_2, P_3 are contextual applications (as "drive no faster than 30 miles per hour" is a contextual application of "move no faster than is both safe and legal"). To be sure, moral universalism *permits* such highly unified anti-contextualist moral conceptions, as exemplified by utilitarianism. But it *also* permits the *critical* contextualist alternative suggested in the last-quoted sentence from Miller: a moral conception holding that fundamental principles P_1, P_2, P_3 apply in contexts C_1, C_2, C_3, respectively, and offering a justification for delimiting the various contexts, and for assigning the various moral principles to them, in these ways.

I find this contextualist moral universalism far more plausible than its anti-contextualist (monistic) alternative. Regarding our general view of moral theorizing, Miller and I may converge then upon an intermediate view – critical contextualism – defined by the rejection of monistic universalism on the one hand and dogmatic contextualism on the other. We both envision different fundamental moral principles applying in different contexts, and we both seek justifications for the delimitation of contexts and the formulation of fundamental principles appropriate to them. We differ in regard to what delimitations, context-specific principles, and justifications we find acceptable.

Because the proposed intermediate view of moral theorizing is unfamiliar, I develop it somewhat further through a discussion of Rawls's work, which provides both an illustration and a violation of the contextualist moral universalism I favor.

4.6 Contextualist moral universalism and John Rawls's moral conception

Rawls wants to confine his theory of justice to a specific context: to the basic structure of a self-contained society existing under the circumstances of justice. His theory commits him to certain moral demands on the political conduct of citizens – they must support and promote a just basic structure. But Rawls wants to leave open what moral principles may apply to their personal conduct. He has been attacked for this aloofness by monistic universalists, such as Gerald Cohen and Liam Murphy.[156] According to them, any fundamental moral principle that applies to social institutions must also apply to personal conduct. Thus, if the difference principle requires that a society's economic order should erase any socioeconomic inequality that does not optimize the lowest socioeconomic position, then individuals must also be required, in their personal conduct, to erase any socioeconomic inequality that does not optimize the lowest socioeconomic position.[157]

Rawls's contextualism can be defended against this critique. Rawls has important reasons for limiting the range of his principles of justice to the basic structure. These reasons – invoking *inter alia* the fact of pluralism as well as the need to avoid overdemandingness and to achieve stability (compliance) – show that basic social institutions should be treated as a separate context to which distinct moral principles apply.[158] These reasons illustrate how limiting the range of moral principles can be justified without the invocation of any deeper, transcontextual principles from which context-specific principles are then derived. The case at hand thus shows how it is possible to justify moral principles as range-limited or context-specific even while also maintaining that they are fundamental. Insofar as the justification for the Rawlsian range limit satisfies the three conditions of moral universalism, his account of the justice of basic social institutions is an instance not merely of critical contextualism, but also, and more specifically, of contextualist moral universalism.

Whereas this Rawlsian separation of contexts instantiates contextualist moral universalism, another separation of contexts, central to his latest work, instantiates its violation. Rawls insists there on applying quite different fundamental principles to national and international institutional schemes, but fails to give an adequate justification for the separation of contexts. This failure occurs on three distinct levels.

First, Rawls strongly rejects the difference principle as a requirement of global justice on the ground that it is unacceptable for one people to bear certain costs of decisions made by another – decisions affecting industrialization or the birth rate, for example.[159] But he fails to explain why this ground should not analogously disqualify the difference principle for national societies as well. Why is it not likewise unacceptable for one province, township, or family to bear such costs of decisions made by another?[160] And if, despite such sharing of costs, the difference principle is the most reasonable one for us to advocate in regard to the domestic economic order, then why is it not also the most reasonable one for us to advocate in regard to the global economic order? Rawls provides no answer.

Rawls also fails to explain how his rejection of the difference principle for the global order accords with his argument in *A Theory of Justice*, which he continues to endorse. There Rawls discusses how a human population of indeterminate size and explicitly conceived as "self-contained" and "a closed system"[161] should institutionally organize itself. His inquiry leads to the difference principle as a requirement of economic justice. He takes this principle to be acceptable – indeed ideal – for the US, even though this society diverges from the task description by not being a self-contained closed system. So why should the difference principle be unacceptable for the world at large, which fits the task description precisely? There is, again, no answer in Rawls.

It might be objected that this unjustified discrepancy is not important. Perhaps Rawls should concede that a global economic order designed to satisfy the difference principle is not, as such, unacceptable. But the goal of such an order is nonetheless morally inappropriate to our world, because many people oppose the difference principle and not unreasonably so.

Against this objection, one needs to point out that such opposition exists at home as well as abroad. Increasingly sensitive to this fact, Rawls continues to propose the difference principle, which he had associated with the ideal of fraternity,[162] as the most reasonable one for the domestic economic order of modern liberal societies including, first and foremost, the US. But he allows that other societies may reasonably subject their national economic regimes to other criteria. And he is even willing to concede that his difference principle is not uniquely reasonable even for the US: his fellow citizens would not be unreasonable if they gave their political support to some other liberal criterion of economic justice.[163] At least according to Rawls's later work, then, a society that deliberately fails to satisfy the difference principle may nonetheless not be unjust. Rather, to count as just (or not-unjust), a national society need merely endorse and (approximately) satisfy *some* not-unreasonable liberal standard of economic justice.

Now if this, rather than the difference principle, is Rawls's minimal criterion of national economic justice, it defines a second level on which the challenge from moral universalism arises: Rawls should either hold that a global order, too, can count as just only if it satisfies this minimal criterion of economic justice or else justify his failure to do so.

Rawls does neither; but he suggests that one reason against applying liberal standards globally is the need to accommodate certain – "decent" – non-liberal societies. (Decent societies are ones to which, Rawls believes, liberal societies should offer reciprocal recognition as full and equal members in good standing within a well-ordered system of states.) This is a strange suggestion because, in our world, nonliberal societies and their populations tend to be poor and quite willing to cooperate in reforms that would bring the global economic order closer to meeting a liberal standard of economic justice. The much more affluent liberal societies are the ones blocking such reforms, and it is not clear how their obstruction can be justified by the concern to accommodate decent societies. Granted, these reforms are not required by decency, decent societies thus could oppose them, and liberal societies might then have reason to accommodate such opposition. But when there exists no decent society actually opposing the reforms, then the concern to accommodate decent societies cannot be a reason for liberal societies to block them contrary to the minimal criterion, and hence to every more specific criterion, of liberal economic justice.

Suppose that the foregoing argument fails or that there are some decent societies opposed to economic reform. If so, the challenge of moral universalism arises one last time on a yet lower level: Rawls should either disqualify as less-than-decent any global economic order that does not meet whatever requirements any national economic order must meet to count as decent or else justify his refusal to do so.

But again, it seems that Rawls wants to insist on an unjustified double standard. He writes that a decent society's "system of law must follow a common good idea of justice that takes into account what it sees as the fundamental interests of everyone in society."[164] Rawls is quite vague on what constraints he takes this condition to place on the national economic order of a decent society. But he does not require the global economic order to meet even these weaker constraints of decency. All he asks is that no peoples should have to live "under unfavorable conditions that prevent their having a just or decent political and social regime."[165] And even this demand does not constrain global economic institutions, but only the conduct of other peoples. We may impose a global economic order that generates strong centrifugal tendencies and ever increasing international inequality, provided we "assist" the societies impoverished by this order just enough to keep them above some basic threshold.[166]

Despite considerable vagueness in his treatment of economic institutions, it seems clear, then, that Rawls endorses double standards on three different levels: in regard to national economic regimes, the difference principle is part of Rawls's highest aspiration for justice; in regard to the global economic order, however, Rawls disavows this aspiration and even rejects the difference principle as unacceptable. Rawls suggests a weaker minimal criterion of liberal economic justice on the national level; but he holds that the global order can fully accord with liberal conceptions of justice without satisfying this criterion. And Rawls suggests an even weaker criterion of economic decency on the national level; but he holds that the global order can be not merely decent, but even just, without satisfying this criterion. Insofar as he offers no plausible rationales for these three double standards, Rawls runs afoul of moral universalism. He fails to meet the burden of showing that his applying different moral principles to national and global institutional schemes does not amount to arbitrary discrimination in favor of affluent societies and against the global poor.

4.7 Rationalizing divergent moral assessments through a double standard

Most citizens of the developed countries reconcile themselves to massive and avoidable poverty abroad by not holding such poverty against the global economic order as they would hold similar poverty within a national society against its domestic economic order. The common and obvious way of rationalizing such a divergence is through a double standard: by subjecting the global economic order to weaker moral demands than any national economic order. Such double standards are widely employed in ordinary and academic discourse. They are often dogmatically taken for granted, perhaps with a general appeal to "our moral convictions" or a general argument for dogmatic contextualism. This is the "third response" to moral universalism, discussed in section 4.5.

Rawls seems willing to defend a double standard in regard to national and global economic justice and thus exemplifies the second response to the universalist challenge. But the defenses he actually provides are incomplete, because he does not face up to the comparative nature of the task. It is not enough, for instance, to provide arguments against a global application of the difference principle. One must also show that these arguments create the desired asymmetry, that they have more weight than analogous arguments against a national application of the difference principle. Rawls does not even begin to do this.

His failure is typical of academic and popular rationalizations of double standards of economic justice. There are reasons for, and reasons against, a strong criterion of economic justice. Discussions of the national economic order tend to highlight the reasons for, discussions of the global order tend to highlight the reasons against. But to justify the desired asymmetry, one must discuss the relevant reasons of both kinds in respect to both contexts. In particular, one must show that some reasons for a strong criterion have more weight in the balance of reasons concerning national than they have in the balance of reasons concerning global economic justice – and/or, conversely, that some reasons for a weak criterion have less weight in the balance of reasons concerning national than they have in the balance of reasons concerning global economic justice.

Arguments for a weak criterion of economic justice typically appeal to cultural diversity or to the autonomy of, or special ties within, smaller groups. Such arguments are often used to justify acquiescence in a global economic order that engenders great poverty and inequality. But all three factors exist within nations as well. And they can then be useful in the defense of a double standard only if one can show them to be significantly less relevant domestically. As we have seen, showing this is not so easy.[167]

In a sense this is a modest result. Many different double standards could be formulated with regard to our topic, and various rationales might be offered for each such formulation. No one can anticipate and refute all conceivable such accounts. But this very impossibility of showing conclusively that no sufficiently large discrepancy of standards can be justified provides a subsidiary reason for what I have presented as an essential element of moral universalism: the assignment of the burden of proof to those who *favor* a double standard. They can bear this burden, as they need only make good on an existential quantifier by formulating *one* version of the desired double standard and then giving a plausible rationale for it. And yet, the *moral* reason remains primary: we owe the global poor an account of why we take ourselves to be entitled to impose on them a global economic order in violation of the minimal moral constraints we ourselves place on the imposition of any national economic order.

If the burden of proof indeed weighs on those favoring a double standard, then the result of my discussion is not so modest after all. We, the affluent countries and their citizens, continue to impose a global economic order under which millions avoidably die each year from poverty-related causes. We would regard it as a grave injustice if such an economic order were imposed within a national society. We must regard our imposition of the present global order as a grave injustice unless we have a plausible rationale for a suitable double standard. We do not have such a plausible rationale.

4.8 Rationalizing divergent moral assessments without a double standard

There is another way of rationalizing the failure of the affluent to hold massive and avoidable poverty abroad against the global economic order as they would hold similar poverty within a national society against its domestic economic order. The next four paragraphs give a summary statement of this rationalization, which invokes the idea of institutional responsibility.

We tend to recoil from an institutional order described as one that is imposed upon people of whom many avoidably are very poor. But let us not be fooled by mere rhetoric. An economic order under which there is a lot of avoidable love sickness is not, for this reason, morally flawed. This example drives home that the moral quality of an institutional order under which avoidable starvation occurs depends on whether and how that order is causally related to this starvation. It depends, that is, on the extent to which starvation could be avoided through institutional modification. And it also depends on the manner in which the institutional order in question engenders more starvation than its best feasible alternative would. Does it, for example, require serfs to do unremunerated work for aristocrats or does it merely fail to tax the more productive participants enough to underwrite an adequate welfare system?

This insight is relevant to our topic. We have been discussing the moral assessment of two kinds of economic order (national and global) that, in the real world, differ greatly in their causal impact. The global economic order plays a marginal role in the perpetuation of extensive and severe poverty worldwide. This poverty is substantially caused not by global, systemic factors, but – in the countries where it occurs – by their flawed national economic regimes and by their corrupt and incompetent elites, both of which impede national economic growth and a fairer distribution of the national product. Such domestic defects are the main reason why these countries become ever poorer in relative and often even in absolute terms and why the burdens of this impoverishment fall upon their poorest citizens most heavily.[168] Excessive poverty and inequality within countries, by contrast, are to a considerable extent traceable to systemic factors and are then, causally and morally, the responsibility of the politically and economically influential elites who uphold the relevant national economic regimes.

We do indeed judge our global economic order, under which a great deal of poverty and inequality persists, less harshly than we would a national economic order associated with similar poverty and inequality data. But these discrepant assessments do not reflect a double standard concerning the significance of extreme poverty and inequality in the moral assessment of global and national regimes. Rather, they reflect a single standard uniformly applied to both kinds of regime, yet a standard that is sensitive not merely to the incidence of avoidable poverty but also to the regime's causal role in its occurrence.

The reconciling force of this empirical rationalization depends on complex economic causalities, on the correct explanation of persisting severe poverty worldwide and of the expansion of global inequality. We must convince ourselves that the global economic order is not a significant causal contributor to these phenomena. Many citizens of the affluent countries are convinced of this, and convinced even that the global economic order could not be modified into a significant causal contributor to the eradication of extreme poverty and inequality. These people believe that, for such progress to occur, the poor countries themselves must get their house in order, must give themselves governments and political institutions that are more responsive to the needs of their populations. With respect to this task, outsiders can help only to a very limited extent. This is so because it would be morally unacceptable to impose what we think of as reasonable leaders or social institutions upon such countries and also because any resolute interference in the internal affairs of poor countries could easily turn out to be counterproductive as corrupt rulers manage further to entrench their rule by denouncing our supposed imperialism or neocolonialism. Sad as it is, our hands are tied. We can try to alleviate world poverty through development assistance, given *ad hoc* by affluent societies and individuals or built into the global order as in the Tobin Tax proposal. But such attempts will not succeed well because we cannot prevent the corrupt elites from siphoning off much of our aid into their own pockets. Perhaps 1.21 percent of our incomes would indeed suffice to raise all the incomes of all human beings to the World Bank's higher poverty line (see n. 122). But, as things stand, there is unfortunately no way of getting such a donation to the world's poorest people in a concentrated way.

Responding to this empirical rationalization, I do not deny the analysis sketched in the preceding paragraph. The eradication of poverty in the poor countries indeed depends strongly on their governments and social institutions: on how their economies are structured and on whether there exists genuine democratic competition for political office which gives politicians an incentive to be responsive to the interests of the poor majority. But this analysis is nevertheless ultimately unsatisfactory, because it portrays the corrupt social institutions and corrupt elites prevalent in the poor countries as an exogenous fact: as a fact that explains, but does not itself stand in need of explanation. "Some poor countries manage to give themselves reasonable political institutions, but many others fail or do not even try. This is just the way things are." An explanation that runs out at this point does not explain very much. An adequate explanation of persistent global poverty must not merely adduce the prevalence of flawed social institutions and of corrupt, oppressive, incompetent elites in the poor countries but must also provide an explanation for this prevalence.

Social scientists do indeed provide deeper explanations responsive to this need. These are, for the most part, "nationalist" explanations which trace flaws in a country's political and economic institutions and the corruption and incompetence of its ruling elite back to this country's history, culture, or natural environment.[169] Because there are substantial differences in how countries, and the incidence of poverty within them, develop over time, it is clear that such nationalist explanations must play a role in explaining national trajectories and international differentials. From this it does not follow, however, that the global economic order does not also play a substantial causal role by shaping how the culture of each poor country evolves and by influencing how a poor country's history, culture, and natural environment affect the development of its domestic institutional order, ruling elite, economic growth, and income distribution. In these ways global institutional factors might contribute substantially to the persistence of severe poverty in particular countries and in the world at large. Section 4.9 shows that this is indeed the case, contrary to the central claim of the empirical rationalization.

4.9 The causal role of global institutions in the persistence of severe poverty

My case can be made by example, and I focus on two highly significant aspects of the existing global order.[170] Any group controlling a preponderance of the means of coercion within a country is internationally recognized as the legitimate government of this country's territory and people – regardless of how this group came to power, of how it exercises power, and of the extent to which it may be supported or opposed by the population it rules.[171] That such a group exercising effective power receives international recognition means not merely that we engage it in negotiations. It means also that we accept this group's right to act for the people it rules and, in particular, confer upon it the privileges freely to borrow in the country's name (international borrowing privilege) and freely to dispose of the country's natural resources (international resource privilege).

The resource privilege we confer upon a group in power is much more than our acquiescence in its effective control over the natural resources of the country in question. This privilege includes the power[172] to effect legally valid transfers of ownership rights in such resources. Thus a corporation that has purchased resources from the Saudis or Suharto, or from Mobuto or Abacha, has thereby become entitled to be – and actually *is* – recognized anywhere in the world as the legitimate owner of these resources. This is a remarkable feature of our global institutional order. A group that overpowers the guards and takes control of a warehouse may be able to give some of the merchandise to others, accepting money in exchange. But the fence who pays them becomes merely the possessor, not the owner, of the loot. Contrast this with a group that overpowers an elected government and takes control of a country. Such a group, too, can give away some of the country's natural resources, accepting money in exchange. In this case, however, the purchaser acquires not merely possession, but all the rights and liberties of ownership, which are supposed to be – and actually *are* – protected and enforced by all other states' courts and police forces. The international resource privilege, then, is the legal power to confer globally valid ownership rights in the country's resources.

Indifferent to how governmental power is acquired, the international resource privilege provides powerful incentives toward coup attempts and civil wars in the resource-rich countries. Consider Nigeria, for instance, where oil exports of $6–10 billion annually constitute roughly a quarter of GDP. Whoever takes power there, by whatever means, can count on this revenue stream to enrich himself and to cement his rule. This is quite a temptation for military officers, and during 28 of the past 32 years Nigeria has indeed been ruled by military strongmen who took power and ruled by force. Able to buy means of repression abroad and support from other officers at home, such rulers were not dependent on popular support and thus made few productive investments toward stimulating poverty eradication or even economic growth.[173]

After the sudden death of Sani Abacha, Nigeria is now ruled by a civilian ex-general, Olusegun Obasanjo, who – a prominent member of the Advisory Council of Transparency International (TI; see n. 243) – raised great expectations for reform. These expectations have been disappointed: Nigeria continues to be listed near the bottom of TI's own international corruption chart.[174] This failure has evoked surprise. But it makes sense against the background of the international resource privilege: Nigeria's military officers know well that they can capture the oil revenues by overthrowing Obasanjo. To survive in power, he must therefore keep them content enough with the status quo so that the potential gains from a coup attempt do not seem worth the risk of failure. Corruption in Nigeria is not just a local phenomenon rooted in tribal culture and traditions, but encouraged and sustained by the international resource privilege.

Nigeria is just one instance of a broader pattern also exemplified by the Congo/Zaire, Kenya, Angola, Mozambique, Brazil, Venezuela, the Philippines, Burma/Myanmar, the oil states of the Middle East, and many smaller resource-rich but poverty-stricken countries.[175] In fact, there is a significant negative correlation, known as the Dutch Disease, between the size of countries' resource sectors and their rates of economic growth. This correlation has a "nationalist" explanation: national resource abundance causes bad government and flawed institutions by encouraging coups and civil wars and by facilitating authoritarian entrenchment and corruption.[176] But this nationalist explanation crucially depends on a global background factor, the international resource privilege, without which a poor country's generous resource endowment would not handicap its progress toward democratic government, economic growth, and the eradication of poverty – certainly not to the same extent.[177]

Similar points can be made about the international borrowing privilege, according to which any group holding governmental power in a national territory – no matter how it acquired or exercises this power – is entitled to borrow funds in the name of the whole society, thereby imposing internationally valid legal obligations upon the country at large. Any successor government that refuses to honor debts incurred by an ever so corrupt, brutal, undemocratic, unconstitutional, repressive, unpopular predecessor will be severely punished by the banks and governments of other countries; at minimum it will lose its own borrowing privilege by being excluded from the international financial markets. Such refusals are therefore quite rare, as governments, even when newly elected after a dramatic break with the past, are compelled to pay the debts of their ever so awful predecessors.

The international borrowing privilege has three important negative effects on the corruption and poverty problems in the poor countries. First, it puts a country's full credit at the disposal of even the most loathsome rulers who took power in a coup and maintain it through violence and repression. Such rulers can then borrow more money and can do so more cheaply than they could do if they alone, rather than the entire country, were obliged to repay. In this way, the international borrowing privilege helps such rulers to maintain themselves in power even against near-universal popular opposition. Second, indifferent to how governmental power is acquired, the international borrowing privilege strengthens incentives toward coup attempts and civil war: whoever succeeds in bringing a preponderance of the means of coercion under his control gets the borrowing privilege as an additional reward. Third, when the yoke of dictatorship can be thrown off, the international borrowing privilege saddles the country with the often huge debts of the former oppressors. It thereby saps the capacity of its fledgling democratic government to implement structural reforms and other political programs, thus rendering it less successful and less stable than it would otherwise be.[178] (It is small consolation that putschists are sometimes weakened by being held liable for the debts of their elected predecessors.)

I have shown how two aspects of the global economic order, imposed by the wealthy societies and cherished also by authoritarian rulers and corrupt elites in the poorer countries, contribute substantially to the persistence of severe poverty. The two privileges crucially affect what sorts of persons jostle for political power and then shape national policy in the poor countries, what incentives these persons face, what options they have, and what impact these options would have on the lives of their compatriots. These global factors thereby strongly affect the overall incidence of oppression and poverty and also, through their greater impact on resource-rich countries, international differentials in oppression and poverty.

This result is not altered by the fact that reforms of the two privileges are not easy to devise and might well, by raising the prices of natural resources, prove quite costly for the affluent consumer societies and for other states dependent on resource imports. I am arguing that the citizens and governments of the wealthy societies, by imposing the present global economic order, significantly contribute to the persistence of severe poverty and thus share institutional moral responsibility for it. I am not yet discussing what we should do about persistent global poverty in light of our moral responsibility for it.[179]

It is easier to disconnect oneself from extensive and severe poverty suffered by wholly innocent people abroad when there are others who clearly are to blame for it. My argument in this section was therefore focused specifically on how the national causal factors we most like to highlight – tyranny, corruption, coups d'état, civil wars – are encouraged and sustained by central aspects of the present global economic order. The argument shows that, those national causal factors notwithstanding, we share causal and moral responsibility. This insight should not lessen the moral responsibility we assign to dictators, warlords, corrupt officials, and cruel employers in the poor countries any more than our initial insight into their moral responsibility should lessen the moral responsibility we assign to ourselves.

The focus of my argument should also not obscure the other ways in which the present global economic order contributes to the persistence of poverty. By greatly increasing international interdependence, this order exacerbates the vulnerability of the weaker national economies to exogenous shocks through decisions and policies made – without input from or concern for the poorer societies – in the US or EU (e.g. interest rates set by the US and EU central banks, speculation-induced moves on commodity and currency markets). Moreover, the components of this global economic order emerge through highly complex intergovernmental negotiations in which the governments and negotiators of the developed countries enjoy a crushing advantage in bargaining power and expertise. Agreements resulting from such negotiations therefore reflect the interests of these rich countries' governments, corporations, and populations – regardless of whether the relevant representatives of the developing countries are corrupt or are selflessly devoted to poverty eradication. And agreements that are good for the rich countries may not be good for the global poor, as is amply demonstrated in the report on the Uruguay Round discussed in section IV of the General Introduction.

4.10 Conclusion

Section 4.9 has shown what is obvious to people in the poor, marginal countries: that the rules structuring the world economy have a profound impact on the global economic distribution just as the economic order of a national society has a profound impact on its domestic economic distribution. The empirical rationalization is not empirically sustainable.

Spreading awareness of its unsustainability could turn out to be of great practical importance in reshaping both the explanatory and the moral debates about world poverty. As it is, the explanatory debate is largely focused on nationalist explanations: on the question of what national economic institutions and policies in poor countries hamper or promote the eradication of domestic poverty. Some argue for free markets with a minimum in taxes and governmental regulations (the

Asian tigers model), others for increased governmental investment in education, medical care, and infrastructure (the Kerala model). This debate is certainly important. But it would also be quite important to examine what *global* economic institutions hamper or promote the eradication of poverty worldwide. Modest such inquiries are familiar: economists and politicians debate alternative structures and missions for the IMF and the World Bank and the international impact of the 1995 Trade-Related Aspects of Intellectual Property Rights (TRIPS) agreement reached within the WTO. But with respect to larger issues, such as the international resource and borrowing privileges and the political mechanisms through which the rules of the world economy are created and revised, the status quo is largely taken for granted as a given background much like the basic natural features of our planet.

As it is, the moral debate is largely focused on the extent to which affluent societies and persons have obligations to help others worse off than themselves. Some deny all such obligations, others claim them to be quite demanding. Both sides easily take for granted that it is as potential helpers that we are morally related to the starving abroad.[180] This is true, of course. But the debate ignores that we are also and more significantly related to them as supporters of, and beneficiaries from, a global institutional order that substantially contributes to their destitution.

If the empirical rationalization fails, if national and global economic regimes are comparable in their workings and impact, then we are after all employing a double standard when we count avoidable extremes of poverty and inequality against national economic regimes only. And we do then face moral universalism's challenge to our easy acceptance of extensive, severe poverty abroad. Without a plausible rationale, our discrepant assessments constitute covert arbitrary discrimination in favor of the wealthy societies and against the global poor.

5

The Bounds of Nationalism

5.0 Introduction

Nationalism is generally associated with sentiments, ideologies, and social movements that involve strong commitments to a nation, conceived as a potentially self-sustaining community of persons bound together by a shared history and culture. Recent empirical and normative discussions have been concentrated on revisionist instances of nationalism, that is, on sentiments, ideologies, and social movements that aim to gain power, political autonomy, or territory for a particular nation. I take a somewhat broader view of nationalism, focusing on persons who have an ordinary patriotic commitment to their own country. Quite content with the status quo, these persons view it as legitimate and even admirable that they and their political leaders

Many thanks to Dagfinn Føllesdal for the kind invitation to join him at the Centre for Advanced Study in Oslo, where this chapter was written in the fall of 1996, to the MIT and NYU Philosophy Departments, where it received friendly yet severe road tests, and to Marko Ahtisaari, Christian Barry, Hilary Bok, Stefan Gosepath, Brian Orend, Guido Pincione, and Ling Tong for further valuable comments and criticisms. Reprinted with permission from the *Canadian Journal of Philosophy*, supplementary volume 22, published by the University of Calgary Press, 1997. There are some minor revisions.

should show a preeminent concern for preserving and enlarging their own collective advantage. Most citizens of the affluent countries – however condescendingly they may regard the revisionist nationalisms of the Serbs, Kurds, Palestinians, Tamils, Irish, and Québécois – are nationalists in this sense, and extreme ones at that.

The prevalence of such conservative nationalism can be explained – psychologically, for instance, or historically. I treat it, however, as a normative position, critically examining the belief that a state's citizens and politicians have such powerful prerogatives and special obligations with respect to the wealth and flourishing of their country and co-nationals. This examination may help moderate conservative nationalism by showing that it has been taken to unjustifiable extremes. Even a slight moderation of this sort could achieve a greater reduction in human misery and premature deaths than could be achieved by the harmonious dissolution of all revisionist nationalist struggles.

We can distinguish straightaway between particularistic and universalistic variants of nationalism. The former hold that nationalist commitments are valuable only when they are commitments to some specific nation (or to one of a specific set of nations). On account of the chauvinist, often racist, distinctions such views invoke, they are not worth serious moral discussion. I concentrate, then, on universalistic variants of nationalism, which assert that all nations can be valuable communities and can, by realizing this potential, generate the same obligations and prerogatives for their members, when they are similarly placed in the relevant respects. What more particular prerogatives and obligations emerge may depend to some extent on the unique history, culture, and/or traditional habitat of this or that nation. But we can leave such complications aside by concentrating on two substantive claims – loosely associated with popular talk of "patriotism" and "priority for compatriots" – which are at the heart of universalistic nationalism:

Common nationalism Citizens and governments may, and perhaps should, show more concern for the survival and flourishing of their own state, culture, and compatriots than for the survival and flourishing of foreign states, cultures, and persons.

Lofty nationalism Citizens and governments may, and perhaps should, show more concern for the justice of their own state and for injustice (and other wrongs) suffered by its members than for the justice of any other social systems and for injustice (and other wrongs) suffered by foreigners.

In discussing these claims, I do not attend to the desirability of there being states at all, but treat their existence, in roughly their present form, as a given. I do, however, address the character of states, which is affected by the scope and strength of its members' obligations vis-à-vis compatriots and of their prerogatives vis-à-vis foreigners.

Some such nationalist priorities are evidently permissible, even desirable; so I accept the two claims to be true as stated. Analogous claims would hold with respect to groups of many other kinds, such as families, religious communities, firms, clubs, and associations.[181] It is also evident that the asserted nationalist priorities cannot plausibly be affirmed as absolute. It cannot be appropriate, for instance, in each and every context to put a compatriot's interest, however minor, ahead of foreigners' interests, however vital. This raises the question of the *weight* of the asserted nationalist priorities. Regarding this question, many have argued that nationalist priorities have less weight than family priorities because nations and states, being more abstract and contingent than families, do not have as much constitutive significance in human lives. Bypassing this issue, I focus on the *scope* of the nationalist priorities, arguing that there are firm limits to their application and hence contexts in which they cannot plausibly be invoked at all. I believe these limits are quite general, constraining the priority agents may give to any group or collective enterprise. These limits constrain even family priorities and thus constrain the asserted nationalist priorities analogously even if nations and states have as much constitutive significance in human lives as families do.

5.1 Common nationalism: priority for the interests of compatriots

Are there any limits on the scope of the priority that citizens and governments may give to their nation and people or, more generally, on the scope of the priority that agents may give to their near and dear? Reflection on a piece of ordinary moral thinking may suggest the beginnings of an affirmative answer. It is within the family that concentration of concern is most clearly desirable and appropriate, and friends of a nationalist concentration of concern often invoke the family as an analogue or metaphor. But acceptable concern for even very close relatives is in fact thought to be quite strictly circumscribed in public life. It is, for instance, not merely illegal, but also deemed highly immoral for a state official to favor her son's firm in the application of regulations or in the awarding of government contracts. Why should this be so? To be sure, the woman, as a citizen and employee, owes loyalty to the state. But she also owes loyalty to her own family. Why, then, should she not balance these two loyalties and help her son in cases where this benefits him at no great cost to the state? And why should we not make a comparative assessment of these benefits and costs and then approve of such partiality and nepotism whenever the beneficiary's gains are sufficiently large relative to the costs?

It is tempting to answer that we understand the role of a state official as providing what Raz has called strong and exclusionary reasons, that is, strong first-order reasons (in one's official capacity) to act conscientiously in the best interest of the state combined with second-order reasons to set aside other first-order reasons that would otherwise be relevant to one's conduct decisions.[182] This is surely a true observation. But it is of no help in our inquiry, because it merely re-describes the phenomenon under examination. The question remains: why should we understand the role of a state official as providing exclusionary reasons?

One clue toward an answer may be provided by the popular metaphor of a "level playing field." Participants in a team sport passionately want their own team to win, and the best of them work very hard for this. However, players also want games to be fair, to be structured so that the better team will tend to win. This requires a level playing field, broadly conceived as including fair rules impartially administered. These may not be entirely separate desires. Players do not merely want to beat the other team – they want to *win by playing well.* Since they care nothing about other forms of "winning," they are not jubilant to learn that a game has been fixed for them in advance. To the contrary, they are disappointed, because fixing the game destroys their chance of winning properly.

To be sure, with lots of money at stake in the major leagues, this portrait of the noble team player is under pressure in two ways. There are the pressures of outright non-compliance: A few players, hoping for fame and advertising revenue, are prepared to do almost anything – on and off the field – to improve their team's score. They would not hesitate, for instance, before a match to infect their opponents with diarrhea or the common cold, if only they could get away with it. And then there are the more subtle and more consequential pressures of compliance redefined: many players, as well as their trainers and fans, now take a strategic attitude toward the rules of the game. They think it alright, for example, falsely to claim a rule violation (so as to induce the referee to penalize their opponents), to conceal or falsely to deny a rule violation (so as to protect their own team from being penalized), and even to commit a violation intentionally (so as to save a dangerous situation or even to cause or to aggravate an opponent's injury).[183] They view these stratagems as part of the game, understanding the rule that prohibits and provides a penalty for doing X as meaning, really, that players are given the option to do X while risking the penalty.[184] With such options open to both sides, compliance redefined is compatible with the idea of a level playing field, albeit a lower one. While my portrait of the noble team player may not, then, be typical of much that goes on in sports today, it nevertheless has, I believe, the kind of reality that matters here. It really is our widely held ideal by reference to which we still judge our athletes. And drawing on it is therefore appropriate to elucidate the political use of the "level playing field" metaphor.

The metaphor suggests that an analogous ideal is operating in public life. In our example, the state official plays a role analogous to that of a referee. She, as well as her son, should ideally be animated by the thought that, if she were to bend the rules in his favor, the game would be spoiled, rendering his "success" meaningless or even shameful. This ideal has wide application, because we all frequently play the role of referee when we act as citizens, voters, jurors, and the like. Consider how the ideal has considerable force even in rather unofficial contexts. By supporting political candidates or even merely through public utterances, many citizens take a stand on whether and how affirmative action should be continued. The ideal requires that they should not base their stance on how affirmative action would affect their own children in particular. And citizens would indeed be widely condemned, by supporters and opponents of affirmative action alike, if they were known to reason along these lines: "We love our children and, if they were girls or black, we would, of course, support affirmative action very strongly. Our children are, however, white boys, whom affirmative action hurts twice over: by reducing their competitive advantage and by increasing the cost of government. We therefore strongly support its demolition." The common condemnation of such reasoning manifests, I believe, a widespread commitment to the analogue of the noble team player ideal. It is widely thought that the sons in both of my examples should desire and strive to *do well in a fair and open competition with others*. And their parents should realize that, even if through partiality they could slant the social order in their children's favor, they would spoil the "game" and thereby deprive their children of any chance for true success.[185]

But wait. Do people really dismiss a good education and income as meaningless so long as some cannot compete for them on fair terms?

Clearly, the ideal of a level playing field in public life is under even greater pressure than its athletic analogue. While it is quite conceivable that a player may have no desire at all to see her team "win" even while she passionately wants it to win properly, it is much harder to conceive of our fictional sons (and their parents) taking no interest in their financial success as such. An extra buck, unlike an extra "win," always is, *pro tanto*, a good thing.

There are more contingent cultural pressures as well. In the US at least, many find it acceptable for companies and individuals to use campaign contributions to influence legislators – for example, to affect their stance on pending legislation or to induce them to intercede with executive officials. But if the rules may be tailored in this way through money, then why not through an old friendship or, indeed, kinship? It is also widely considered acceptable for legislators from underprivileged minorities vigorously to promote the collective interests of "their people." And if prioritizing the interests of Hispanics is alright for Hispanic legislators, then why should it not be alright for Hispanic citizens to do the same? And if trying to affect the rules in favor of one's ethnic group is alright for Hispanics, then why not for whites as well? It is not only a general de-moralization of the culture that gnaws away at the level playing field ideal, but also the Anglo-American persuasion that an adversarial clash of conflicting partialities is conducive to substantive fairness. This sentiment makes it possible for partiality – paradigmatically illustrated by prosecutors and defense attorneys doing their utmost to win their cases – to appear as a sacred mission and duty that is required for the sake of the very impartiality that it also persistently assaults through compliance redefined. But even here definite limits are recognized: lawyers who try to succeed by bribing the judge or by stealing their opponents' evidence are roundly condemned for their excessive dedication.

To be sure, it is hard in public life, certainly much harder than in sports, for ordinary moral thinking to draw the line between acceptable conduct that seeks success in the game and dubious conduct that seeks to slant the playing field – and hard, also, to distinguish acceptable conduct that seeks to make the playing field more level in favor of one's group from dubious conduct that seeks to slant the playing field in favor of one's group in ways that also happen to make it more level. It is also hard to maintain allegiance to the apparently hopelessly unrealistic ideal that officials and citizens in public life should bracket all their particular interests. In light of these facts, it is not surprising that persons differ in how they understand the ideal of a level playing field which rules out certain kinds of partiality altogether.

There is still greater international variation, as even the national cultures of developed Western states differ widely in how much explicit and tacit public tolerance they display for various forms of corruption and nepotism. It is surprising, however, that within and increasingly also beyond these countries there is widespread support for the general idea that fairness requires of persons, and especially of officials, that in certain public contexts they set aside any loyalty to their near and dear, including even their very closest family members.[186] Though there is considerable diversity of opinion on *how* acceptable partiality is limited in scope, there is firm and widespread agreement *that* it is so limited when the basic justice of the larger playing field is at stake.

It may be possible to deepen this agreement by stating outer bounds, or minimum conditions that any institutional order must meet for it to be considered minimally fair. The widely acclaimed *UDHR* sets forth certain human rights as fulfilling this function. Its Article 28 reads: "Everyone is entitled to a social and international order in which the rights and freedoms set forth in this Declaration can be fully realized." In the case of national regimes ("social order"), the logical addressees of this entitlement are the officials and citizens of the society in question. They face outer bounds on what they may do or tolerate by way of efforts to slant the playing field in favor of special interests. Their society must be structured so as to afford all members secure access to the objects of their human rights.[187] In most societies, more is expected from citizens and especially from officials. My point is surely not that all partiality not endangering human rights is alright and should be tolerated – only the converse: partiality by officials and citizens is certainly *not* alright when it seeks to shape a society's ground rules or their administration so as to endanger the secure access by some to the objects of their human rights.

This minimal constraint on the scope of acceptable partiality, which, I have argued, would find wide international acceptance even in reference to close family ties, should also limit the scope of nationalist partiality, which differs from family partiality by being rooted more in collective self-interest and less in meaningful personal ties. Of course, this limit on the scope of common nationalism is not widely accepted today. But its rejection smacks of inconsistency. How can we despise those who seek to slant the national playing field in favor of themselves and their relatives and yet applaud those who seek to slant the international playing field in favor of themselves and their compatriots? How can we ask our officials to put their own family's finances out of their minds when deliberating about the domestic economic order (e.g. the tax code) and yet expect those same officials to have their own nation's finances uppermost in their minds when deliberating about the global economic order?

To illustrate what accepting this minimal constraint would mean in practice, let me present what I see as a paradigm violation of the outer bounds of permissible partiality. It was the basic principle of Part XI of the 1982 *UN Convention on the Law of the Sea* that natural resources on the ocean floors beneath international waters "are the common heritage of mankind" (Article 136), to be used "for the benefit of mankind as a whole . . . taking into particular consideration the interests and needs of developing States [through an] equitable sharing of financial and economic benefits" (Article 140), which was to have been effected by sharing of seabed mining technologies and profits (Annex III, Articles 5 and 13) under the auspices of the International Seabed Authority, or ISBA (Annexes III and IV). Three successive US administrations have tried quite hard to secure the great benefits of the treaty in "protecting and promoting the wide range of U.S. ocean interests"[188] without the sharing scheme. Shortly before the *Convention* was to come into force (on November 28, 1996), the Clinton Administration succeeded in having the sharing provisions replaced by a superseding *Agreement*.[189] This *Agreement* endorses the US view that the common-heritage principle means that the oceans and their resources "are open to use by all in accordance with commonly accepted rules."[190] Accordingly, it frees mining companies from having to share seabed mining technologies[191] and greatly reduces the sharing of profits.[192] The *Agreement* further accommodates US demands by "1) guaranteeing a U.S. seat in the Council [the executive organ of the ISBA]; 2) allowing ourselves and a few other industrialized nations acting in concert to block decisions in the Council."[193]

In managing to renegotiate the *UN Convention on the Law of the Sea* – by pressing the Reagan era threat of founding a competing seabed resources scheme with a few like-minded countries[194] – the Clinton Administration won a great victory for the US and any other countries that will have the capital and technologies for profitable seabed mining.[195] The reaction in these wealthy countries was quiet relief: their governments raised no objections and their media largely ignored the event. The rulers of the poorer countries went along as well to avoid being excluded. It is the global poor, in any case, who will bear the real loss from this further slanting of the playing field. They are the ones who can least afford to be shut out from this common heritage of humankind. For the sake of what for us are distant and trivial advantages,[196] Clinton has taken us a great step away from an "international order in which the rights and freedoms set forth in this [*UDHR*] can be fully realized."[197] His decision, and our acquiescence in it, stand as a paradigm violation of the outer bounds of permissible partiality.[198]

Did Clinton merely do what he had to do as the elected guardian of the US national interest? One might think that nationalist priority should be limited for individuals, but not for governments whose very point it is to safeguard the interests of their nation. Though not unpopular, this view fares no better than the analogous view about lawyers whose very point it is, within an adversarial system, to safeguard the interests of their clients. A democratically constituted government can indeed plausibly be conceived as the agent of its people. But allowing such agents to give unlimited priority to the interests of their clients runs into a fatal trilemma. For such clients

- either: must then be permitted to give the same unlimited priority to their own interests even when acting in their own behalf (without an agent),
- or: must then be prohibited from appointing an agent (here: government) to represent their collective interest,
- for otherwise: they would be able to circumvent moral constraints that the interests of others impose on their conduct merely by acting through an agent rather than directly.

All three of these possibilities are implausible. There are firm constraints on what persons and groups within a larger social system may do by way of tailoring its rules, or corrupting the application of these rules, in their own favor. They may appoint agents to safeguard their interests, but these agents are bound by the same constraints. Clinton could not permissibly do for his constituents what they could not permissibly have done for themselves.[199] And if it is not the case, therefore, that democratically constituted governments, who are truly the agents of their people, may give unlimited priority to the interests of their state and its citizens, then, surely, undemocratic governments must not do so either.

A more informal way of confirming this result involves comparing Clinton's hypothesized defense with that of the parliamentary delegation of a middle-class party which says that it is merely doing what it has to do in the best interest of its constituents when it proposes that children from families paying no income taxes be barred from public benefits,[200] such as school lunches or government-guaranteed student loans: "It would be wrong for our constituents themselves to slant the playing field in their favor in this way. But we, as their chosen representatives, may and even must do just that. We must be single-mindedly devoted to advancing the interests of our constituents." This sort of reasoning would hardly find support. And those who reject it while accepting Clinton's defense must then implicitly rely on the moral significance of the distinction between nationalist and other forms of partiality. But why this distinction should be morally significant remains a mystery.

Why this distinction is *thought to be* morally significant is less mysterious. Those who have the opportunity to reflect upon morality publicly, in the media or in academic discourse, are, by and large, privileged persons in the more affluent countries. In these countries, the domestic poor have at least some capacity to articulate their claims and some power to make their voices heard. The parliamentary delegation I have imagined would provoke considerable protest and social unrest. The global poor, who labor all day for a few dollars a month, are unable to cause us the slightest inconvenience and unable even to alert us to their plight. Thanks to our military superiority, they fall outside what Rawls has called the circumstances of justice, following Hume: "Were there a species of creatures intermingled with men, which . . . were possessed of such inferior strength, both of body and mind, that they were incapable of all resistance, and could never . . . make us feel the effects of their resentment; . . . the restraints of justice and property . . . would never have place in so unequal a confederacy."[201]

One might think that the prevailing tolerance for common nationalism can be justified by reference to the idea that no one should ask us to subordinate our pursuit of our national interest to a concern for a minimally just international order so long as other countries are not practicing similar self-restraint. This thought invokes a "sucker exemption": an agent is not morally required to comply with rules when doing so would lead to his being victimized ("made a sucker") by non-compliers. The morally relevant difference between nationalist partiality and, say, family partiality lies, then, in the currently prevailing levels of non-compliance and compliance redefined. We must honor tight limits on the scope of family partiality insofar as most of our compatriots practice similar self-restraint; but we may violate even the outer bounds on the scope of nationalist partiality because this is what other states are doing as well. If the facts of our situation were reversed, we would be free to violate even the outer bounds on the scope of family partiality while having to honor tight limits on the scope of our common nationalism.

Does such an appeal to a sucker exemption furnish a plausible defense? It is true, of course, that international relations have historically been brutal. The main players – the governments of militarily and/or economically powerful societies and lately also the larger multinational corporations – negotiate and re-negotiate the rules of the game among themselves with each pressing vigorously for its own advantage, using war and the threat of war when this seems opportune and showing no concern for the interests or even survival of the weakest "players." The brutality of the international scene may indeed support the principle that societies and their governments may in pursuit of their national interest seek to achieve or uphold an unjust global order (one under which, avoidably, the human rights of many cannot be fulfilled), if other societies and their governments would otherwise slant the global playing field against them. Invoking this principle, a rich society may decline to introduce unilateral reforms to protect the world's poorest populations (e.g. a national law requiring that its mining firms share with the global poor some of the value of the seabed resources they harvest) on the ground that doing so would put it at a competitive disadvantage against its peers. But if each such society so defended itself by pointing to the others, the reasonable response would surely be to ask them all to work out a multilateral reform that affects all of them equally and thus does not alter their competitive positions vis-à-vis one another. Each should propose some suitable reforms and should also conditionally promise to support their implementation if the others will do so as well.[202] Such initiatives would not only promote a more level global playing field, but would also build mutual trust and cooperation, ensuring that the sucker exemption would, in time, cease to apply.

Another appeal to the sucker exemption would claim that we may uphold the extreme inequalities of the present world order because, if the rich societies instituted a more level playing field, then many of the presently poor societies, who are inclined unjustly to slant the playing field in their favor and against us, would over time become powerful enough to do so. This appeal also strikes me as implausible. There are indeed many authoritarian and aggressive governments in the less developed countries. But this fact is in large measure due to our highly unjust world order, and thus cannot serve as its justification. Relative poverty breeds corruptibility and corruption, which tend to degrade or destroy democratic institutions in the poorer societies. Absolute poverty and ignorance make it easy to manipulate people into nationalist resentment. There is every reason to believe that, as the rich countries begin to show genuine concern for world poverty and cooperate in its eradication, more benign and reasonable sentiments and political institutions would develop in the poorer countries.

In the last five paragraphs, I have tried to respond to two ways of defending the refusal to impose the same outer bounds on the scope of nationalist partiality which we unhesitatingly impose upon the scope of other kinds of partiality. Perhaps these responses were too brief to be convincing. Or perhaps there are better defenses of the asymmetry than the two I have tried to rebut. None of this should detract from the challenge to common nationalism I have laid down in this section. In conducting our foreign policy, and especially in shaping the global order regulating international politics and the world economy, we have taken partiality to extremes that we would find intolerable in any other context. Despite its grievous effects upon the global poor, this exceptional tolerance for *nationalist* partiality is widely approved. But how can this exception be justified?

5.2 Lofty nationalism: the justice-for-compatriots priority

I have suggested that the affluent in the developed countries may be practicing a morally untenable nationalism by coercively upholding a badly slanted global order in which the human rights of millions of foreigners are unfulfilled. In response to this line of argument, it is often asserted that we should forgo grand theorizing about global justice until we have achieved justice at home. This response invokes the second nationalist priority claim. Though rarely articulated, let alone explicitly defended, this claim seems to express a prejudice that is widely held, as can be gauged from the fact that participants in academic and popular discourse on justice overwhelmingly focus on assessing the ground rules of their own society, while the moral assessment of our global order is largely ignored.[203]

Such lofty nationalism may well be important in explaining why the widespread common nationalism, which section 5.1 has criticized as excessive, is so rarely challenged. Our moralists implicitly assume that, even if extensive and severe misery were produced by a heavily slanted global order that we help shape and uphold, such misery would manifest a wrong suffered by foreigners and hence would be of less urgency for us than wrongs suffered by compatriots. If this diagnosis is correct, then the project of section 5.1 – showing how common nationalism is limited in scope – cannot be fully effective without the project of the present section: showing the limits of lofty nationalism.

As in the discussion of common nationalism, I leave aside the issue of weight and thus do not ask how much greater wrongs suffered by foreigners must be than wrongs suffered by compatriots in order for their eradication, at equal cost, to be equally urgent for us. Instead, I focus on the issue of scope and argue that there are contexts in which the priority asserted by lofty nationalism does not hold at all.

The examination of lofty nationalism, too, may begin from reflection on a piece of ordinary moral thinking. It is widely believed that negative duties have greater weight than their positive counterparts, if these even exist. Thus killing a person for the sake of some gain is widely thought to be morally worse than failing, for the sake of a like gain, to rescue him. And one is deemed negatively obligated not to commit small thefts and yet not positively obligated to prevent such even when doing so is safe and easy. The distinction between negative and positive duties is complicated and has been drawn in various ways. I try to draw it, within the domain of interpersonal responsibilities, so as to vindicate its moral significance, that is, the popular idea that, given equal stakes for all involved, negative duties have greater weight. I propose, then, to call *negative* any duty to ensure that others are not unduly harmed (or wronged) through one's own conduct and to call *positive* the remainder: any duty to benefit persons or to shield them from other harms. This negative/positive distinction is doubly moralized, because its application requires us to decide whether A's conduct *harms* P (relative to some morality-stipulated baseline) and, if so, harms P *unduly*.

The importance in ordinary moral thinking of this distinction suggests that our initial formulation of lofty nationalism requires some refinement. When wrongs (including injustice) are produced by oneself, then showing concern for such wrongs means trying to reduce one's undue harming of others (and perhaps also to mitigate undue harms one can no longer prevent). When wrongs are produced by third parties, then showing concern for such wrongs means trying to benefit others by stopping these wrongs (or perhaps also by mitigating their effects).

Once we rethink lofty nationalism to take account of this distinction, we find that the permissibility of giving priority to the near and dear is quite dubious in the case of negative duties. This is so even with family ties. Few would mind that, if I come upon a group of children who have been hit by a speeding driver, I attend to my own child first and foremost, even if I could do more toward reducing the harm another child will have suffered. But this judgment changes if we alter the case so that I am the reckless driver. In this case, it would seem wrong to give such priority to my own child. The priority for compatriots fails even more clearly in analogous cases, when, for instance, I have made conflicting commitments to a compatriot and to a foreigner. Here it seems clear that, if the foreigner stands to lose more from my breach of commitment, I should break my promise to the compatriot. Or consider a runaway trolley case (popular among philosophers) where you must choose between crashing the trolley into a group of foreigners or into a somewhat smaller group of compatriots. Again it would seem that one should minimize the harm one will cause others, irrespective of their nationality. And acting in this way is not viewed as disloyal to one's country and does not therefore detract from national fellow feeling and shared solidarity.

Consider also comparative moral judgments. Is it morally worse to beat up a compatriot than a foreigner?[204] Is it morally worse to defraud a poor family in one's own country than an equally poor family abroad? The much celebrated priority for compatriots does not seem to have force in these cases.

The same point can be made about the conduct of governments. It is no better, morally, for a government to jail without charge, or to expropriate, a foreign visitor than one of its citizens. In fact, there are various harms which it is worse for a government to impose upon foreigners than upon compatriots. Goodin lists seven cases of this sort, which are recognized in international law. In discussing these cases, Goodin invokes a distinction between negative and positive duties, stating that "special relationships have this curious tendency to strengthen positive duties while weakening negative ones."[205] I do not share the diagnosis of an inverse priority, which this sentence suggests for negative duties. In my view, negative duties are not, and are not thought to be, weakened by special relationships as such. Rather, some of them can be partly waived through *consent* under conditions of *fair reciprocity*. Relevant harms, such as expropriation or conscription, must be allocated pursuant to a procedure that is consented to by those subject to it and this allocation must be fair so that (at least) participation in the scheme is not irrational *ex ante*.[206] The citizens of a society may then democratically authorize their government to expropriate or conscript under specified conditions. Yet, through such an authorization they may render only *themselves*, not foreigners, liable to be harmed in these ways. This is how a government may come to practice a kind of anti-nationalist priority that works against compatriots. The moral situation is thus not quite the one Goodin's sentence suggests: it is not the case that special relationships imply weakened negative duties, as can be illustrated by a special relationship that fails to satisfy the two provisos. The implication goes only the other way: weakened negative duties imply a special relationship – for example, the special relationship of reciprocity and joint consent which obtains when the two provisos are satisfied. The contra-positive of this second conditional is: absence of a special relationship implies that negative duties fully apply. This crucial point, which Goodin rightly stresses, can explain why no society may render innocent foreigners liable to conscription or expropriation and why no government may conscript or expropriate them: foreigners do not stand to gain from such a scheme (reciprocity). Nor have they consented to it – we would have a strange notion indeed of moral duties if we held that those bound by them can weaken or eliminate these duties unilaterally.

This discussion shows that the thesis of lofty nationalism is plausible only in regard to concern for third-party wrongdoing. It is certainly permissible, and perhaps also morally desirable, for such concern to be strongest for the near and dear and to fade outward through a series of concentric circles. But the strength of an agent's moral reason not to harm another unduly does not vary with the potential victim's relational closeness to the agent, and, in particular, does not vary with the potential victim's status as a compatriot or foreigner. Combining these findings with our starting point – the deeply entrenched view that any moral duty not to wrong another person, or not to harm him unduly, is much weightier than any corresponding duty to protect him against like wrongs from other sources – we can conclude that, holding fixed what is at stake for all parties, ordinary moral thinking is committed to a hierarchy of moral reasons which has the following form:

(1) Negative duties not to wrong (unduly harm) others;
(2a) Positive duties to protect one's next of kin from wrongdoing,
:
(2n) Positive duties to protect one's compatriots from wrongdoing,
:
(2z) Positive duties to protect unrelated foreigners from wrongdoing.[207]

Acceptable lofty nationalism, as well, is then clearly limited in scope. The task it is stressing – to protect our compatriots from injustice and other wrongdoing – can distance us from undue harms foreigners suffer only insofar as these harms are not our own doing. In this case, our morality does indeed allow a priority for compatriots and, more generally, a priority for the near and dear. It is morally more important to stop injustices and other wrongs committed against our compatriots than to stop such injustices and wrongs committed against foreigners by third parties; and, more generally, it is morally more important to attend to the needs of our compatriots than to give like assistance to foreigners. In the other case, however, when the undue harms foreigners suffer are our own doing, foreigners and compatriots are on a par. Injustices and other wrongs we commit against foreigners have the same weight as like injustices and other wrongs we commit against compatriots (and we have more moral reason to stop either of these than like injustices and other wrongs done to our compatriots by third parties).[208] In this way, the moral claims foreigners have on us constrain our pursuit of justice at home. Honoring these constraints is morally required and thus shows no disloyalty to our country and, so understood, does not undermine shared feelings of allegiance and community.

Many think about the wrongs, including injustice, that foreigners suffer in our world in terms of positive duty and thus put them at the very bottom of their list. They think: "The extreme deprivation of so many children abroad surely manifests an injustice to some extent, and one I could help alleviate. But injustice and other wrongs are rife in my own country and community as well, and I should give priority to combating these, even if those abroad are considerably greater."[209] This may be quite the right way to think when foreigners are suffering home-grown wrongs and even when they are severely disadvantaged in their dealings with us through no fault of ours. But it may *not* be the right attitude when they are being harmed through a badly slanted global order in whose continuous shaping and coercive imposition we are materially involved. Such harms may engage not merely our vague positive duty to help those badly off and worse off than ourselves, but also our sharper and much weightier *negative* duty not to harm others unduly, either single-handedly or in collaboration with others. And this duty is no weaker toward foreigners than it is toward compatriots.

Whether or not we accept such a negative duty in regard to the justice of our global order makes a momentous moral difference. If we do not, we may place any injustice suffered by the global poor at the bottom of our list (2z). If we do, we place some of it at the very top (1). The amount of harm that might be effected by such an upgrade is large, as hundreds of millions are affected by, and some 18 million die each year through, poverty and oppression.

Given the importance of the issue, it is strange that it is so easily taken for granted on all sides – even by those who have most forcefully presented global poverty as a moral task[210] – that such poverty is for us, First World citizens, a matter of positive duty. My main concern here, once again, is to challenge those who hold this consensus belief to reflect upon it. But I also try, in what follows, to show how problematic this belief is.

One author who supports this consensus view is John Rawls – amazingly with regard to not only international but also domestic justice. Agreeing that "it seems plausible to hold that, when the distinction is clear, negative duties have more weight than positive ones,"[211] he explicitly classifies our natural duty of justice as *positive*.[212] This implies that the natural duty of justice (along with the "positive" natural duties to mutual aid and to mutual respect) has less weight than our "negative" natural duties (not to injure and not to harm the innocent). Rawls defines the natural duty of justice as having two aspects. He writes that it "requires us to support and to comply with just institutions that exist and apply to us [and] to further just arrangements not yet established."[213]

As an alternative to Rawls's two-aspect position, let us examine the views that

(a) in some cases at least, just institutions that apply to oneself generate weighty *negative* duties of compliance;
(b) in some cases at least, significant and continuing participants in an unjust institutional order have weighty *negative* duties to promote its reform and/or to protect its victims (while any corresponding duties of non-participants would indeed be positive).

Since (b) is what matters most, I defend (a) only in outline, merely to show that Rawls's position is problematic across the board. Suppose we are born into a world in which a just institutional order is already in place. And suppose we owe one another a merely positive moral duty to comply with this regime: non-compliance as such does not count as harming others unduly, though it is good to comply as it is good to help others. When positive duties to comply and to help conflict, it would, then, seem to be at least permissible (perhaps desirable or even mandatory) to choose the course of conduct that, all things considered, is better for others – for instance, to cheat on one's taxes in order to help someone in need whenever the gain to the recipient(s) outweighs the loss, if any, to one's fellow citizens.[214] This is surely not the prevailing view. More importantly, this view also undermines a major desideratum within Rawls's theory: just institutions cannot be *stable*, that is, cannot maintain themselves on the basis of the moral motives of their participants, if these participants see their duty to support and to comply with the institutions of their society as on a par with beneficence or charity.[215]

The foregoing can show at most that our moral duty to comply with just institutions is believed, like negative duties, to have more weight than the standard positive duties,[216] and that this belief is necessary for the possibility of a just social order based on moral motives. But is the belief plausible? How can we show a person who does not wish to consent to the just order we are maintaining that her noncompliance would unduly harm others?

Kant's justification of perfect duties and of the imposition of coercive legal institutions suggests a plausible line of argument.[217] His basic idea is that persons are entitled to equal freedom and should therefore constrain their freedom so that the freedom of each is consistent with the equal freedom of all. Acting beyond this limit, one invades the rightful freedom of others, thus violating a negative duty: a person unduly harms others when the success of his conduct implies that like conduct by others is constrained.

Since a consistent and equal distribution of freedom can be achieved in various ways, we need shared institutions to avoid invading one another's freedom. And we have a *negative* duty to comply with such existing institutions, whenever noncompliance can succeed only if like noncompliance by others is constrained. Obtaining more resources than one is entitled to under an existing just property scheme, or free-riding on an existing institution like promising, harms others unduly, because one's success depends on others not being allowed, or not allowing themselves, a like liberty.[218] If this Kantian strategy can be made to work, then central cases of noncompliance with just institutions can plausibly be classified as violations of a negative duty. This would defeat the view that the first part of Rawls's natural duty of justice can unequivocally be classified as positive.[219]

It is easier to defend (b). When undue harms are mandated or authorized by a society's social institutions (e.g. its laws) and when state officials inflict these harms or protect and aid those who do, then citizens who uphold these institutions through their political consent and economic support contribute to the harms. The horrendous harms inflicted by the Nazis, for instance, were not possible without the economic contributions of many citizens through the tax system, nor without the legitimacy that Nazi laws and officials derived from the consent many citizens expressed by participating in legal and political institutions, by attending rallies, by enlisting in the armed forces, etc.[220] By lending such support, these citizens, too, violated their *negative* duty not to harm others unduly.[221]

It does not follow that one must stop contributing to the economy of an unjust society – though it may come to that in extreme cases.

One can often continue to contribute and yet avoid collaborating in the undue harming of others by taking compensating action: by making as much of an effort, aimed at protecting the victims of injustice or at institutional reform, as would suffice to eradicate the harms, if others followed suit.[222]

The reflection on the Nazi case suffices to establish the existential claim in (b). But does it carry over to the case of unjust *economic* institutions that are *global* in scope? Only if it does, can the vast evil of global poverty engage our *negative* duty not to harm others unduly, and thus command a place at the top, rather than the bottom, of our priority list.

Here is a straightforward way of arguing that the conclusion carries over: "Insofar as our global poor are worse off than the poorest under some alternative feasible global economic order would be, the existing global economic order is unjust. By imposing this order upon them, we are therefore harming them unduly." This easy argument invites controversy on two points. First, it invokes a conception of justice that is highly controversial, especially when applied to the world at large. Presupposing that an economic order is just only if *no* alternative would engender less severe poverty, the easy argument assumes the full burden of defending a globalized version of Rawls's difference principle.[223] Second, since any social order requires a certain degree of coercion (imposition) in its creation and maintenance, the easy argument also assumes that we have a negative duty not to help create and not to collaborate (without making compensating efforts) in the maintenance of any social order that is less than perfectly just. But this assumption is disputable as even imperfect social institutions may render all their participants better off than anyone would be in their absence.[224] How can one be *harming* others unduly by imposing upon them imperfect economic institutions that *raise* all participants' standard of living? (Compare: how can one be unduly harming an unconscious accident victim merely by doing less than one could do by way of improving her situation?)

The controversial assumptions of the easy argument are not beyond defense. But we should first examine whether they are really necessary. The attacks on the two assumptions suggest two ideas toward a more widely acceptable argument. We should not overgeneralize by dissolving our question – whether the extensive and severe global poverty we face today engages our negative duty not to harm others unduly – into the much broader question whether *any* avoidable degree of global poverty does so. And we should try to avoid the controversial appeal to *relative* harms, involving comparisons across alternative economic orders, by appealing instead to a more robust noninstitutional baseline.

The latter idea points in the direction of a Lockean account of economic justice. I indeed present the following argument as a reconstruction of Locke's account – though what matters, of course, is the soundness of the argument, not that of my reading. Locke assumed that, in a pre-institutional state of nature, persons have equal moral claims on all natural resources. He specified this equal claim as the freedom to take possession of any unowned land, water, minerals, fruits, animals, etc., subject to the so-called Lockean proviso that each person's unilateral appropriations in a state of nature must leave "enough, and as good" for others.[225] Locke thought of this constraint not as a positive duty of kindness or beneficence, but as an enforceable negative duty strictly owed to others. And this makes sense, as those who take more harm others by cutting into their fair shares. We can put this point in terms of the Kantian idea I invoked before to support a negative duty of compliance with just institutions: taking while leaving enough and as good for others is compatible with their freedom to do the same and thus does not harm them unduly. But taking more than this can succeed only if others' freedom to do so as well is constrained. Quite apart from whether Locke or Kant would have appreciated it, this affinity is welcome, because it shows that, insofar as our duty of justice is a negative one, its two aspects – compliance with, and promotion of, just institutions – can be grounded in one fundamental moral principle.

There is a compelling reason against making the Lockean proviso sacrosanct. For it may be possible for human beings to create and uphold social institutions that *both* permit disproportional unilateral appropriation *and* render all participants economically better off than people would be in a state of nature. To accommodate this possibility, Locke argues that human beings may create and enforce economic institutions that permit disproportionate unilateral appropriation – provided everyone *rationally* consents to (i.e. gains from) their introduction. One might call this constraint on institutions the *second-order* Lockean proviso, because it governs not changes in the property status of resources (acquisitions and transfers), but changes in the rules that govern changes in the property status of resources.[226]

Locke holds that creation of the institution of money, which he claims happened "out of the bounds of society and without compact,"[227] suspends the Lockean proviso in a way that satisfies the second-order proviso. He writes that "the Invention of Money, and the tacit Agreement of Men to put a value on it, introduced (by Consent) larger

Possessions, and a Right to them."[228] And he goes to some length to show that this invention, though it suspends the enough-and-as-good constraint, does make everyone economically better off than anyone would be in a state of nature – that "a King of a large fruitful territory [in the Americas] feeds, lodges, and is clad worse than a day Laborer in England."[229]

Locke's reference to a king in a state of nature suggests that he wants to define his baseline by reference to the best lives that can be lived in a state of nature. But it might be said that a Lockean account really supports a less restrictive baseline, because it could be rational to consent to social institutions that make everyone merely better off than persons in such a state of nature would be *on average*.[230] Yet Locke is clearly right to require that social institutions must lift each participant, even the lowly day laborer, above the baseline. Merely keeping the average above this baseline is not enough: a social order cannot be justified to its present participants by appeal to the actual or hypothetical consent of their ancestors.[231] And if we tell slaves or English day laborers or the present global poor that *they* could have rationally agreed *ex ante* (in ignorance of their social position at birth) to institutions under which some may be worse off than persons in a state of nature, they can plausibly reply that this hypothetical consent could not possibly have been *theirs*, since they never had a real chance to occupy the better positions.[232]

Locke's reasoning thus leads to the demand that any social order must not merely increase economic aggregates or the average standard of living, but must also distribute this gain so as to afford everyone access to an economic position that is superior to what persons, at least on average, would have in a Lockean state of nature. We are harming others unduly if we impose upon them a social order under which they do not have access to such a minimal economic position. In this way, Locke's reasoning can support some of the human rights I have proposed, in section 5.1, as minimum conditions on any institutional order.

To be sure, it is rather unclear how an appropriate state of nature should be imagined and what human lives within it would then be like. Locke assumes that most conveniences and all modern technologies would be lacking in such a state, which could thus sustain only a much smaller human population. But he also assumes that these people would have access to sufficient food, clean water, clothing, and shelter. Despite huge economic progress in aggregate, a substantial fraction of humankind are today deprived of such access, even while they are also being forced to comply with existing economic institutions, to observe the property rights that others assert over all the wealth of this world. On Locke's account, they are clearly being harmed – and unduly so: their extreme poverty is foreseeable, avoidable, and cannot be justified by anything they have done (they certainly did not squander their share, but were excluded from birth, if not from conception). And even those who find Locke's assumptions about the state of nature too optimistic cannot with any confidence tell these poor people that they are better off than people would be in a pre-institutional state of nature and that we are therefore not harming them by imposing on them this global economic order and the extreme and increasing international economic inequality it engenders.

If all this were said in reference to national economic regimes, it would provoke little opposition in the rich societies. Most of us reject as unjust the economic institutions of Brazil, for instance,[233] and agree that the wealthy elite of that country, by imposing these institutions with the avoidable poverty they produce,[234] is unduly harming many of them.[235] But very few of us who accept these conclusions about Brazil are willing to draw parallel conclusions about our global economic order, which is much more inegalitarian even than Brazil's.[236] The discussion of lofty nationalism, too, concludes then with a problematic asymmetry of judgments. We accept a weighty negative duty not to impose a *national* economic system that avoidably engenders extreme poverty. Yet, we *fail* to accept a like negative duty with respect to the *global* economic system that we impose, shape, and dominate. This failure is surely convenient. If we accepted such a negative duty, global poverty would fall outside the scope of lofty nationalism and its eradication would move to the top of our moral priority list. But convenience alone does not explain why we find it so very easy to think of global poverty in terms of positive duty.

5.3 Explanatory nationalism: the deep significance of national borders

This ease can be explained, I believe, by our "nationalist" way of looking at the world as a plurality of interacting national systems and, more specifically, at the world economy as a plurality of national economies that interact through trade, loans, and foreign investment. This view permeates the way economists and the financial media tend to analyze global poverty. They present it as a set of national phenomena explainable mainly by bad domestic policies and institutions that stifle, or fail to stimulate, national economic growth and engender national economic injustice. It is difficult to design policies and institutions that promote both growth and economic justice (and the experts differ on how this should best be done), but some countries have succeeded rather well, and so could the others, if only they had better economic institutions and pursued better economic policies. If the governments of presently poor countries had done better in these regards, there would now be much less poverty in the world; and, if such governments were to do better from now on, severe poverty would gradually disappear.

This dominant view is quite true on the whole. But it is also totally one-sided. For it holds fixed, and thereby entirely ignores, the economic and geopolitical context in which the national economies and governments of the poorer countries are placed. The modern state, after all, is itself an institution. The land surface of our planet is divided into a number of clearly demarcated and nonoverlapping national territories. Human beings are matched up with these territories, so that (at least for the most part) each person belongs to exactly one territory. Any person or group effectively controlling a preponderant share of the means of coercion within such a territory is recognized as the legitimate government of both the territory and the persons belonging to it. It is entitled to rule "its" people through laws, orders, and officials, to adjudicate conflicts among them, and also to exercise ultimate control over all resources within the territory ("eminent domain"). It is also entitled to represent these persons against the rest of the world: to bind them vis-à-vis outsiders through treaties and contracts, to regulate their relations with outsiders, to declare war in their name, to represent them through diplomats and emissaries, and to control outsiders' access to the country's territory. In this second role, a government is considered continuous with its predecessors and successors: bound by the undertakings of the former, and capable of binding the latter through its own undertakings.

This global context is of crucial importance for explaining the incidence of unfulfilled human rights and the persistence and severity of world poverty. Explanations by reference solely to national factors and international differences leave important questions open. They leave open why national factors (institutions, officials, policies, culture, climate, natural environment, level of technical and economic development) have *these* effects rather than others. It is quite possible that, in the context of a different global order, the same national factors, or the same international differences, would have quite a different impact on human living conditions.[237] Such explanations also leave open why national factors are the way they are in the first place.

Global factors significantly affect national policies and institutions, especially in the poorer and weaker countries. It is quite possible that, in a different global environment, national factors that tend to generate poverty, or tend to undermine the fulfillment of human rights more generally, would occur much less frequently or not at all.[238]

Such questions are not especially subtle, and economists are well aware of them in other contexts. They recognize the explanatory importance of global institutional factors, for example, when they try to assess the effects of alternative global trading regimes (Bretton Woods, WTO, etc.) on trade flows and global economic growth. Why are there no systematic attempts to analyze the effects of alternative global institutions on the incidence of poverty? I will not speculate. But it is possible, at least, that the popularity of explanatory nationalism is related to how it distorts our ordinary moral analysis of world poverty.

Explanatory nationalism sends a message that has become deeply entrenched in common sense. It makes us look at poverty and oppression as problems whose root causes and possible solutions are domestic to the foreign countries in which they occur. To be sure, we deplore the misery abroad and recognize a positive moral duty to help out with aid and advice. When poverty is due to natural causes, we demand that "there should be certain provisions for mutual assistance between peoples in times of famine and drought and, were it feasible, as it should be, provisions for ensuring that in all reasonably developed liberal societies people's basic needs are met."[239] Insofar as "the great social evils in poorer societies are likely to be oppressive government and corrupt elites,"[240] we may be able to help by exerting some pressure on the rulers – perhaps through loans, trade, or diplomacy. But, since we see no causal link between global factors and the incidence of oppression, corruption, and poverty, we do not even ask whether those who shape global institutions and, more generally, the global context in which the poorer countries are placed have a negative moral responsibility for world poverty.

Some quick reflections may show the importance of such causal links. A large portion of the huge quantities of natural resources we consume is imported, much of it from repressive, undemocratic countries. We deplore this lack of democracy and wonder what we might do to help. But, as good explanatory nationalists, we see no connection between the international transaction and the domestic tyranny. The former involves us, but is a fair exchange at market prices; the latter is unjust, but we, not being party to it, bear no responsibility for its injustice. Once we structure our world view in this way, it becomes very hard to ask the right questions. What entitles a small global elite – the citizens of the rich countries *and* the holders of political and economic power in the resource-rich developing countries – to enforce a global property scheme under which we may claim the world's natural resources for ourselves and can distribute these among ourselves on mutually agreeable terms? How, for instance, can our ever so free and fair agreements with tyrants give us property rights in crude oil, thereby dispossessing the local population and the rest of humankind? How can there be a moral difference between paying the Saudi clan or General Sani Abacha – the Nigerian strongman who kept the winner of the annulled 1993 election in jail and has executed numerous political opponents – and stealing the oil outright? In fact, paying Abacha inflicted a second undue harm upon the poverty-stricken Nigerian population: not only is the oil taken away for our consumption (and much environmental damage done) without their consent, but their tyrant is also propped up with funds he can spend on arms and soldiers to cement his rule (cf. n. 173). What is more, we are offering a prize to every would-be autocrat or junta anywhere. Whoever can gain effective power by whatever means will have the legal power to incur debts in the country's name and to confer internationally valid ownership rights in the country's resources. And having done all this, we lavish condescending pity on impoverished populations for their notorious "failure to govern themselves democratically"!

As ordinary citizens of the rich countries, we are deeply implicated in these harms. We authorize our firms to acquire natural resources from tyrants and we protect their property rights in resources so acquired. We purchase what our firms produce out of such resources and thereby encourage them to act as authorized. In these ways we recognize the authority of tyrants to sell the natural resources of the countries they rule. We also authorize and encourage other firms of ours to sell to the tyrants what they need to stay in power – from aircraft and arms to surveillance and torture equipment.[241] We might instead work out an international treaty declaring that rulers who hold power contrary to their country's constitution and without democratic legitimation cannot sell their country's resources abroad nor borrow in its name. Such a treaty would not merely end our complicity. It would also dramatically reduce the rewards and hence the frequency of coups d'état and dictatorship in the poor countries.[242]

Once we think about present human misery in global terms, other reforms come readily to mind – for example, a treaty by which states would commit themselves to outlaw bribes paid by their firms to foreign officials. Such a reform would evidently render officials in poor countries more responsive to domestic interests. By greatly reducing a now customary "perk" of official positions, it would also alter the pool of office-seekers toward more public-spirited candidates.[243]

That these global factors really have an important influence is indicated by the fact that resource-rich developing countries tend to have slower economic growth. The factors we examined can explain this. The fact that the *de facto* ruler of a resource-rich developing country can sell these resources, or use them as loan collateral, provides strong incentives to gain power in such a country, by whatever means. And, since the officials of such countries have resources to sell and money to spend, it is also more lucrative to corrupt them than their resource-poor peers. For these reasons, ample resources can become an obstacle to growth, because they foster coups, oppression, and corruption (as Nigeria illustrates). That they have this effect is, however, due to the global factors I have mentioned.[244]

Explanatory nationalism traces present human misery to bad national policies and institutions in the poor countries. I have given one response: these national policies and institutions are indeed often quite bad; but the fact that they are can be traced to global policies and institutions. It is worth showing briefly how global factors would be of great explanatory importance even if the national policies and institutions of poor countries were optimal.

Many governments of poor countries face an acute shortage of investment capital for providing education, safe drinking water, sewers, electricity, road, rail, and communication links, etc., which could boost economic development. To raise revenues, such governments may well decide, as some economists are urging them to do, to provide tax incentives for foreign investment in the construction of sweatshops or sex tourism resorts. To be sure, work in a Central American *maquila* or an Asian brothel is badly paid and quite unpleasant. But, as things stand, many poor persons and their families depend on such work for their livelihood. Encouraging such investment may then truly be part of the best development strategy for many of the poorer countries. But this is so only because and insofar as these countries and regions lack other sources of investment capital and the power to mandate minimum working conditions on their own soil. Many of them cannot generate domestic investment capital because they struggle under a mountain of foreign debt accumulated by previous dictators and military rulers and must service these debts on pain of being shut out of the international financial markets. And, given their dependence on foreign investment capital, they cannot mandate minimally decent working conditions, because foreign firms can easily shift their investments elsewhere. Global institutional reforms could solve these problems through international law or treaties: by creating a source of investment capital to foster economic development in the poorest regions,[245] and by creating global minimum standards for working conditions.

I conclude that explanatory nationalism and the moral world view based on it do not fit the real world. Global factors are all-important for explaining present human misery, in four main ways. Such factors crucially affect what sorts of persons shape national policy in the poor countries, what incentives these persons face, what options they have, and what impact the implementation of any of their options would have on domestic poverty and human-rights fulfillment. Current policies of the rich countries and the global order they impose greatly contribute to poverty and unfulfilled human rights in the poor countries and thereby inflict severe undue harms on many. These harms could be dramatically reduced through even relatively minor international reforms.

5.4 Conclusion

I have argued that – acceptable common and lofty nationalism notwithstanding – much of the massive poverty and oppression in the poorer countries engages our negative duty to avoid harming others unduly. Standard defenses that challenge the adverb "unduly" have little chance of success: the global poor have done nothing to deserve their position – in fact, most of them are children. Politicians and the more affluent citizens of the rich countries know at least in broad outlines what living conditions are imposed upon the global poor, and we also know, or at least should know and can easily find out, how our national laws and policies affect these conditions either directly or through global institutions. We can then try to initiate appropriate changes in national policies or global institutions – for example, by publicizing their nature and effects and by developing feasible paths of reform. We can also take compensating action through volunteer work or contributions to effective relief organizations (such as the World Food Program, UNICEF, Oxfam, Médecins sans Frontières, or Amnesty International) that help protect the victims of current policies and institutions.[246] By continuing to support the current global order and the national policies that shape and sustain it without taking compensating action toward institutional reform or shielding its victims, we share a negative responsibility for the undue harms they foreseeably produce.

Some will wonder how we can possibly be collaborating in the starvation of millions, if we have never chosen to do any such thing and our lives feel perfectly fine, morally, from the inside. Many Nazi sympathizers wondered likewise. They, too, had never chosen to support war and genocide, but had merely continued to do their jobs, to follow orders, perhaps to attend rallies. Yet, by acting in these ways, they did contribute to the massacres. Given what they knew about the ongoing war and genocide and their own causal roles, they ought to have thought, and chosen, and then acted differently.[247] Or so we now tend to believe. And if this is how we think about most Germans in the early 1940s, then this is how we must surely think about ourselves, seeing that we enjoy so much more freedom to inform ourselves and to act politically.

The point of this parallel is not to raise issues of blame or guilt, which I am leaving aside throughout, nor to liken our conduct to that of Nazi sympathizers. The common point is thoughtlessness. Poverty so extensive and severe as to cause 18 million deaths a year requires a reflective moral response from each and every one of us. It requires that we morally situate ourselves in respect to it and choose how to act or fail to act in the face of it. That the academic justice industry has, by and large, ignored this phenomenon is a stunning failure[248] – which I have tried to explain by reference to the deeply ingrained lofty nationalism of these moralists as reinforced in turn by the explanatory nationalism propagated by their more hard-nosed economist colleagues.

If we do stop to think and if we do conclude that we have been involved in the undue harming of the global poor, some misguided communitarians and patriots will say that it is magnificent and valuable to love and to benefit one's own country and compatriots even if doing so means death to myriad outsiders. But we do not face this kind of choice. Our countries can flourish quite well without depriving the global poor. And our national solidarity and fellow feeling can thrive lavishly even without our readiness to deprive them – just as your loving bond with your children can thrive fully even without your willingness to kill to get them all the latest toys. We can honor our negative duties and still build the most splendid republic that lofty nationalists, communitarians, and patriots might ever desire. Whether we can build such a republic while the dying continues is at least doubtful.

6

Achieving Democracy

6.0 Introduction

Democracy means that political power is authorized and controlled by the people over whom it is exercised, and this in such a way as to give these persons roughly equal political influence. Democracy involves voting – on political issues or on candidates for political offices – in accordance with the general idea of one-person-one-vote. But genuine democracy involves a lot more besides. Votes must feature alternatives that give voters a genuine choice. People must have a way of influencing the agenda (political issues and options) or the list of candidates. Voters must be shielded from pressure and retaliation by government officials and private citizens alike; they must, more

This chapter first appeared in *Ethics & International Affairs* 15, 1 (2001): 3–23. It originated as a lecture given in honor of my friend Otfried Höffe on the occasion of his honorary doctorate, in August 2000, from the Pontifícia Universidade Católica in Pôrto Allegre, Brazil. For important comments, which I have tried to accommodate in this written version, I thank my respondent Wilson Mendonça as well as Alvaro de Vita, Sônia Filipe, Otfried Höffe, Thomas Kesselring, and Alessandro Pinzani. I also gratefully acknowledge support through a grant from the Research and Writing Initiative of the Program on Global Security and Sustainability of the John D. and Catherine T. MacArthur Foundation.

generally, be safe from extreme economic need and from arbitrary physical violence and psychological duress, any of which might make them excessively dependent on others. Voters must be free to assemble and discuss, and free also to inform themselves, which presupposes freedom of the press and of the other mass media. Political power must be exercised pursuant to standing, public rules so that the consequences of electoral results on political decisions can be assessed and at least roughly predicted by voters. Last but not least, democracy requires certain dispositions and conduct on the part of citizens: a readiness to accept majority decisions and a commitment to exercise their responsibilities as voters by informing themselves about candidates and political issues and by going to the polls.[249]

Democratic government might take many institutional forms that are consistent with these core requirements. Some of these are instantiated in present or historical democratic states. These actual political systems fall short of being fully democratic in some respects – democracy is a scalar predicate, as political systems can be more or less democratic in multiple dimensions. A rough and vague distinction can nonetheless be drawn between broadly democratic states and the rest, which I blandly label "authoritarian."

Many countries have become democratic, or more democratic, in recent years. Most of these new democracies seem weak and fragile, and the trend may not last. Still, the phenomenon has been remarkable enough to spawn a burgeoning literature – composed mostly in the rich and well-established democracies – offering political analysis and advice to newly democratic states.[250] This chapter fits this "transition-to-democracy" genre, but its analysis pays far more attention than is commonly done to the global context within which national democratic regimes succeed or fail, and the advice I offer fledgling democracies consequently has a strong foreign-policy component. In the former respect, this chapter is continuous with another body of work which argues that the global order maintained by the rich democracies and their foreign policies is a significant contributor to the lack of democracy elsewhere.[251] I am sympathetic to such work in that I share its goal of global institutional reform toward achieving a more democratic *global* order.[252] Still, this chapter is not focused on the critique or reform of the rich democracies or of the global order they impose. Rather, its focus is on what the political leaders of a fledgling democracy can and should do – *other than* repeating justified yet ineffective demands upon the rich democracies. For dramatic effect, I use "we" and "us" in reference to such political leaders of a fledgling democracy; but I am in fact a German citizen living in Manhattan. If this chapter is worth reading nonetheless, it is because of how its analysis and advice differ from the mainstream.

6.1 The structure of the problem faced by fledgling democracies

Let us imagine ourselves in a typical transition-to-democracy scenario. We are associated with a fledgling democratic government newly installed or restored after a period of undemocratic and repressive rule. We must work to establish the essentials of democratic government, of course, including civil and political rights and the rule of law; but we must also come to terms with the enemies of democracy and in particular with the former authoritarian rulers and their supporters. The transition-to-democracy literature focuses on these two tasks and, often, on more specific questions about how a fledgling democracy ought to cope with the legacy of an authoritarian past. To what extent should we recognize as valid economic transactions and administrative policies executed pursuant to the laws of the authoritarian predecessor regime? To what extent should we expose and punish the crimes of former rulers and their supporters? And what measures should we take to compensate surviving victims of the preceding regime, to recognize their suffering and to restore their dignity?[253]

These questions are about coping with the past, and backward-looking considerations bear on them – for instance, considerations concerning compensatory and retributive justice. And yet, intelligent answers to these questions must also take the future into account. Of the many future-oriented considerations that may come into play, let us concentrate on the most weighty: those that concern the impact of our conduct (that of the new democratic government) on the prospects for democracy. These specific considerations may be grouped under three distinct headings.

The first and most obvious set of such considerations concerns the immediate resistance or support generated by particular policies we might pursue. Prominent here are dangers that may emanate from remnants of the authoritarian predecessor regime. These dangers may be negligible when this prior regime is thoroughly destroyed and discredited, as in the cases of Nazi Germany, South Africa, and some of the communist regimes in eastern Europe. But these dangers have been quite serious in other cases, as when military juntas have turned over power to civilians and returned to their barracks, notably in

Latin America and also recently in Nigeria. In such situations, any attempt to expose and punish abuses that officers committed during the period of military rule is fraught with the danger of provoking elements of the military to rebel and even to seize power once again. Yet, on the other hand, we may face possible resistance also from the victims of the predecessor regime. They may be strongly opposed to leaving prior abuses unpunished, and their opposition, too, may endanger the new democratic order.

A second, somewhat less obvious set of future-oriented considerations concerns the incentive effects produced by our decisions understood as inaugurating or continuing a standing practice. For example, by making no attempt to expose and punish the former authoritarian rulers, we may send a signal to potential predators that any future undemocratic acquisition and exercise of governmental power will run no serious risk of punishment. This signal may encourage, or insufficiently *dis*courage, coup attempts and may thereby undermine the stability of our and of future democratic governments. Yet, on the other hand, by displaying a disposition severely to punish former such rulers who have ceded power without an all-out fight, we may encourage future authoritarian rulers desperately to cling to power by any means, including extreme ruthlessness and violence.[254] This second set of considerations is broader and more principled than the first. Attending to the effects our conduct has through the dispositions it displays, these considerations expand our perspective beyond the present democratic period to all other democratic periods into the indefinite future.

The third set of future-oriented considerations expands the perspective once again – in spatial rather than temporal dimensions. When predators assess the risks and rewards of their undemocratic acquisition or exercise of governmental power or weigh the costs and benefits of stepping down, they are mindful not only of the (possibly quite sparse) evidence about how previous authoritarian rulers in their own country have fared. They are likely also to take account of the fate of authoritarian rulers in other, similarly situated countries. The way we deal with our former repressive rulers thus also sends a signal abroad and will therefore, by influencing the calculations of actual and potential authoritarian rulers there, affect the prospects for democracy in other countries. An example of this recently played out in South Korea, which has been criticized for treating its former military rulers too harshly. The critics protest that such severe treatment will make it harder to get other authoritarian rulers – those in Burma and Cambodia, for example – to step down.

Now one may think that a fledgling democratic government should focus exclusively on entrenching democracy at home and thus should pay no attention to how its decisions affect the prospects for democracy elsewhere. But there are two reasons for paying attention to the third set of future-oriented considerations. First, giving no weight to how our decisions affect the prospects for democracy elsewhere is myopic in that the prospects for democracy in our country are likely to be affected by whether other countries are democratic or not. Thus, the more of Latin America is governed democratically, the more stable any one of its democracies is likely to be. Second, exclusive concentration on the aim of entrenching democracy at home is likely to be collectively self-defeating. *Each* fledgling democratic government is likely to be less successful with regard to this aim than it would be if *all* of these democratic governments also gave some weight to the entrenchment of democracy elsewhere.[255]

The distinction of these three sets of considerations bearing on the prospects for democracy may become clearer by showing how it exemplifies a general point about strategic rationality, which can also be illustrated in more familiar small-scale contexts. How should you behave when you are blackmailed for ransom by a kidnapper? The first set of considerations suggests that you should deal with the kidnapper so as to maximize the prospects for the safe return of your child. The second set of considerations suggests that you should also think about the signal that your conduct in this case (illustrating how you are disposed to act) sends to persons who may be ready to blackmail you similarly in the future. Your willingness to meet extravagant demands for the safe return of your child could make your children favorite kidnap targets. The third set of considerations suggests, in addition, that your conduct in this case may also affect the kidnap risk to which children other than your own are exposed. Your willingness to meet extravagant demands may attract more people to a career in the kidnapping business.

A general way of stating how the future-oriented considerations in the second and third sets are broader than those in the first is this: actors who optimize locally, at each decision point, may not succeed in optimizing globally, over time. This is so because such actors influence how the world goes not merely through their conduct (which, we assume, is optimal), but also through their disposition to optimize which, if known, may well encourage harmful or unhelpful conduct by others. Suppose some generals know that, if they seize and hold power by force and then lose it again sometime later, they will be dealt with in whatever way optimizes the prospects for democracy, and suppose they predict that our optimal response to this eventuality would then be to let them go unpunished. Our known disposition of "local" democratic optimization would then *encourage* such generals to take power undemocratically, or would at least fail to *dis*courage them from doing so. (The same disposition may also encourage them to use their power, while they have it, to change the situation so as to make it less opportune for us to punish them later.) A disposition on our part flexibly to do what is best for democracy in our country may well, then, not be best for democracy in our country – just as your disposition always flexibly to do what is best for your children's safety may not be best for your children's safety.

Juxtaposing these two topics (rational response to potential kidnappings and to potential coups d'état) does not merely help clarify the relevant threefold distinction. It also highlights the importance of the second and third sets of considerations. That getting your children to stop screaming by giving them a piece of candy will tend to cause them to scream more often in order to receive more candy – this thought is almost too obvious for words. That meeting the demands of kidnappers and hijackers will tend to increase the incidence of kidnappings and hijackings – this thought, too, is rarely missed. But the thought that reconciliation with, and amnesty for, former authoritarian rulers will tend to encourage the undemocratic acquisition and repressive exercise of political power – this thought is often missed in more journalistic contributions to the transition-to-democracy literature.

While it is clear that we should pay attention to the second and third sets of considerations, it is much less clear how these considerations should affect our policies. The only straightforward case is that where the former authoritarian rulers have clung to power with violence and ruthlessness as long as they could and were thoroughly defeated. In cases of this sort, all considerations point toward severe punishment. The authoritarian rulers were, despite their best efforts, defeated, and thus pose no serious threat to the present democratic order (first set of considerations). They displayed behavior that should be severely discouraged for the future. And they displayed no behavior – such as stepping down gracefully – that we have reason to encourage. In such cases, we should, then, aim at a quite severe punishment – while also spreading the word, perhaps, that this punishment would have been less severe if they had agreed to relinquish power without all the bloodshed.

Apart from this straightforward case, there are no easy answers. It all depends on how one estimates the various incentive effects and probabilities – and on whether and how one discounts the future and discounts transnational externalities. The resulting uncertainty is good news for many politicians who can defend whatever response they like as being driven by a sincere and sophisticated concern for the prospects of democracy. It is good news also for the pundits in academia and the media, who can go on rehearsing the old arguments without risk of ever being refuted. But it is bad news for the prospects of democracy: the more uncertain it is what a commitment to democracy demands, the less agreement there will be among those who, sincerely or not, profess such a commitment.

6.2 Reducing the expected rewards of coups d'état

My attempt to break new ground takes the just-developed framework of future-oriented considerations beyond issues of coping with the past. Our fledgling democratic government has some power to shape the incentives that in turn will influence conduct on which the future survival and stability of democratic institutions depend. So my general question is: beyond coping well with the past, what *else* can a fledgling democratic government do to entrench democracy and, in particular, to discourage the undemocratic acquisition and exercise of power for the future?

My response focuses not so much on measures that make a coup d'état more difficult as on measures that render even a successful coup less lucrative. In some respects such measures are analogous to those employed by business corporations to discourage hostile takeover bids. But there is an important disanalogy between the two cases. Those who seek to take over a corporation can ordinarily do this only in accordance with its existing charter and bylaws, which they can change only *after* a successful takeover. Those who seek to take over a country, by contrast, can do so by force and, if successful, can then undo many of the measures we may have put in place to discourage their takeover.

This disanalogy may seem to show that there is no interesting parallel at all. But I don't think that this is so. The reason why those who want to take over a corporation must abide by its present rules is that these rules are backed by the coercive apparatus of a more comprehensive social system. If gangsters succeed in seizing control of Microsoft headquarters, Bill Gates can simply call the police and have them evicted. In fact, the police are known to be preauthorized and disposed to do this, which in turn discourages gangsters from making any such attempt in the first place. Measures to deter takeovers must, then, involve some mechanism that survives a successful takeover and continues to reduce the payoff that the predators reap from their success.

Modeled on my Microsoft example, the simplest way of transferring this deterrence idea to the case of countries is to create some international analogue to the police, which a fledgling democratic government could preauthorize to intervene in the event that it is overthrown by a predator. Unsurprisingly, leading American political scientists have volunteered the US for this noble role. They have proposed treaties through which small countries – notably those in the Caribbean – would preauthorize military interventions against themselves in the event that a future government significantly violates democratic principles (Tom Farer) or human rights (Stanley Hoffmann).[256] The point of such treaty preauthorizations would be to facilitate outside interventions in defense of democracy and thereby to deter coup attempts, thus making less frequent the occasions that trigger the preauthorization. Preauthorizing a military intervention against one's own country is, then, akin to the business world's poison pills and golden parachutes in this respect. Their point is that predators should be less likely to strike as the expected payoff associated with victory is reduced.

The proposal by Farer and Hoffmann is not likely to be widely adopted. The main reason is that many democrats in the developing countries, and in Latin America especially, are suspicious of US foreign policy and US military interventions, which historically have often supported the enemies of democracy rather than its friends. It is unlikely, then, that fledgling democratic governments would find the US a sufficiently reliable guarantor of their democratic institutions or would be able to convince their peoples of the wisdom of preauthorizing military interventions by the US. Still, preauthorized military interventions by the UN or under the auspices of regional bodies like the Organization of American States may be a different matter, especially if the preauthorizing government itself had significant influence on specifying the conditions under which the authority to intervene would become effective and on composing the agency that would decide whether these conditions are met.

6.3 Undermining the borrowing privilege of authoritarian predators

There are other, better ways of affecting the dispositions of foreign states in ways that would, without violence, reduce the rewards of, and would thereby tend to discourage, an undemocratic takeover. One such measure is a constitutional amendment requiring that debts incurred by future unconstitutional governments – by rulers who will acquire or exercise power in violation of our democratic constitution – must not be serviced at public expense. The idea behind this amendment is to bring it about that successful predators will be able to borrow less, and this at higher interest rates. If it can achieve this purpose, the amendment would stabilize our fledgling democratic order by reducing the payoff associated with a successful coup d'état and thereby weakening the incentives for attempting such a coup in the first place.

Now it is true that predators can, after a successful coup, simply declare the amendment suspended – or the whole constitution, for that matter. However, should they eventually lose power, their successor government can nonetheless refuse repayment of their debts on the grounds that the coup was illegal, that the constitution was never rightfully suspended, and that creditors had fair notice that the people of our country were not assuming responsibility for any debts incurred by their authoritarian rulers.

Could our constitutional amendment enable such a successor government to fend off demands by foreign creditors that it service the debts incurred by its unconstitutional predecessor? To be sure, governments of the rich democracies – with the help of international financial institutions they control – have often supported their banks by bringing severe pressure to bear on fledgling democratic governments to repay the debts of their authoritarian predecessors. But if the constitutional amendment were in place, governments of the rich democracies would find it far more embarrassing to give such support to their banks, which would therefore no longer be able to count on such help from their governments.

Imagine the following scenario. Phase One: the Brazilian people, through their elected representatives, ask foreign banks not to lend money to future unconstitutional rulers of themselves and also constitutionally bind any future government of theirs not to repay such debts. Phase Two: a military junta takes power in Brazil by force, suspends the constitution, and receives large loans from Citibank. Phase Three: Brazil's constitution is restored, and the new democratic government refuses to service the debts to Citibank. Citibank complains to the US government. Would the US, under such circumstances, exert pressure on the new Brazilian government to assume responsibility for the junta's debt, for example by threatening otherwise to shut Brazil out of the international financial system?

Serious public-relations problems, both at home and abroad, could arise from exerting such pressure, and governments of the rich democracies may therefore find it prudent to refrain. It could not be taken for granted, at least, that they would intercede on behalf of their banks. By creating uncertainty about the outcome in Phase Three, our constitutional amendment would thus increase the risks associated with lending to authoritarian predators in Phase Two. In light of these greater risks, banks in Phase Two would make less money available to our unconstitutional successors, and this on less favorable terms. This foreseeable fact of reduced access to credit, in turn, would weaken the incentives of potential authoritarian predators in Phase One to attempt a coup in the first place. The proposed constitutional amendment thus stabilizes our democratic order by reducing the expected rewards of overthrowing it.

The key idea of the proposed constitutional amendment is that it should reduce the ability of any future authoritarian governments, but not that of democratic governments, to borrow abroad. Three important problems must be solved in order to achieve these intended asymmetric effects.

6.3.1 The criterial problem

While the loss of constitutionally democratic government is quite obvious in some cases (e.g. when there is a military coup), other cases are more doubtful and thus subject to controversies, real or contrived. Such more difficult cases may, for instance, involve allegations that some government has engaged in massive electoral fraud, has unreasonably postponed elections, has placed excessive limits on opposition activities, or has greatly exceeded its constitutional powers in other ways. Such allegations can be presented to the domestic judiciary, of course, for internal resolution. But the opponents of the government may allege that this domestic judiciary has lost its integrity and independence, that deciding judges have been corrupted, intimidated, dismissed, or killed by the government or its supporters. The prospect of such hard cases, in which it is doubtful or controversial whether a particular government does or does not count as legitimate under our constitutional amendment, disturbs its intended asymmetric effects. Banks will be reluctant to lend to *any* government of a country that adopts the proposed amendment because they will worry that repayment may be – reasonably or unreasonably – refused in the future on the ground that the government receiving the loan was not legitimate under the terms of the amendment.

To avoid such ambiguities and doubts, a fledgling democracy should officially, preferably within the text of the amendment itself, empower some external agency to settle such controversies quickly and authoritatively in the manner of a court. This agency should not be another government, or group of governments, as such judgments by governments would often be, and even more often be suspected or accused of being, influenced by self-serving political concerns or by political pressures and incentives.[257] More suitable would be an international panel, composed of reputable, independent jurists living abroad who understand our constitution and political system well enough to judge whether some particular group's acquisition and exercise of political power is or is not constitutionally legitimate.

If several fledgling democracies pass variants of the proposed constitutional amendment, they can initiate the creation of a standing Democracy panel under the auspices of the UN. This Panel should have at its disposal sufficient personnel to monitor elections and other pertinent developments in the participating countries in order to be able to decide quickly whether any of them is governed in violation of the constitutional rules it had democratically imposed upon itself. The prospect of quick and authoritative decisions of this kind would strengthen the amendment's deterrent effect on potential authoritarian predators and their potential lenders.[258] Yet, the panel's existence would also safeguard the ability of democratic governments to borrow abroad, as each participating country assumes full responsibility for debts incurred by any of its governments in power that has not been declared unconstitutional by the Democracy Panel.

As its name suggests, the Democracy Panel should monitor only countries with broadly democratic constitutions. It should not, for instance, support the entrenchment of authoritarianism by agreeing to monitor a constitutional amendment that forbids governments to repay the loans of future governments that rule in violation of an existing *un*democratic constitution. The Democracy Panel requires, then, not merely diverse *specific* criteria for the constitutional legitimacy of governments of the various countries it agrees to monitor, but must also have one *general* criterion for deciding whether a country that is, or requests to be, monitored (still) has a *broadly democratic* constitution. This single general criterion can be formulated by the governments setting up the Democracy Panel. Its application, however, should be left entirely to the jurists on the panel. By assigning to themselves the task of judging one another's democratic credentials, the governments of participating countries would expose themselves to severe political pressures (as when a superpower is eager to have a "friendly" client government officially recognized as "broadly democratic"), as well as to suspicions and accusations of having been influenced by inappropriate political motives and pressures. Of course, participating governments may find it necessary to modify the general criterion later on, and so should agree from the start on a procedure for revising it. However, they should also agree to a significant time lag between the adoption of a revision and its entering into force. Under no circumstances should a revision be applied retroactively to a case that was pending at the time of its adoption.

There is much to be said about how the general criterion for a broadly democratic constitution should be formulated. I can here only add two points to this chapter's opening paragraphs. First, the word "constitution" must be understood as including more than the canonical constitutional text, which may be beautifully democratic and yet widely ignored in practice. The general criterion therefore must be sensitive to whether the written constitution really governs the conduct of all branches of government and how particular constitutional provisions are actually interpreted and applied. The general criterion should guide the Democracy Panel to focus on what basic rules are actually operative in the society under examination. Second, one may ask whether a country's constitution should count as broadly democratic if essential parts of it are protected from democratic amendment. Here I am inclined to think that the answer should depend on how restrictive the relevant constitutional provisions are. If they merely entrench a broad commitment to democracy (as is the case with the "untouchable" Articles 1 and 20 of the German *Grundgesetz*), then these provisions should not disqualify a constitution from being counted as "broadly democratic."

It is possible for a broadly democratic constitution to be – through a sequence of constitutionally legitimate alterations – subverted into an authoritarian one. If this happens, the Democracy Panel should resign its authority at the point when the constitution in question ceases to be broadly democratic. It should not allow itself to be lured into the service of a (however popular) constitutional authoritarianism. It is also possible, of course, that a constitutionally democratic country that had adopted a version of the proposed amendment later would repeal it democratically. In this case, the Democracy Panel should accept that its authorization to judge the constitutional credentials of the country's governments has been withdrawn and should cease its monitoring of the country in question. Finally, the Democracy Panel should also be instructed to allow for the possibility that a government, although it came to power in violation of a constitution that includes the proposed amendment, may later legitimate itself through a new broadly democratic constitution. If this new constitution has wide popular support, the Democracy Panel should accept it as having superseded the old constitution.

A Democracy Panel of the kind I have sketched would not be expensive to run. At the limit, even a single small and poor country could afford to put such a panel together by finding some distinguished international lawyers willing to serve – though it is to be hoped, of course, that additional and unconditional financial support would be offered by the UN, by some more affluent democratic states, and by some governmental and nongovernmental international organizations. If constituted and instructed in accordance with the ideas sketched above, the Democracy Panel would significantly reinforce the intended asymmetrical effects of the proposed constitutional amendment.

6.3.2 The tit-for-tat problem

In countries where democracy is fragile, there is a possibility that authoritarianism will reemerge despite passage of the proposed constitutional amendment. If this were to happen, the new authoritarian government might well find it prudent to refuse to service the debts incurred by its democratic predecessors. Unable to borrow in the name of the whole country anyway, it has little to lose by such a refusal and also has a special need to preserve the more limited funds at its disposal.

Anticipating that possible authoritarian successors of ours may well refuse to service the debts we incur, foreign banks will be more reluctant to lend to us as well. By adopting the proposed constitutional amendment, our fledgling democratic government is thus liable to undermine its own ability to borrow abroad along with the ability of its potential authoritarian successors. The amendment may therefore render our fledgling democratic government less stable than it would be if we continued the going practice under which a country's democratic and authoritarian governments assume responsibility for each other's debts. In the end, *all* Brazilian governments, authoritarian or democratic, could be hurt by the amendment – contrary, once again, to its intended asymmetric effects.

This difficulty could be neutralized through an International Democratic Loan Guarantee Fund ("Democracy Fund" for short), which temporarily services the debts of countries with broadly democratic constitutions, as recognized by the Democracy Panel, in the event and *only* in the event that unconstitutional rulers of such countries refuse to do so. The existence of the Democracy Fund does not alter the fact that authoritarian rulers – no matter how illegal and illegitimate their acquisition and exercise of political power may be domestically – are obligated under international law to service their country's public debts abroad and should be subject to sanctions if they fail to do so. The sole point of the Democracy Fund is to neutralize precisely the risk that the constitutional amendment under discussion might otherwise add to the ordinary risks of lending money to countries with fledgling democratic governments.

To be fully credible, the Democracy Fund must have the ability to mobilize sufficient funds to service the debts incurred by fledgling democratic governments in the event of their unconstitutional overthrow. To achieve such full credibility, it is desirable that the Democracy Fund be backed jointly by many democratic societies, including rich and stable ones that have not adopted and see no need to adopt the proposed constitutional amendment. It is true that the enduringly stable democracies will then contribute to a facility from which they will probably never profit directly. This financial contribution by these mostly wealthy democracies would, however, be well justified in view of the resulting global gain for democratization, which would be associated with a reduction in wars, civil wars, and human-rights problems and hence with a reduced need for the absorption of refugees and other humanitarian initiatives.

Moreover, the financial contributions required to sustain the Democracy Fund might well be quite small. This is so because the more financial backing democratic states give to this fund, the less it may actually have to spend. If the Democracy Fund is fully credible, then fledgling democracies can, by passing the amendment, discourage potential predators without weakening their own position (access to credit). A fully credible Democracy Fund may thus greatly reduce the number of successful coups d'état that might lead to claims against it. And there is another reason why the Democracy Fund may in the end prove quite cheap to run: the fund should be entitled to reclaim, once democracy returns, any money it expends on servicing the debts of a temporarily authoritarian country. This is important because the existence of the Democracy Fund should not create a moral hazard by giving democratic governments an incentive to orchestrate coups against themselves in order to ease their country's debt burden at the expense of other democratic states.

The Democracy Fund can thus safeguard the desired asymmetric incentive structure. The ability of any authoritarian government to borrow is diminished by the prospect that it will be displaced by a democratic successor forbidden to repay its debts; but the ability of any democratic government to borrow is not diminished by the risk that it will be displaced by an authoritarian successor.

When affluent democracies back the Democracy Fund, they do good by strengthening the credibility of this fund and hence the creditworthiness of fledgling democratic governments. They do good also by signaling their democratic loyalties to banks that might lend to authoritarian predators, thereby discouraging such loans and thus reinforcing the intended effect of our constitutional amendment. Affluent democracies could do even better in this latter respect – quite apart from whether or not they back the Democracy Fund – by publicly promising not to bring pressure to bear in behalf of any of their banks that will choose to lend to our future authoritarian rulers. While pursuing the constitutional amendment, our fledgling democratic government should then also approach the governments of the rich democracies with the request that they publicly promise to respect our democratically promulgated amendment and publicly warn their banks that they will not consider our country liable for debts incurred by its future unconstitutional rulers.

6.3.3 The establishment problem

It is not likely that the governments of the most powerful states would readily agree to back the Democracy Fund, to respect our constitutional amendment, and to warn their banks. It is more likely, in fact, that some of these governments would even bring pressure to bear on us not to proceed with the amendment. In doing so, they may urge that it is important for the stability of the international financial system that lenders be able to rely on governments to repay the debts of their predecessors, irrespective of what they believe, or pretend to believe, about these predecessors' legitimacy.

On the level of argument, we can respond to such pressure by pointing out that our constitutional amendment will have no negative effects on the stability of the international financial system and on our own ability to borrow so long as the rich democracies help sustain the full credibility of the Democracy Fund. Even if this response fails to win their backing for the Democracy Fund, it highlights the nice point that it is *only on account of their refusal* that our amendment engenders instability. This point reduces the pressure rich democracies can bring to bear against our plan without risking losses in the arena of world public opinion.

The foreseeable refusal of various rich democracies to support our amendment and the Democracy Fund does not show the idea to be impractical. The capital facility needed for the Democracy Fund can be financed through contributions by democratic developing countries, by the more progressive developed democracies, by international organizations, and by contributions from banks and multinational corporations. Moreover, risks could be greatly reduced through reinsurance and through securitization (whereby private investors assume some of the risk in exchange for a fixed premium).

Obviously, the entire plan, Democracy Panel and Democracy Fund included, has a better chance of succeeding if it is pursued jointly by several democratic developing countries. If such cooperation turns out to be infeasible, it makes sense nonetheless for a single such country to pass the amendment, provided its present democratic government can cope with the expected reduction in its ability to borrow.[259] This unilateral step makes sense because it would build moral momentum. It would highlight that, in the existing global economic order, poor populations are held responsible for debts incurred by their thoroughly illegitimate rulers and are thus often forced, after having suffered an extended ordeal of brutal oppression, to pay – with interest – for the weapons that were used against them. It would highlight that this international practice contributes to the frequency of undemocratic government in the developing countries and that people in these countries are seeking to change that practice. A single developing country could get the ball rolling, might induce other developing countries to follow its example, might get a Democracy Panel organized, and might finally build sufficient support for the Democracy Fund.[260]

6.3.4 Synthesis

Let me briefly relate this discussion back to the three sets of future-oriented considerations distinguished in section 6.1. It is natural for a fledgling democratic government to be primarily concerned with its own survival, stability, and influence. Reasoning in terms of this first set of considerations alone, we may well find that we have no compelling reason to spend scarce political capital on an attempt to undermine the international borrowing privilege. Getting the constitutional amendment passed is likely to require considerable political effort that might instead be expended on other goals. And even if such an effort were to succeed, the benefit of our amendment (discouraging potential authoritarian predators by reducing their expected access to foreign loans they could use for their own enrichment and the entrenchment of their rule) may be balanced by its drawback (reducing our own access to credit – the "tit-for-tat problem").

The case in favor of the amendment initiative becomes much stronger, however, once we bring in the second and third sets of considerations, thus broadening our concern beyond the prospects of *this* fledgling democratic government to the prospects of democratic institutions in the long run and in the developing world at large. Governments of the developing countries have, for the most part, been corrupt, authoritarian, and often brutal. In the wealthy countries, this problem is seen as the responsibility of the people in the developing world, often attributed to their lacking the courage to resist oppression or the cultural sophistication to distinguish between the might of their rulers and their right to rule. In truth, however, the *developed* countries are the chief upholders of the might-is-right principle. It is they who insist that the mere fact that someone holds effective power over us – regardless of how he came to power, of how he exercises power, and of the extent to which he is opposed by the people he rules – gives him the right to incur legally binding international obligations in our behalf. Their imposition of this principle creates a strong and continuous headwind against democracy in the developing countries. By focusing attention on this principle and its pernicious effects, and by seeking the support of other countries and their citizens toward its repeal, we have a good chance to achieve a great and lasting advance for democracy in the developing world. Expending the political capital of a fledgling democratic government on this project may not be the individually optimal strategy for each, but it is very likely to be the collectively optimal strategy for all, especially if full weight is also given to the concern to secure democracy for future generations. To make enduring progress toward democracy, the democrats in the developing world must look beyond our diverse spatially and temporally limited stability problems and unite in the attack on the root causes of our vulnerability to oppressive government. To facilitate such unity, we should set an example here and now by working to pass the proposed constitutional amendment.

6.4 Undermining the resource privilege of authoritarian predators

There is another peaceful way of affecting the dispositions of other states in ways that would reduce the rewards of, and would thereby tend to deter, undemocratic takeovers. This is a constitutional amendment in which our country declares that only its constitutionally democratic governments may effect legally valid transfers of ownership rights in public property and forbids any of its governments to recognize ownership rights in property acquired from a preceding government that lacked such constitutional legitimacy. Now, of course, once they have seized power, authoritarian rulers can hand over public property to anyone they like. But recipients of such property are, through the amendment, put on notice that their ownership rights will be contested once democracy returns. This will tend to reduce the revenue authoritarian rulers can raise through sales of public property, thus making it harder for them to enrich themselves and to entrench their rule. And this in turn reduces the attractions of a coup attempt, thus tending to enhance the stability of our fledgling democratic regime.

In attempting to explain and support this proposal, let me first point out that the sale of public property really is an important causal contributor to the incidence of undemocratic government. It has been well known among economists for quite some time that there is a significant *negative* correlation between a developing country's resource endowment and its rate of economic growth. Offhand, this is surprising. One would think that being well endowed with natural resources is good for a country's economic growth prospects, putting at its disposal a stream of export revenues that can be used for productivity-enhancing investments. It turns out, however, that the availability of such a revenue stream also has the effect of attracting predators, so that resource-rich countries are more likely to be victimized by coup attempts, civil wars, and authoritarian governments, which tend to reduce economic growth. The fact that the *de facto* rulers of resource-rich developing countries can sell these resources, or use them as loan collateral, provides strong incentives to seek power in such a country, by whatever means. And, since the officials of such countries have resources to sell and money to spend, it is also more lucrative to corrupt them than their resource-poor peers. For these reasons, ample resources become an obstacle to growth, because they foster coups, civil wars, oppression, and corruption.

The empirical connection I have just asserted has been documented in detail by two Yale economists, Ricky Lam and Leonard Wantchekon. The empirical part of their paper specifically supports the hypothesis that the causal connection between resource wealth and poor economic growth – the so-called Dutch Disease[261] – is mediated through reduced chances for democracy. The authors' cross-country regression analysis shows that "a one percentage increase in the size of the natural resource sector [relative to GDP] generates a decrease by half a percentage point in the probability of survival of democratic regimes. . . . In order to improve economic performance, one has to limit . . . elite discretion over the process of rent distribution."[262] The purpose of the second proposed amendment is precisely to "restrict elite discretion over the process of rent distribution" – at least insofar as such elites lack democratic legitimation.

Could this further proposal possibly work? The second proposed amendment might well have a salutary effect by reducing the price an authoritarian government could fetch for immovable domestic public property, such as government-owned land or buildings. In these cases there is a real danger that a successor government, recognizing its constitutional obligation, will deprive buyers of their possessions on the grounds that they had been acquired through what they should have known were invalid transactions. But how could the amendment succeed with regard to the much more important case of movable goods such as natural resources, which can easily be exported?[263] Is there any chance that the second proposed amendment would induce foreign governments and legal systems not to recognize ownership rights conferred by any future authoritarian government?

At first blush, this does not seem likely. The rich democracies may not like a plan that diminishes the opportunities of their banks to make profitable loans to authoritarian governments of developing countries; but this change is for them no more than a minor irritant. The prospect of not being able to acquire ownership rights in natural resources controlled by such authoritarian governments is, by contrast, catastrophic. The economies of the rich democracies are heavily dependent on importing such resources and would be severely hurt if they could import only from democratically governed countries. Just imagine what would happen if the affluent countries had to meet their crude oil import needs through purchases solely from democratically governed countries! The price of crude oil would be more volatile and much higher,[264] sharply reducing prosperity and economic growth in the developed world.[265]

To make the problem more vivid, let me once again embed it in a concrete example. Suppose the current democratic government of Nigeria passes the second proposed constitutional amendment. A few years later, the country suffers yet another military coup – Nigeria has been ruled by unelected military officers for 28 of the last 34 years – and the Democracy Panel determines that the new military ruler has no legitimate authority under Nigeria's own constitution. Would the governments and courts of the US, Great Britain, and the Netherlands conclude that Shell can then no longer acquire ownership rights in crude oil through contracts with, and payments to, this new military ruler? And would these governments and courts allow a subsequent democratic government of Nigeria to sue Shell for the value of any Nigerian crude oil Shell "bought" from the military strongman?

I confess that the answer to these questions is No. The second proposed amendment would not work this sort of miracle. And yet, it should be passed nonetheless. It should be passed, first and foremost, because it clarifies the moral situation. We live within a global economic order that is structured in accordance with the interests of the affluent high-consumption countries and coercively imposed by them. An important feature of this order – highlighted by the second proposed amendment – is the international resource privilege: the privilege of any person or group exercising effective power within a country to confer internationally valid legal ownership rights in its natural resources. This general privilege is of great benefit to authoritarian rulers and a strong incentive to any predators aspiring to this role. More important for its persistence, however, is the fact that this privilege is also very much in the interest of the rich consumer societies. It guarantees them a reliable and steady supply of resources, because they can acquire internationally valid legal ownership rights in such resources from anyone who happens to exercise effective power in a foreign country – without regard to how this ruler acquired or exercises power, without regard to how he can be expected to spend the sale revenues, and without regard to how strongly his subjects may be opposed to him or to his sales. And this privilege also greatly reduces the price of such resources – because no supplier is excluded (e.g. for lack of democratic legitimation) and also because authoritarian rulers, produced and entrenched by the international resource and borrowing privileges, tend to maximize sales in the short term in order to serve their own personal interests, whereas democratic supplier governments serving the needs of a country's present and future people would be more inclined to budget its resources for maximum long-term benefit.[266]

The second proposed constitutional amendment would focus attention on these issues and could thus help change the attitudes of citizens in the more affluent countries toward the plight of the poorer populations. The now prevalent attitude of condescending pity for peoples somehow unable to get their act together, allowing themselves to be ruled by autocrats who ruin their economies, may give way to a realization of how the rich democracies have a causal and moral responsibility for the great difficulty of establishing and maintaining stable democratic regimes in the poorer countries. As more persons in the affluent societies recognize their involvement and responsibility, they may change their behavior as consumers, reducing their use of products that incorporate resources purchased from authoritarian governments. Such shifts will not have much of an economic effect – natural resources are, for the most part, quite fungible. But they will have a political effect, making it increasingly difficult for the governments of the rich democracies to collude with authoritarian rulers by enforcing ownership rights acquired from them and thereby recognizing these rulers' legal power to confer internationally valid ownership rights in their country's property.

The previous paragraph suggests why I have not chosen a narrower title for this chapter, such as "Achieving Democracy in the Developing World." There is a serious democracy deficit also in the affluent countries, whose citizens have not approved, and for the most part do not even understand, very important foreign policies and international practices that are conducted and upheld in their name. To be sure, many of these citizens may find it convenient to be ignorant and aloof in this way and may endorse in a general way that their government should conduct whatever foreign policy is best for them. But democracy requires more than such general endorsement. Democracy involves the fulfillment not only of important rights, but also of important responsibilities of citizens. To the extent that citizens abandon their responsibility to control the power that is exercised in their name, their country is less than fully democratic. Most citizens of the affluent states are abandoning this responsibility insofar as they choose to understand very little about how the vast quantities of imported resources they consume are acquired and about the impact that the terms of such acquisitions have in the countries where these resources originate.

A challenge to the international resource privilege would make these issues harder to avoid and thus would produce a gain for democracy in the affluent countries. And people in the developing world would surely suffer less harm if people in the developed countries paid more attention to their political responsibilities regarding foreign affairs. Even if the latter will be too selfish to agree to modify the international resource privilege, they will at least better understand how they are causally connected to poverty and oppression in the developing world. They will better understand that they and their countries face here not merely opportunities for occasional charitable contributions, but severe harms to which their economic practices and policies are substantially contributing and which they therefore have a weighty duty to mitigate.

6.5 Conclusion

The currently popular topic of democratic transition covers some very vexed issues that are extremely difficult to resolve in a general way. But it also covers some less complicated issues with respect to which considerable real progress could be made. Those who really care about democracy and economic progress in the developing countries might do well to focus, for now, on these less complicated issues and, in particular, on formulating measures that would reduce the economic payoffs from, and thus incentives toward, authoritarian rule. It is clear, I believe, that measures of the kind I have described could be devised, though doing so in full detail would surely require careful attention to more complexities than I could cope with here. The greatest obstacles we face are not intellectual but political, as authoritarian rulers and the developed consumer societies have a very powerful common interest in blocking reforms that would enhance the prospects for democracy in the developing countries.

7

Cosmopolitanism and Sovereignty

7.0 Introduction

The human future suddenly seems open. This is an inspiration; we can step back and think more freely. Instead of containment or détente, political scientists are discussing grand pictures: the end of history, or the inevitable proliferation and mutual pacifism of capitalist democracies. And politicians are speaking of a new world order. My inspiration is a little more concrete. After developing a rough, cosmopolitan specification of our task to promote moral progress, I offer an idea for gradual global institutional reform. Dispersing political authority over nested territorial units would decrease the intensity of the struggle for power and wealth within and among states, thereby reducing the incidence of war, poverty, and oppression. In such a multilayered

This chapter has benefited from incisive comments and suggestions by Andreas Føllesdal, Bonnie Kent, Ling Tong, and my fellow participants at the Ethicon East/West Dialogue Conference on the Restructuring of Political and Economic Systems (Berlin, January 1991). It first appeared in *Ethics* 103, 1 (October 1992): 48–75, I have revised some passages with the benefit of more recent literature and of the evolving Yale doctoral dissertation, "Sovereignty and Global Justice," by Eric Cavallero. But I have made no effort to change the tone of the chapter, which reflects the spirit of 1990, the year of its original composition.

institutional order, borders could be redrawn more easily to accord with the aspirations of peoples and communities.

7.1 Institutional cosmopolitanism based on human rights

Three elements are shared by all cosmopolitan positions. First, *individualism*: the ultimate units of concern are *human beings*, or *persons*[267] – rather than, say, family lines, tribes, ethnic, cultural, or religious communities, nations, or states. The latter may be units of concern only indirectly, in virtue of their individual members or citizens. Second, *universality*: the status of ultimate unit of concern attaches to *every* living human being *equally* (cf. n. 90) – not merely to some subset, such as men, aristocrats, Aryans, whites, or Muslims.[268] Third, *generality*: this special status has global force. Persons are ultimate units of concern *for everyone* – not only for their compatriots, fellow religionists, or suchlike.

Let me separate three cosmopolitan approaches by introducing two distinctions. The first is that between legal and moral cosmopolitanism. *Legal* cosmopolitanism is committed to a concrete political ideal of a global order under which all persons have equivalent legal rights and duties – are fellow citizens of a universal republic.[269] *Moral* cosmopolitanism holds that all persons stand in certain moral relations to one another. We are required to respect one another's status as ultimate units of moral concern – a requirement that imposes limits on our conduct and, in particular, on our efforts to construct institutional schemes. This view is more abstract, and in this sense weaker than, legal cosmopolitanism. It may support the latter for certain empirical circumstances, but it may, for different circumstances, support less uniform arrangements such as a system of autonomous states or even a multitude of self-contained communities. Here I present a variant of moral cosmopolitanism before examining below whether this position supports reforms that would bring our global order closer to the ideal of legal cosmopolitanism.

The central idea of moral cosmopolitanism is that every human being has a global stature as an ultimate unit of moral concern. Such moral concern can be fleshed out in countless ways. One may focus on subjective goods and ills (human happiness, desire fulfillment, preference satisfaction, or pain avoidance) or on more objective ones (such as human-need fulfillment, capabilities, opportunities, or resources). Also, one might relativize these measures, for instance by defining the key ill as *being worse off than anyone need be*, as *being dominated by others*, or as *falling below the mean* – which is equivalent to replacing straightforward aggregation (sum-ranking or averaging) by a maximin or egalitarian standard. In order to get to my topic quickly, I do not discuss these matters, but simply opt for a variant of moral cosmopolitanism that is formulated in terms of *human rights* with straightforward aggregation.[270] In doing so, I capture what most other variants likewise consider essential. And my further reflections can, in any case, easily be generalized to other variants of moral cosmopolitanism.

My second distinction lies *within* the domain of the moral. It concerns the nature of the moral constraints to be imposed. An *institutional* conception postulates certain fundamental principles of social *justice*. These apply to institutional schemes and are thus second-order principles: standards for assessing the ground rules and practices that regulate human interactions. An *interactional* conception, by contrast, postulates certain fundamental principles of *ethics*. These principles, like institutional ground rules, are first-order in that they apply directly to the conduct of persons and groups.

Interactional cosmopolitanism assigns direct responsibility for the fulfillment of human rights to other individual and collective agents, whereas institutional cosmopolitanism assigns such responsibility to institutional schemes. On the latter view, the responsibility of persons is, then, indirect – a shared responsibility for the justice of any practices one helps to impose. One ought not to cooperate in the imposition of a coercive institutional order that avoidably leaves human rights unfulfilled without making reasonable efforts to aid its victims and to promote institutional reform.[271]

Institutional and interactional conceptions are compatible and thus may be combined in a mutually complementary way.[272] Here I focus, however, on a variant of institutional cosmopolitanism while leaving open the question of its supplementation by a variant of interactional cosmopolitanism. I hope to show that making the institutional view primary leads to a more plausible and more pertinent overall morality. To do this, let me begin by exploring how the two approaches yield different understandings of human rights and their fulfillment. On the interactional view human rights impose constraints on conduct, while on the institutional view they impose constraints, in the first instance, upon shared practices. The latter approach has two straightforward limitations. First, its applicability is contingent, in that human rights are activated only through the emergence of social institutions. Where such institutions are lacking, human rights are merely latent, incapable of being either fulfilled or unfulfilled. Thus, if we accept a purely institutional conception of human rights, then we need some additional moral conception to formulate moral constraints on conduct in a disorganized state of nature.

Second, the cosmopolitanism of the institutional approach is contingent as well, in that the *global* moral force of human rights is activated only through the emergence of a *global* institutional order, which triggers obligations to promote any feasible reforms of this order that would enhance the fulfillment of human rights. So long as there is a plurality of self-contained cultures, the responsibility for unfulfilled human rights does not extend beyond their boundaries. (On the interactional approach suggested by Luban, by contrast, human rights would impose duties on persons anywhere to give possible aid and protection in specified cases of need.) It is only because all human beings are now participants in a single, global institutional order – involving such institutions as the territorial state, a system of international law and diplomacy, as well as a global economic system of property rights and markets for capital, goods, and services – that all unfulfilled human rights have come to be, at least potentially, everyone's responsibility.[273]

These two limitations do not violate generality. Each person has a duty toward *every* other not to cooperate in imposing an unjust institutional order upon her, even while this duty triggers human-rights-based obligations only to fellow participants in the same institutional scheme. This is analogous to how the duty to keep one's promises is general even while it triggers obligations only toward persons to whom one has actually made a promise.

We see here how the institutional approach makes available an appealing intermediate position between two interactional extremes. It goes beyond simple libertarianism, according to which we may ignore harms that we do not directly bring about, without falling into a utilitarianism of rights, which commands us to take account of all relevant harms whatsoever, regardless of our causal relation to them (cf. n. 101).

Consider, for example, a human right not to be enslaved. On an interactional view, this right would constrain persons, who must not enslave one another. On an institutional view, the right would constrain legal and economic institutions: ownership rights in persons must not be recognized or enforced. This leads to an important difference regarding the moral role of those who are neither slaves nor slaveholders. On the interactional view, such third parties have no responsibility toward existing slaves, unless the human right in question involved, besides the negative duty not to enslave, also a positive duty to protect or rescue others from enslavement. Such positive duties have been notoriously controversial. On the institutional view, by contrast, those involved in upholding an institutional order that authorizes and enforces slavery – even those who own no slaves themselves – count as cooperating in the enslavement, in violation of a *negative* duty, unless they make reasonable efforts toward protecting slaves or promoting institutional reform. The institutional view thus broadens the circle of those who share responsibility for certain deprivations and abuses beyond what a simple libertarianism would justify, and it does so without having to affirm positive duties.

To be sure, promoting institutional reform is doing something (positive). But the obligation to do so may nonetheless be negative for those who would otherwise, through their involvement in upholding the relevant institutional order, be harming its victims. This is analogous to how the libertarians' favorite negative duty may entail positive obligations: one must do what one has promised or contracted to do pursuant to one's negative duty not to promise/contract without performing. In both cases, the negative duty gives rise to positive obligations only through prior voluntary conduct: one's promise, or one's involvement in upholding a coercive institutional order.

The move from an interactional to an institutional approach thus blocks one way in which today's rich and mighty in the world's affluent regions like to see themselves as morally disconnected from the fate of the poor in the developing countries. It overcomes the claim that one need only refrain from violating human rights directly, that one cannot reasonably be required to become a soldier in the global struggle against human-rights violators and a comforter of their victims worldwide. This claim is not refuted but shown to be irrelevant. We are asked to be concerned about avoidably unfulfilled human rights not simply insofar as they exist at all, but only insofar as they are produced by coercive social institutions in whose imposition we are involved. Our negative duty not to cooperate in the imposition of unjust coercive institutions triggers obligations to protect their victims and to promote feasible reforms that would enhance their fulfillment of human rights.

One may think that a shared responsibility for the justice of any social institutions one is involved in imposing cannot plausibly extend beyond our national institutional order, in which we participate as citizens, and which we can most immediately affect. But such a limitation is untenable. The existing global institutional order is neither natural nor God-given, but shaped and upheld by the more powerful governments and by other actors they control (such as the EU, NATO, UN, WTO, OECD, World Bank, and IMF). At least the more privileged and influential citizens of the more powerful and approximately democratic countries bear then a collective responsibility for their governments' role in designing and imposing this global order and for their governments' failure to reform it toward greater human-rights fulfillment.

There are two main strategies for attempting to limit the practical importance of this shared responsibility. A more philosophical strategy seeks to show that any institutional order should be held responsible only for deprivations it *establishes*, that is, mandates or at least authorizes. A human-rights standard should then classify such an order as acceptable so long as no severe deprivations are established by it, irrespective of any severe deprivations this order merely – however predictably and however avoidably – engenders. And we should therefore not count against the current global order the fact that it tends to engender a high incidence of war, torture, and starvation, because nothing in the existing written or unwritten international ground rules calls for such deprivations; they actually forbid both torture and the waging of aggressive war. The prominence of these evils therefore indicates no flaw in our global order and, *a fortiori*, no violation of negative duties on our part (though we may be responsible if our own government engages in torture or an unjust war).

This position is implausible. It would be irrational to assess social institutions without regard to the effects they predictably engender – irrational, for instance, to design a penal code or a tax code without regard to the effects it will actually produce through, for example, the compliance and reward incentives it provides. Longer jail terms may lower crime rates thus reducing aggregate jail time, and lower tax rates may expand the tax base thus increasing tax revenues – or they may have the opposite effect. A legislature would not be doing its job if it made such decisions without regard to their engendered consequences. It would be similarly irresponsible to think about the design and reform of global institutions without regard to *their* engendered consequences.

It does not follow that a plausible standard for assessing social institutions must treat established and engendered consequences on a par. A human right to physical security, for instance, though it should be sensitive to the risks an institutional order may impose on (some of) its participants through the high crime rate it engenders, should certainly be *more* sensitive to the risks it produces through officially authorized or even mandated assaults. (We should not, to give a simple illustration, authorize a "reform" of police procedures that would cause an extra 90 assaults by police against suspects, even if its contribution to deterrence would also reduce by 100 the number of similarly severe assaults by criminals against citizens.) These differentiations can and should be incorporated into any plausible conception of human rights, which should avoid, then, the kind of purely recipient-oriented view of deprivations that is embodied in consequentialist and contractualist (veil-of-ignorance) theorizing. With these differentiations in place, we can count engendered deprivations (such as poverty in a market system or insecurity due to crimes) as relevant to the fulfillment of human rights without committing to a purely recipient-oriented assessment of social institutions that would assign to engendered deprivations the same weight as it assigns to equally severe established deprivations.[274]

The sensitivity of the institutional approach to engendered deprivations suggests a further contrast to the interactional approach, concerning the way each understands what it means for a human right to be unfulfilled. It cannot plausibly be required of an institutional order, for example, that it reduce the incidence of criminal assaults to zero. This would be impossible; and approximating such an ideal as closely as possible would require a police state. The institutional approach thus should count a person's human right to physical security as fulfilled if the integrity of her body is *reasonably* secure.[275] This entails that, even in the presence of a shared institutional order, some of what count as human rights violations on the interactional view (e.g. certain assaults) do not count as unfulfilled human rights on the institutional view (because the victims enjoy a high level of physical security which made the assault they actually suffer highly unlikely). Conversely, some of what count as unfulfilled human rights on the institutional view (e.g. inadequate protection associated with a considerable risk of assault) may not register on the interactional view (because some insufficiently protected persons are not actually assaulted).

A second, more empirical strategy for attempting to limit the practical importance of our shared responsibility for global institutions seeks to downplay the extent to which our global institutional order is causally responsible for current deprivations:

> Unfulfilled human rights and their distribution have local explanations. In some countries torture is rampant, while it is virtually non-existent in others. Some regions are embroiled in frequent wars, while others are not. In some countries democratic institutions thrive, while others bring forth a succession of autocrats. And again, some poor countries have developed rapidly, while others are getting poorer year by year. Therefore our global institutional order has very little to do with the deplorable state of human-rights fulfillment on earth.[276]

This challenge appeals to true premises but draws an invalid inference. Our global institutional order can obviously not figure in the explanation of *local* variations in the underfulfillment of human rights, but only in the *macro*explanation of its *global* incidence. This parallels how Japanese culture may figure in the explanation of the Japanese suicide rate or how the laxity of US handgun legislation may figure in the explanation of the North American homicide rate, without thereby explaining particular suicides/homicides or even intercity differentials in rates. In these parallel cases the need for a macroexplanation is obvious from the fact that there are other societies whose suicide/homicide rates are significantly lower. In the case of *global* institutions, the need for a macroexplanation of the overall incidence of unfulfilled human rights is less obvious because – apart from some rather inconclusive historical comparisons – the contrast to observable alternative global institutional schemes is lacking. Still, it is highly likely that there are feasible (i.e. practicable and accessible) alternative global regimes that would tend to engender lower rates of deprivation. This is clear, for example, in regard to economic institutions, where our experience with various national and regional schemes suggests that free markets must be regulated or complemented in certain ways if extreme poverty, entailing effective exclusion from political participation as well as from educational and medical opportunities, is to be avoided. This supports a generalization to the global plane, to the conjecture that the current global economic order must figure prominently in the explanation of the fact that our world is one of vast and increasing international inequalities in income and wealth, with consequent huge differentials in national rates of infant mortality, life expectancy, disease, and malnutrition. Such a macroexplanation does not explain why one poor country is developing rapidly while another is not. It explains why so few are while so many are not.

Let me close the more abstract part of the discussion with a sketch of how this institutional view might understand social and economic human rights and how it might thus relate to the notion of distributive justice. A man sympathetic to the moral claims of the poor, Michael Walzer, has written: "the idea of distributive justice presupposes a bounded world, a community, within which distributions take place, a group of people committed to dividing, exchanging, and sharing, first of all among themselves."[277] This is precisely the picture of distributive justice that Robert Nozick has so vigorously attacked. To the notion of dividing he objects that "there is no *central* distribution, no person or group entitled to control all the resources, jointly deciding how they are to be doled out."[278] And as for the rest, he would allow persons to do all the exchanging and sharing they like, but would strongly reject any enforced sharing effected by some redistribution bureaucracy.

The institutional approach involves a conception of distributive justice that differs sharply from the one Walzer supports and Nozick attacks. Here the issue of distributive justice is not how to distribute a given pool of resources or how to improve upon a given distribution but, rather, how to choose or design the economic ground rules that regulate property, cooperation, and exchange and thereby condition production and distribution. (On the particular view I defend, for example, we should aim for an economic order under which each participant would be able to meet her basic social and economic needs.) A conception of distributive justice understood in this way, as providing a standard for the moral assessment of alternative feasible schemes of economic institutions, is prior to both production and distribution occurring under such schemes and therefore involves neither the idea of an already existing pool of stuff to be doled out nor the idea of already owned resources to be *re*-distributed.

The institutional conception of distributive justice also does not presuppose the existence of a community of persons committed first of all to share with one another. Rather, it has a far more minimal rationale: we face a choice of economic ground rules that is partly open – not determined by causal necessity, nor preempted by some God-given or natural or neutral order that we must choose irrespective of its effects. This choice has a tremendous impact on human lives, an impact from which persons cannot be insulated and cannot insulate themselves. Our present global economic order produces a stable pattern of widespread malnutrition and starvation among the poor, with some 18 million persons dying each year from poverty-related causes, and there are likely to be feasible alternative regimes that would not produce similarly severe deprivations. If this is so, the victims of such avoidable deprivations are not merely poor and starving, but impoverished and starved through an institutional order coercively imposed upon them. There is an injustice in this economic order, which it would be wrong for its more affluent participants to perpetuate. And that is so quite independently of whether we and the starving are united by a communal bond or committed to sharing resources with one another – just as murdering a person is wrong irrespective of such considerations. This is what the assertion of social and economic human rights amounts to within the proposed institutional cosmopolitanism.[279]

This institutional cosmopolitanism does not, as such, entail crisp practical conclusions. One reason for this is that I have not – apart from allusions to the *UDHR* – given a full list of well-defined human rights together with relative weights or priority rules. Another reason is that this institutional cosmopolitanism bears upon the burning issues of the day only in an indirect way, mediated by empirical regularities and correlations about how existing institutional schemes, compared to feasible modifications thereof, tend to affect the incidence of unfulfilled human rights (as roughly indicated by rates of infant mortality, child abuse, crime, war, malnutrition, poverty, personal dependence, and exclusion from education or health care).

The intervention of such empirical matters, and the openness of the notion of human rights, do not mean that no conclusions can be drawn about the burning issues – only that what we can conclude is less precise and less definite than one might have hoped.

7.2 The idea of state sovereignty

Before discussing how we should think about sovereignty in the light of the proposed institutional cosmopolitanism, let me define this term, in a somewhat unusual way, as a two-place relation: A is *sovereign* over B if and only if

(1) A is a governmental body or officer ("agency"), and
(2) B are persons, and
(3) A has unsupervised[280] and irrevocable authority over B
  (a) to lay down rules constraining B's conduct, or
  (b) to judge B's compliance with rules, or
  (c) to enforce rules against B through preemption, prevention, or punishments, or
  (d) to act in B's behalf toward other agencies (ones that do or do not have authority over B) or persons (ones whom A is sovereign over, or not).

A has *absolute sovereignty* over B if and only if

(1) A is sovereign over B, and
(2) no other agency has any authority over A or over B which is not both supervised and revocable by A.

Any A having (absolute) sovereignty over some B can then be said to be an (absolute) sovereign (the one-place predicate).[281]

Central to contemporary political thought and reality is the idea of the autonomous territorial state as the preeminent mode of political organization. In the vertical dimension, sovereignty is very heavily concentrated at a single level – it is states and only states that merit separate colors on a political map of our world. For nearly every human being, and for almost every piece of territory, there is exactly one government with preeminent authority over, and primary responsibility for, this person or territory. And each person is thought to owe primary political allegiance and loyalty to this government with preeminent authority over him or her. Such governments check and dominate the decision-making of political subunits, as well as supranational decisions which tend to be made through intergovernmental bargaining.[282]

From the standpoint of a cosmopolitan morality – which centers on the fundamental needs and interests of individual human beings, and of *all* human beings – this concentration of sovereignty at one level is no longer defensible. What I am proposing instead is not the idea of a centralized world state, which is really a variant of the preeminent-state idea. Rather, the proposal is that governmental authority – or sovereignty – be widely dispersed in the vertical dimension. What we need is *both* centralization *and* decentralization – a kind of second-order decentralization away from the now dominant level of the state. Thus, persons should be citizens of, and govern themselves through, a number of political units of various sizes, without any one political unit being dominant and thus occupying the traditional role of state. And their political allegiance and loyalties[283] should be widely dispersed over these units: neighborhood, town, county, province, state, region, and world at large. People should be politically at home in all of them, without converging upon any one of them as the lodestar of their political identity.[284]

Before defending and developing this proposal by reference to the institutional cosmopolitanism set forth above, let me address two types of objection to any vertical division of sovereignty.

Objections of type 1 dispute that sovereignty can be divided at all. The traditional form of this objection rests on the belief that a *juridical condition* (as distinct from a lawless state of nature) presupposes an absolute sovereign. This dogma of absolute sovereignty arises (e.g. in Hobbes and Kant) roughly as follows. A juridical condition, by definition, involves a recognized decision mechanism that uniquely resolves any dispute. This mechanism requires some agency because a mere written or unwritten code (constitution, holy scripture) cannot settle disputes about its own interpretation. But so long as this agency is limited or divided – whether horizontally (i.e. by territory or by governmental function) or vertically (as in my proposal) – a juridical condition has not been achieved because there is no recognized way in which conflicts over the precise location of the limit or division can be authoritatively resolved. A genuine state of peace requires then an agency of last resort – ultimate, supreme, and unconstrained. Such an agency may still be limited by codified or uncodified obligations. But these can obligate merely *in foro interno* (in conscience) because to authorize subjects, or some second agency, to determine whether the first agency is overstepping its bounds would enable conflicts about this question for which there would be no reliable legal path of authoritative resolution.[285]

This argument, which – strictly construed – would require an absolute world sovereign, has been overtaken by the historical facts of the last 200 years or so, which show conclusively that what cannot work in theory works quite well in practice. Law-governed coexistence is possible without a supreme and unconstrained agency. There is, it is true, the possibility of *ultimate* conflicts: of disputes in regard to which even the legally correct method of resolution is contested. To see this, one need only imagine how a constitutional democracy's three branches of government might engage in an all-out power struggle, each going to the very brink of what, on its understanding, it is constitutionally authorized to do. From a theoretical point of view, this possibility shows that we are not insured against, and thus live in permanent danger of, constitutional crises. But this no longer undermines our confidence in a genuine division of powers: we have learned that such crises need not be frequent or irresolvable. From a practical point of view, we know that constitutional democracies can endure and can ensure a robust juridical condition.

This same point applies in the vertical dimension as well. Just as it is nonsense to suppose that, in a juridical condition, sovereignty *must* rest with one of the branches of government, it is similarly nonsensical to think that in a multilayered order sovereignty *must* be concentrated on one level exclusively. As the history of federalist regimes clearly shows, a vertical division of sovereignty can work quite well in practice, even while it leaves some conflicts over the constitutional allocation of powers without a reliable legal path of authoritative resolution.

Objections of type 2 oppose, more specifically, any *vertical* dispersal of sovereignty. There are certain vertically indivisible governmental functions that constitute the core of sovereignty. Any political unit exercising these core functions must be dominant – free to determine the extent to which its subunits may engage in their own local political decision-making, even while its own political process is immune to regulation and review by larger political units of which it forms a part. If there is to be any vertical distribution of sovereignty at all, it must therefore be lopsided in favor of those governments in the vertical order, which have authority over the core functions. The political units coordinate to these dominant governments, and only they, deserve the title of "country" or "state" (excepting the use of this word within the US).

To be assessable, such a claim stands in need of two clarifications, which are rarely supplied. First, when one thinks about it more carefully, it turns out to be surprisingly difficult to come up with examples of indivisible governmental functions. Eminent domain, economic policy, foreign policy, judicial review; the control of natural resources, security forces, education, health care, and income support; the regulation and taxation of resource extraction and pollution, of work and consumption, can all be handled at various levels and indeed *are* so handled in existing federal regimes and confederations. So what are the governmental functions that supposedly are vertically indivisible? And, second, is their indivisibility supposed to be derived from a conceptual insight, from empirical exigencies, or from moral desiderata? And which ones?

Since I cannot here discuss all possible type 2 objections, let me concentrate on one paradigm case. Walzer claims that the authority to fix membership, to admit and exclude, is at least part of an indivisible core of sovereignty: "At some level of political organization something like the sovereign state must take shape and claim the authority to make its own admissions policy, to control and sometimes to restrain the flow of immigrants."[286] Walzer's "must" does not reflect a conceptual or empirical necessity, for in those senses the authority in question quite obviously *can* be divided – for example, by allowing political units on all levels to veto immigration. It is on moral grounds that Walzer rejects such an authority for provinces, towns, and neighborhoods: it would "create a thousand petty fortresses."[287] But if subunits are to be precluded from controlling the influx of new members, then immigration must be controlled at the state level: "Only if the state makes a selection among would-be members and guarantees the loyalty, security, and welfare of the individuals it selects, can local communities take shape as 'indifferent' associations, determined only by personal preference and market capacity."[288] The asserted connection is again a moral one. It is certainly factually possible for local communities to exist as indifferent associations even while no control is exercised over migration at all; as Walzer says, "the fortresses too could be torn down, of course."[289] Walzer's point is, then, that the insistence on openness (to avoid a thousand petty fortresses) is asking too much of neighborhoods, unless the state has control over immigration: "The distinctiveness of cultures and groups depends upon closure. . . . If this distinctiveness is a value . . . then closure must be permitted somewhere."[290]

But is the conventional model really supported by the rationale Walzer provides? To be sure, Walzer is right to claim that the value of protecting cohesive neighborhood cultures is better served by national immigration control than by no control at all.[291] But it would be served even better if the state could admit only immigrants who are planning to move into a neighborhood that is willing to accept them. Moreover, since a neighborhood culture can be as effectively destroyed by the influx of compatriots as by that of immigrants, neighborhoods would do even better, if they had some authority to select from among prospective domestic newcomers or to limit their number. Finally, neighborhoods may often want to bring in new members from abroad – persons to whom they have special ethnic, religious, or cultural ties – and they would therefore benefit from a role in the national immigration control process that would allow them to facilitate the admission of such persons. Thus there are at least three reasons for believing that Walzer's rationale – cohesive neighborhood cultures ought to be protected without becoming petty fortresses – is actually *better* served by a division of the authority to admit and exclude than by the conventional concentration of this authority at the level of the state.

7.3 Some main reasons for a vertical dispersal of sovereignty

Having dealt with some preliminary obstacles, let me now sketch four main reasons that favor, over the status quo, a world in which sovereignty is widely distributed vertically.

7.3.1 Peace and security

In the existing global order, interstate rivalries are settled ultimately through military competition, including the threat and use of military force. Moreover, within their own territories, national governments are free to do virtually anything they like. Such governments therefore have very powerful incentives and very broad opportunities to develop their military might. This is bound to lead to the further proliferation of nuclear, biological, chemical, and conventional weapons of mass destruction. And in a world in which dozens of competing governments control such weapons, the outbreak of devastating wars is only a matter of time. It is unlikely that national control over weapons of mass destruction can be abolished within the existing world order – through a disarmament program that depends upon the voluntary acceptance and compliance of each and every national government, for example. The continuation of this order would thus probably lead to more and more national governments gaining the capacity to trigger a major catastrophe, and possibly to attempts by some preemptively to disarm others. Nonproliferation and gradual abolition of weapons of mass destruction presuppose a substantial centralization of authority and power at the global level – in violation of the prevalent idea of state sovereignty. Such centralization can best be accomplished in the context of a multilayered global order, that is, in the course of a process of second-order decentralization. If such global institutional reform process also reduced repression and economic injustice, its disarmament component might well win broad support from peoples and governments – provided it increases the security of all on fair terms that are effectively adjudicated and enforced. The attempt to advance disarmament in this way would in any case be far less dangerous than continuing the status quo.

7.3.2 Reducing oppression

In the current global order, national governments are effectively free to control "their" populations in whatever way they see fit. Many make extensive use of this freedom by torturing and murdering their domestic opponents, censoring information, suppressing and subverting democratic procedures, prohibiting emigration, and so forth. These massive violations of human rights could be reduced through a vertical dispersal of sovereignty over various layers of political units that would check and balance one another as well as publicize one another's abuses.

7.3.3 Global economic justice

The magnitude and extent of current economic deprivations[292] call for reforms of the prevailing global economic order. One plausible reform would involve a global levy on the use of natural resources to support the economic development in the poorest areas. Such a levy would assure the poor of their fair share of the value of natural resources extracted and would also encourage conservation. Reforms for the sake of economic justice would again involve some centralization – though without requiring anything like a global welfare bureaucracy.[293]

Global economic justice is an end in its own right, which requires, and therefore supports, some reallocation of political authority. But it is also quite important as a means toward the first two objectives. War and oppression result from the contest for power within and among political units, which tends to be the more intense the higher the stakes. In fights to govern states, or to expand their borders or spheres of influence, far too much is now at stake by way of control over people and resources. We can best lower the stakes by dispersing political authority among several levels *and* by institutionally securing economic justice at the global level.

This important point suggests why my first three considerations – though each supports some centralization – do not on balance support a centralized world state. While such a world state could lead to significant progress in terms of peace and economic justice, it also poses significant risks of oppression. Here the kind of multilayered order I propose has the great advantages of affording plenty of checks and balances and of assuring that, even when some political units turn tyrannical and oppressive, there will always be other, *already fully organized* political units – above, below, or on the same level – which can render aid and protection to the oppressed, publicize the abuses, and, if necessary, fight the oppressors. The prospect of such organized resistance would have a deterrent effect as governments would understand that repression is more likely to reduce than enhance their power.

There are two further important reasons against a centralized world state. Cultural and social diversity are likely to be far better protected when the interests of cultural communities at all levels are represented (externally) and supported (internally) by coordinate political units. And the order I propose could be reached *gradually* from where we are now (through what I have called second-order decentralization), while a centralized world state – involving, as it does, the annihilation of existing states – would seem reachable only through revolution or in the wake of some global catastrophe.

7.3.4 Ecology/democracy

Modern processes of production and consumption are liable to generate significant negative externalities that, to a large and increasing extent, transcend national borders. In a world of competing autonomous states, the internalization of such externalities is generally quite imperfect because of familiar isolation, assurance, and coordination problems. Treaties among a large number of very differently situated actors require difficult and time-consuming bargaining and negotiations, which often lead to only very slight progress, if any. And even when treaties are achieved, doubts about the full compliance of other parties tend to erode each party's own commitment to make good-faith efforts toward compliance.

One may object that this fourth reason goes beyond my institutional cosmopolitanism, because there is no recognized human right to a clean and healthy environment. Why should people not be free to live in a degraded natural environment if they so choose? In response: perhaps they should be, but for now they will not have had a choice. The degradation of our natural environment inescapably affects us all. And yet, most people are effectively excluded from any say about this issue which, in the current state-centric model, is regulated by national governments unilaterally or through intergovernmental bargaining heavily influenced by huge differentials in economic and military might.

This response suggests replacing *Ecology* with a deeper and more general fourth reason labeled *Democracy*: persons have a right to an institutional order under which those significantly and legitimately[294] affected by a political decision have a roughly equal opportunity to influence the making of this decision[295] – directly or through elected delegates or representatives.[296] Such a human right to equal opportunity for political participation also supports greater local autonomy in matters of purely local concern than exists in most current states or would exist in a world state, however democratic.[297] In fact, it supports just the kind of multilayered institutional order I have proposed.

Before developing this idea further, let me consider an objection. One might say, against a human right to equal opportunity for political participation, that what matters about political decisions is that they be correct, not that they be made democratically by those concerned. But this objection applies only to political choices that are morally closed and thus *can* be decided correctly or incorrectly. I believe that we should reject a view on which almost all political choices are viewed as morally closed (with the correct decision determined, perhaps, through utility differentials), but I have no space here adequately to defend this belief. Moreover, even when political choices are morally closed, the primary and ultimate responsibility for their being made correctly should lie with the persons concerned. To be sure, some other decision procedure – such as a group of experts – may be more reliable for this or that kind of decision, and such procedures (judges, parliaments, cabinets, central banks, etc.) should then be put in place. This should be done, however, by the affected people delegating, or abstaining from, such decisions. It is ultimately up to them, and not to self-appointed experts, to recognize the greater reliability of, and to institutionalize, alternative decision-making procedures.

Given a human right to equal opportunity for political participation so conceived, the proper vertical distribution of sovereignty is determined by considerations of three kinds. The first favor decentralization, the second centralization, while the third may correct the resulting balance in either direction.

First, decision-making should be decentralized as far as possible. This is desirable in part for minimizing the decision-making burdens upon individuals. But there are more important reasons as well. Insofar as decisions are morally closed, outsiders are more likely to lack the knowledge and sensitivities to make responsible judgments – and the only practicable and morally acceptable way of delimiting those who are capable of such judgments is by rough geographical criteria. Insofar as decisions are morally open, the goal must be to optimize persons' equal opportunity to influence the social conditions that shape their life. This opportunity should not be diluted for the sake of enhancing persons' opportunities to influence decisions of merely local significance elsewhere. Perhaps political units should be free to trade such opportunities by mutual consent for the sake of creating common decision-making mechanisms. (Here one must bear in mind that such exchanges are likely to reflect the differential bargaining power of the parties and may thus aggravate existing inequalities.) Such discretionary centralization may be rational, for example, in cases of conflict between local and global rationality (tragedy-of-the-commons cases: fishing, grazing, pollution) and also in regard to desired projects that require many contributors because they involve coordination problems or economies of scale, for example, or because they are simply too expensive (construction and maintenance of transportation and communication systems, research and technology, space programs, and so forth).

Considerations of the second kind favor centralization insofar as this is necessary to avoid excluding persons from the making of decisions that significantly and legitimately affect them. The practical unavoidability of such decisions follows directly from Kant's insight that human beings cannot avoid affecting one another: through direct contact and through their impact upon the natural world in which they coexist. The relevant decisions concern two – possibly three – types of issues.[298] First, inhabiting the same natural environment and being significantly affected by what others do to it, our human right to equal opportunity for political participation extends to regulating the use of this environment. In the present global order, most people have no political influence over how the common environment is treated, on resource extraction, for example, or pollution.[299] Second, since the lives of human beings are very significantly shaped by prevailing social institutions – those defining property rights and markets, for instance, and those structuring child rearing and the exercise of political authority – our human right to equal opportunity for political participation extends to the choice and design of such institutions. The existing international order engenders dangerous arms races, oppressive governments, as well as extreme poverty and inequality which greatly affect all human beings; yet most people have no political influence on the structure of these institutional rules. A right to participate in deciding issues of the third type is more controversial. There are contexts, one might say, in which we act as a species and thus should decide together how to act. Examples might be planned modifications of the human gene pool, conduct toward other biological species (extinction, genetic engineering, cruelty), treatment of the cultural heritage of humankind (ancient skeletons and artifacts, great works of art and architecture, places of exceptional natural beauty), and ventures into outer space. In all these cases it would seem wrong for one person, group, or state to take irreversible steps unilaterally.

The significance of considerations of the second kind depends heavily upon empirical matters, though it does so in a rather straightforward and accessible way. These considerations in favor of centralization have clearly become much more significant over the past few centuries. This is so partly because of rising population density, but much more importantly because of heightened global interdependence. Such interdependence is to some extent due to vastly more powerful technologies, which bring it about that what a population does within its own national territory – stockpiling weapons of mass destruction, cutting down vegetation essential for the reproduction of oxygen, emitting pollutants that are destroying the ozone layer and cause global warming – now often imposes very significant harms and risks upon outsiders. These externalities bring into play the political human rights of these outsiders, thereby morally undermining the conventional insistence on an absolute right to national self-determination. Such technologies have also facilitated today's truly global capital and commodities markets which quickly communicate crashes and crises from any region to any other and enable even minor shocks – the devaluation of the Thai currency, a change in British interest rates, or a commodity futures trading frenzy in Chicago – literally to make the difference between life and death for large numbers of people half a world away, in Africa, for instance, where many countries are heavily dependent on foreign loans and on exports of minerals and cash crops. This is not to say that such interdependence is bad as such (it can hardly be scaled back in any case); but it does require democratic centralization of political decision-making: As persons become ever more heavily affected by the structure of the global economic order, they have an ever stronger moral claim to an equal opportunity for political participation in shaping this order. This claim is not fulfilled when its design is determined by free bargaining among states. For such negotiations do not satisfy the equal-opportunity principle so long as many people are excluded from effective political participation within their state, and many states are much too weak significantly to affect the outcome of such negotiations (e.g. in the context of the WTO).[300]

Taken by themselves, considerations of the first two kinds yield the result that any political decision should rest with the democratic process of a political unit that (i) is as small as possible but still (ii) includes as equals all persons significantly and legitimately affected by this decision. In the real world, these two desiderata must be balanced against each other because there cannot always be an established political unit that includes all and only those significantly affected. A matter affecting the populations of two provinces, for example, might be referred to the national parliament or be left to bargaining between the two provincial governments. The former solution serves (ii) at the expense of (i), involving many persons who are not legitimately affected. The latter solution serves (i) at the expense of (ii), giving the persons legitimately affected not an equal opportunity to influence the matter, but one that depends on the relative bargaining power of the two provincial governments.

Considerations of the first two kinds would suffice on the ideal-theory assumption that any decisions made satisfy all moral constraints with regard to both procedure (the equal-opportunity requirement) and output (human rights). But this assumption is never strictly true. And so consideration of a third kind come into play: what would emerge as the proper vertical distribution of sovereignty from a balancing of the first two considerations alone should be modified – in either direction – if such modification significantly increases the democratic nature and reliability of the decision-making. Let me briefly outline how considerations of this third kind might make a difference.

On the one hand, one must ask whether it would be a gain for human-rights fulfillment on balance to transfer decision-making authority "upward" to larger units – or, perhaps more plausibly, to make the political process of smaller units subject to regulation and/or review by the political process of the next more inclusive one. Such authority would allow the larger political unit, solely on human-rights grounds, to require revisions in the structure of the political process of the subunit and/or to invalidate its political decisions, and perhaps also to enforce such revisions and invalidations. Even when such a regulation and review authority really does protect human rights, it has some costs in terms of the political human rights of the members of the subunit. But then, of course, the larger unit's regulation and review process may itself be unreliable and thus may produce unfulfilled human rights either by overturning unobjectionable structures or decisions (at even greater cost to the political human rights of members of the subunit) or by forcing the subunit to adopt structures and decisions that directly lead to unfulfilled human rights.

On the other hand, there is also the less familiar inverse question: whether the third consideration might support a move in the direction of *de*centralization. Thus one must ask to what extent the political process of a larger unit is undemocratic or unreliable, and whether it might be a gain for human-rights fulfillment on balance to transfer decision-making authority "downward" to its subunits – or to invest the political process of such subunits with review authority. Such an authority might, for instance, allow provincial governments, solely on human-rights grounds, to block the application of national laws in their province. This authority is justified if and only if its benefits (laws that were passed in an undemocratic manner or would have led to unfulfilled human rights are not applied) outweigh its costs (unobjectionable laws are blocked in violation of the political rights of members of the larger unit).

How such matters should be weighed is a highly complex question, which I cannot here address with any precision. Let me make two points nonetheless. First, a good deal of weight should be given to the actual views of those whose human rights are unfulfilled and invoked in justification of a vertical shift in authority. If most blacks in some state of the US would rather suffer discrimination than see their state government constrained by the federal government, then the presumption against such an authority should be much weightier than if the opposition came only from whites. This is not to deny that victims of injustice may be brainwashed or may suffer from false consciousness of various sorts. But it must be shown that this is so; and thus it is harder to make the case for instituting a regulation and/or review authority when its purported beneficiaries are opposed to it.

Second, commonalities of language, religion, ethnicity, or history are irrelevant. Such commonalities do not give people a claim to be part of one another's political lives, nor does the lack of such commonalities argue against restraints. Their presence or absence may still, however, have empirical significance. Thus suppose that the members of some political subunit share religious or ethnic characteristics that in the larger unit are in the minority (e.g. a Muslim province within a predominantly Hindu country). Historical experience with such cases may well suggest that a regulation and review authority by the larger unit would probably be frequently abused or that a review authority by the subunit would tend to enhance human-rights fulfillment overall. The relevance of such information brings out that the required balancing does not depend on value judgments alone. It also depends on empirically grounded expectations about how alternative arrangements would actually work in one or another concrete context.

Considerations of the third kind are also relevant to determining where decisions about the proper allocation of decision-making should be made. For example, there may be disputes between an agency of a larger political unit and an agency of one of its subunits over which of them should be in charge of some specific set of decisions. And the question is then which agency of which political unit ought to be in charge of settling such disputes. Here, again, a particular locus of decision-making must be justified by showing that it is likely to be more reliable in terms of human-rights fulfillment than its alternatives.

Nothing definite can be said about the ideal number of levels or the exact distribution of legislative, executive, and judicial functions over them. These matters might vary in space and time, depending on the prevailing empirical facts relevant to the second and third considerations (externalities, interdependence; unreliability problems) and on persons' preferences as shaped by the historical, linguistic, religious, or other cultural ties among them. Democracy may take many forms, as the human right to equal opportunity for political participation leaves room for a wide variety, hence regional diversity, of decision-making procedures – direct or representative, with or without political parties, and so on. This right does require, however, that the choice and implementation of any such procedure within a political unit be accepted by the majority of its citizens.

7.4 The shaping and reshaping of political units

One great advantage of the proposed multilayered order is that it can be reached gradually from where we are now. This requires moderate centralizing and decentralizing moves involving the strengthening of political units above and below the level of the state. In some cases, such units will have to be created, and so we need some idea about how the geographical shape of new political units is to be determined. Or, seeing that there is considerable dissatisfaction about even the geographical shape of existing political units, we should ask more broadly: what principles ought to govern the geographical delimitation of political units on any level?

Guided again by the human right to equal opportunity for political participation, I suggest these two procedural principles as a first approximation:

1 The inhabitants of any contiguous territory may decide, through some majoritarian or supermajoritarian procedure, to join an existing political unit whose territory is contiguous with theirs and whose population is willing – as assessed through some majoritarian or supermajoritarian procedure – to accept them as members.[301] This liberty is subject to two conditions: the territory of the newly enlarged political unit must have a reasonable shape; and any newly contracted political unit must either remain viable in a contiguous territory of reasonable shape or be willingly incorporated, pursuant to this same liberty, into another political unit or other political units.[302]

2 The inhabitants of any contiguous territory of reasonable shape, if sufficiently numerous, may decide, through some majoritarian or supermajoritarian procedure, to constitute a new political unit. This liberty is constrained in three ways. First, there may be subgroups whose members are free, pursuant to principle 1, to reject membership in the unit to be formed in favor of membership in another political unit. Second, there may be subgroups whose members are free, pursuant to principle 2, to reject membership in the unit to be formed in favor of forming their own political unit.[303] And third, any newly contracted political unit must either remain viable in a contiguous territory of reasonable shape or be willingly incorporated, pursuant to the first clause of principle 1, into another political unit or other political units.

It will be said that acceptance of such principles would trigger an avalanche of applications. It is surely true that many existing groups are unhappy with their current membership status. There is a significant backlog, so to speak, that might pose a serious short-term problem. But once this backlog had been worked down, attempts at redrawing political borders would become much less frequent as most people would then be content with their political affiliations and most borders would be supported by stable majorities.

Moreover, with the advocated vertical dispersal of sovereignty, conflicts over borders would lose much of their intensity. In our world, many such conflicts are motivated by morally inappropriate considerations – especially the following two. There is competition over valuable or strategically important territories and groups because control over them importantly affects the distribution of international bargaining power (economic and military potential) for the indefinite future. And there are attempts by the more affluent (white South Africans, Slovenes, northern Italians) to separate themselves from people poorer than themselves in order to circumvent widely recognized duties of distributive justice among compatriots.[304] Under the proposed multilayered order – in which the political authority currently exercised by national governments is both constrained and dispersed over several layers, and in which economic justice is institutionalized at the global level and thus inescapable – territorial disputes on any level would be only slightly more intense than disputes about provincial or county lines are now. It is quite possible that my two principles are not suitable for defining a right to secession in our present world of excessively sovereign states.[305] But their plausibility will increase as the proposed second-order decentralization progresses.[306]

Finally, the incidence of applications can be reduced through two plausible amendments. First, the burden of proof, in appealing to either of the two principles, should rest with the advocates of change, who must map out an appropriate territory, mobilize the support of its population, and so forth. This burden would tend to discourage frivolous claims. Second, it may be best to prescribe some supermajoritarian procedure (requiring, say, that proponents must outnumber opponents plus nonvoters in two referenda one year apart). Some such provision would help prevent areas changing back and forth repeatedly (with outside supporters moving in, perhaps, in order to tip the scales).

Let me briefly illustrate how the two principles would work in the case of nested political units. Suppose the Kashmiris agree that they want to belong together as one province but are divided on whether this should be a province of India or of Pakistan. The majority West

Kashmiris favor affiliation with Pakistan, the East Kashmiris favor affiliation with India. There are four plausible outcomes: a united Kashmiri province of Pakistan (P), a united Kashmiri province of India (I), a separate state of Kashmir (K), and a divided Kashmir belonging partly to Pakistan and partly to India (D). Since the East Kashmiris can, by principle 2, unilaterally insist on D over P, they enjoy some protection against the West Kashmiri majority. They can use this protection for bargaining, which may result in outcome K (if this is the second preference on both sides) or even in outcome I (if that is the second preference of the West Kashmiris while the East Kashmiris prefer D over P).[307]

The conventional alternatives to voluntaristic principles for settling the borders of political units reserve a special role either for historical states and their citizens (compatriots) or for nations and their members (fellow nationals). The former version is inherently conservative, the latter potentially revisionist (by including, e.g. the Arab, Kurdish, and Armenian nations and by excluding multinational states like the Soviet Union or the Sudan). The two key claims of such a position are: (a) only (encompassing) groups of compatriots/fellow nationals have a right to self-government in one political unit; (b) the government of such a unit may extend its rule even to areas inhabited by unwilling subgroups of compatriots/fellow nationals, who are to have at best a right of individual emigration.[308] Those who hold such a conventional position are liable to reject the cosmopolitan view as excessively individualist, contractualist, or voluntaristic. Examples of this sentiment are easy to find: "the more important human groupings need to be based on shared history, and on criteria of nonvoluntaristic (or at least not wholly contractarian) membership to have the value that they have."[309] Insofar as this is an empirical claim – about the preconditions of authentic solidarity and mutual trust, perhaps – I need not disagree with it.[310] If indeed a political unit is far more valuable for its members when they share a common descent and upbringing (language, religion, history, culture), then people will recognize this fact and will themselves seek to form political units along these lines. It is quite possible that the groups seeking to change their political status under the two principles would for the most part be groups characterized by such unchosen commonalities.

But would I not allow any other group to change its political status, even if this means exchanging a more valuable for a less valuable membership? Margalit and Raz ridicule this idea through their examples of "the Tottenham Football Club supporters," "the fiction-reading public," and "the group of all the people whose surnames begin with a 'g' and end with an 'e.'"[311] Yet these cases – apart from being extremely unlikely to arise – are ruled out by the contiguity requirement, which a "voluntarist" can and, I think, should accept in light of the key function of government: to support common rules among persons who cannot avoid influencing one another through direct interaction and through their impact upon a shared environment. A more plausible example would then be that of the inhabitants of a culturally and linguistically Italian border village who prefer an *ex hypothesi* less valuable membership in France over a more valuable membership in Italy. Here I ask: do they not, France willing, have a right to err? Or should they be forced to remain, or to become, Italians against their will?

This example brings out the underlying philosophical value conflict. Institutional moral cosmopolitanism is committed to the freedom of individual persons and therefore envisions a pluralist global order. Such an institutional order is compatible with political units whose membership is homogeneous with respect to some partly unchosen features (nationality, ethnicity, native language, history, religion, etc.), and it would certainly engender such units. But it would do so only insofar as persons *choose* to share their political life with others who are like themselves in such respects. It would not entitle persons to partake in one another's political life merely because they share certain unchosen features.

One strategy for justifying the conventional alternative involves rejecting the individualist premise that only human beings are ultimate units of moral concern.[312] One could then say that, once the moral claims of states/nations are taken into account alongside those of persons, one may well find that, all things considered, justice requires institutional arrangements that are inferior, in human-rights terms, to feasible alternatives – institutional arrangements, for example, under which the interest of Italy in its border village would prevail over the villagers' interest in deciding about their own citizenship.

This justificatory strategy faces two main problems. It is unclear how states/nations can have interests or moral claims that are not reducible to interests and moral claims of their members (which can be accommodated within a conception of human rights). This idea smacks of bad metaphysics,[313] and also is dangerously subject to political and ideological manipulations, as exemplified by Charles de Gaulle, who was fond of adducing the interests of *la nation* against those of his French compatriots. Moreover, it is unclear why this idea should work here, but not in the case of other kinds of sub- and supranational political units, nor in that of religious, cultural, and athletic entities. Why need we not also take into account the moral claims of Catholicism, art, or soccer?

These problems suggest the other justificatory strategy, which accepts the individualist premise but then formulates the political rights of persons with essential reference to the state/nation whose members they are. This strategy has been defended, most prominently, by Michael Walzer, albeit in a treatise that focuses on international ethics (interactions) rather than international justice (social institutions). Walzer approvingly quotes Westlake: "The duties and rights of states are nothing more than the duties and rights of the men who compose them," adding "the rights . . . [to] territorial integrity and political sovereignty . . . belong to states, but they derive ultimately from the rights of individuals, and from them they take their force. . . . States are neither organic wholes nor mystical unions."[314]

The key question is, of course, how such a derivation is supposed to work. There are two possibilities. The direct route would be to postulate either a human right to be jointly governed with one's compatriots/fellow nationals,[315] or a human right to participate in the exercise of sovereignty over one's compatriots/fellow nationals. The former of these rights is implausibly demanding upon others (the Bavarians can insist on being part of Germany, even if all the other Germans were to want nothing to do with them) and would still fail to establish claim (b), unless it were also unwaivable – a duty, really. The latter right is implausibly demanding upon those obligated to continue to abide by the common will merely because they have once, however violently, been incorporated into a state or merely because they have once shared solidarity and sacrifices.

The indirect, instrumental route would involve the empirical claim that human rights (on a noneccentric definition) are more likely to be fulfilled, or are fulfilled to a greater extent, if there is, for each person, one political unit that decisively shapes her life and is dominated by her compatriots/fellow nationals. This route remains open on my cosmopolitan conception (via the third consideration), though the relevant empirical claim would not seem to be sustainable on the historical record.

If this empirical claim indeed fails, then the institutional moral cosmopolitanism here proposed would favor a global order in which sovereignty is widely distributed vertically while the geographical shape of political units is determined, in accordance with principles 1 and 2, by the autonomous decisions of the person concerned.

7.5 Conclusion

From our angle, the world seems in good shape. We live in clean and healthy surroundings, economically and physically secure under an alliance of governments that have "won the Cold War." We have every reason to be content with the global order we have shaped. But resting content with it is doubly myopic. It ignores that we are only 15 percent of humankind: much larger numbers must live, despite hard work, on incomes with $^1/_{50}$ the purchasing power of ours and hence in constant confrontation with infant mortality, child labor, hunger, squalor, and disease. Fully one-third of all human beings still die from poverty-related causes. In view of such massive deprivations and unprecedented inequalities, we cannot decently avoid reflection on global institutional reform.

Resting content with the status quo also ignores the future. More and more, the transnational imposition of externalities and risks is becoming a two-way street, as no state or group of states, however rich and well armed, can effectively insulate itself from external influences – from military and terrorist attacks, illegal immigrants, epidemics and the drug trade, pollution and climate change, price fluctuations as well as scientific, technological, and cultural innovations.

Bringing these potentially highly disruptive risks and externalities under effective control requires a global institutional reform with significant reductions in national sovereignty. To be morally acceptable and politically feasible, such reform must be capable of functioning without heavy and continuing enforcement and hence must bring to poorer societies not merely a reduction in their formal sovereignty, but also economic sufficiency and democratic governance. This chapter was meant to show how the main elements of such a global institutional reform might be conceived and how they might be given an interculturally sharable justification in terms of a cosmopolitan human-rights standard.

8

Eradicating Systemic Poverty: Brief for a Global Resources Dividend

8.0 Introduction

In three previous essays I have sketched and defended the proposal of a Global Resources Dividend or GRD.[316] This proposal envisions that states and their governments shall not have full libertarian property rights with respect to the natural resources in their territory, but can be required to share a small part of the value of any resources they decide to use or sell. This payment they must make is called a dividend because it is based on the idea that the global poor own an inalienable stake in all limited natural resources. As in the case of

This chapter first appeared in the *Journal of Human Development* 2, 1 (2001): 59–77. This journal's website is www.tandf.co.uk. Earlier work on the Global Resources Dividend was supported by a 1993–4 Laurance S. Rockefeller fellowship at the Princeton University Center for Human Values. I would also like to thank those who have commented on lecture versions presented at the 1994 Global Stewardship Conference at the University of Maryland, at a 1994 conference in memory of Professor Tscha Hung in Beijing, at a 1995 colloquium on international justice in Graz, and at a 1996 colloquium at the Zürich Ethik Zentrum – in particular, Rudolf Haller, Ted Honderich, Peter Koller, Anton Leist, Alexander Somek, Paul Streeten, and Susan Wolf. The final version has benefited from additional comments by Marko Ahtisaari, Christian Barry, David Crocker, Sidney Morgenbesser, Brian Orend, Peter Unger, and Steffen Wesche. Their good objections have led to substantial clarifications.

preferred stock, this stake confers no right to participate in decisions about whether or how natural resources are to be used and so does not interfere with national control over resources, or eminent domain. But it does entitle its holders to a share of the economic value of the resource in question, if indeed the decision is to use it. This idea could be extended to limited resources that are not destroyed through use but merely eroded, worn down, or occupied, such as air and water used for discharging pollutants or land used for farming, ranching, or buildings.

Proceeds from the GRD are to be used toward ensuring that all human beings can meet their own basic needs with dignity. The goal is not merely to improve the nutrition, medical care, and sanitary conditions of the poor, but also to make it possible that they can themselves effectively defend and realize their basic interests. This capacity presupposes that they are freed from bondage and other relations of personal dependence, that they are able to read and write and to learn a profession, that they can participate as equals in politics and in the labor market, and that their status is protected by appropriate legal rights which they can understand and effectively enforce through an open and fair legal system.

The GRD proposal is meant to show that there are feasible alternative ways of organizing our global economic order, that the choice among these alternatives makes a substantial difference to how much severe poverty there is worldwide, and that there are weighty moral reasons to make this choice so as to minimize such poverty. With the benefit of some critical responses[317] and spirited defenses,[318] I include here a more concise statement of the proposal and its justification.

8.1 Radical inequality and our responsibility

One great challenge to any morally sensitive person today is the extent and severity of global poverty.[319] There are two ways of conceiving such poverty as a moral challenge to us: we may be failing to fulfill our *positive* duty to help persons in acute distress; and we may be failing to fulfill our more stringent *negative* duty not to uphold injustice, not to contribute to or profit from the unjust impoverishment of others.

These two views differ in important ways. The positive formulation is easier to substantiate. It need be shown only that they are very badly off, that we are very much better off, and that we could relieve some of their suffering without becoming badly off ourselves. But this ease comes at a price. Some who accept the positive formulation think of the moral reasons it provides as weak and discretionary and thus do not feel obligated to promote worthy causes, especially costly ones. Many feel entitled, at least, to support good causes of their choice – their church or alma mater, cancer research or the environment – rather than putting themselves out for total strangers half a world away, with whom they share no bond of community or culture. It is of some importance, therefore, to investigate whether existing global poverty involves our violating a *negative* duty. This is important for us, if we want to lead a moral life and important also for the poor, because it makes a great difference to them whether we affluent do or do not see global poverty as an injustice we help maintain.

Some believe that the mere fact of *radical inequality* shows a violation of negative duty. Radical inequality may be defined by reference to five conditions:[320]

1 The worse-off are very badly off in absolute terms.
2 They are also very badly off in relative terms – very much worse off than many others.
3 The inequality is impervious: it is difficult or impossible for the worse-off substantially to improve their lot; and most of the better-off never experience life at the bottom for even a few months and have no vivid idea of what it is like to live in that way.
4 The inequality is pervasive: it concerns not merely some aspects of life, such as the climate or access to natural beauty or high culture, but most aspects or all.
5 The inequality is avoidable: the better-off can improve the circumstances of the worse-off without becoming badly off themselves.

World poverty clearly exemplifies radical inequality as defined. But I doubt that these five conditions suffice to invoke more than a merely positive duty. And I suspect most citizens of the developed West would also find them insufficient. They might appeal to the following parallel. Suppose we discovered people on Venus who are very badly off, and suppose we could help them at little cost to ourselves. If we did nothing, we would surely violate a positive duty of beneficence. But we would not be violating a negative duty of justice, because we would not be *contributing* to the perpetuation of their misery.

This point could be further disputed. But let me here accept the Venus argument and examine what *further* conditions must be satisfied for radical inequality to manifest an injustice that involves violation of a negative duty by the better-off. I see three plausible approaches to this question, invoking three different grounds of injustice: the *effects of shared social institutions*, *the uncompensated exclusion from the use of natural resources*, and *the effects of a common and violent history*. These approaches exemplify distinct and competing political philosophies. We need nevertheless not decide among them here if, as I argue, the following two theses are true. First, *all three approaches classify the existing radical inequality as unjust and its coercive maintenance as a violation of negative duty*. Second, *all three approaches can agree on the same feasible reform of the status quo as a major step toward justice*. If these two theses can be supported, then it may be possible to gather adherents of the dominant strands of Western normative political thought into a coalition focused on eradicating world poverty through the introduction of a Global Resources Dividend or GRD.

8.2 Three grounds of injustice

8.2.1 The effects of shared social institutions

The first approach[321] puts forward three additional conditions:

6 There is a shared institutional order that is shaped by the better-off and imposed on the worse-off.
7 This institutional order is implicated in the reproduction of radical inequality in that there is a feasible institutional alternative under which such severe and extensive poverty would not persist.
8 The radical inequality cannot be traced to extra-social factors (such as genetic handicaps or natural disasters) which, as such, affect different human beings differentially.

Present radical global inequality meets condition **6** in that the global poor live within a worldwide states system based on internationally recognized territorial domains, interconnected through a global network of market trade and diplomacy. The presence and relevance of shared institutions is shown by how dramatically we affect the circumstances of the global poor through investments, loans, trade, bribes, military aid, sex tourism, culture exports, and much else. Their very survival often crucially depends on our consumption choices, which may determine the price of their foodstuffs and their opportunities to find work. In sharp contrast to the Venus case, we are causally deeply involved in their misery. This does not mean that we should hold ourselves responsible for the remoter effects of our economic decisions. These effects reverberate around the world and interact with the effects of countless other such decisions and thus cannot be traced, let alone predicted. Nor need we draw the dubious and utopian conclusion that global interdependence must be undone by isolating states or groups of states from one another. But we must be concerned with how the rules structuring international interactions foreseeably affect the incidence of extreme poverty. The developed countries, thanks to their vastly superior military and economic strength, control these rules and therefore share responsibility for their foreseeable effects.

Condition 7 involves tracing the poverty of individuals in an explanatory way to the structure of social institutions. This exercise is familiar in regard to national institutions, whose explanatory importance has been powerfully illustrated by domestic regime changes in China, eastern Europe, and elsewhere. In regard to the global economic order, the exercise is unfamiliar and shunned even by economists. This is due in part, no doubt, to powerful resistance against seeing oneself as connected to the unimaginable deprivations suffered by the global poor. This resistance biases us against data, arguments, and researchers liable to upset our preferred world view and thus biases the competition for professional success against anyone exploring the wider causal context of world poverty. This bias is reinforced by our cognitive tendency to overlook the causal significance of stable background factors (e.g. the role of atmospheric oxygen in the outbreak of a fire), as our attention is naturally drawn to geographically or temporally variable factors. Looking at the incidence of poverty worldwide, we are struck by dramatic local changes and international variations, which point to local explanatory factors. The heavy focus on such local factors then encourages the illusion that they completely explain global poverty.[322]

This illusion conceals how profoundly local factors and their effects are influenced by the existing global order. Yes, a culture of corruption pervades the political system and the economy of many developing countries. But is this culture unrelated to the fact that most affluent countries have, until quite recently, allowed their firms to bribe foreign officials and even made such bribes tax-deductible (see n. 243)? Yes, developing countries have shown themselves prone to oppressive government and to horrific wars and civil wars. But is the frequency of such brutality unrelated to the international arms trade,[323] and unrelated to international rules that entitle anyone holding effective power in such a country to borrow in its name and to sell ownership rights in its natural resources?[324] Yes, the world is diverse, and poverty is declining in some countries and worsening in others. But the larger pattern of increasing global inequality is quite stable, reaching far back into the colonial era.[325] The affluent countries have been using their power to shape the rules of the world economy according to their own interests and thereby have deprived the poorest populations of a fair share of global economic growth – quite avoidably so, as the GRD proposal shows.

Global poverty meets condition **8** insofar as the global poor, if only they had been born into different social circumstances, would be just as able and likely to lead healthy, happy, and productive lives as the rest of us. The root cause of their suffering is their abysmal social starting position which does not give them much of a chance to become anything but poor, vulnerable, and dependent – unable to give their children a better start than they had themselves.

It is because the three additional conditions are met that existing global poverty has, according to the first approach, the special moral urgency we associate with negative duties, so that we should take it much more seriously than otherwise similar suffering on Venus. The reason is that the citizens and governments of the affluent countries – whether intentionally or not – are imposing a global institutional order that foreseeably and avoidably reproduces severe and widespread poverty. The worse-off are not merely poor and often starving, but are *being* impoverished and starved under our shared institutional arrangements, which inescapably shape their lives.

The first approach can be presented in a consequentialist guise, as in Bentham, or in a contractualist guise, as in Rawls or Habermas. In both cases, the central thought is that social institutions are to be assessed in a forward-looking way, by reference to their effects. In the present international order, billions are born into social starting positions that give them extremely low prospects for a fulfilling life. Their misery could be justified only if there were no institutional alternative under which such massive misery would be avoided. If, as the GRD proposal shows, there is such an alternative, then we must ascribe this misery to the existing global order and therefore ultimately to ourselves.

8.2.2 Uncompensated exclusion from the use of natural resources

The second approach adds (in place of conditions **6–8**) only one condition to the five of radical inequality:

9 The better-off enjoy significant advantages in the use of a single natural resource base from whose benefits the worse-off are largely, and without compensation, excluded.

Currently, appropriation of wealth from our planet is highly uneven. Affluent people use vastly more of the world's resources, and they do so unilaterally, without giving any compensation to the global poor for their disproportionate consumption. Yes, the affluent often pay for the resources they use, such as imported crude oil. But these payments go to other affluent people, such as the Saudi family or the Nigerian kleptocracy, with very little, if anything, trickling down to the global poor. So the question remains: what entitles a global elite to use up the world's natural resources on mutually agreeable terms while leaving the global poor empty-handed?

Defenders of capitalist institutions have developed conceptions of justice that support rights to unilateral appropriation of disproportionate shares of resources while accepting that all inhabitants of the earth ultimately have equal claims to its resources. These conceptions are based on the thought that such rights are justified if all are better off with them than anyone would be if appropriation were limited to proportional shares.

This pattern of justification is exemplified with particular clarity in John Locke.[326] Locke is assuming that, in a state of nature without money, persons are subject to the moral constraint that their unilateral appropriations must always leave "enough, and as good" for others, that is, must be confined to a proportional share.[327] This so-called Lockean Proviso may, however, be lifted with universal consent.[328] Locke subjects such a lifting to a second-order proviso, which requires that the rules of human coexistence may be changed only if all can *rationally* consent to the alteration, that is, only if everyone will be better off under the new rules than anyone would be under the old. And he claims that the lifting of the enough-and-as-good constraint through the general acceptance of money does satisfy this second-order proviso. A day laborer in England feeds, lodges, and is clad better than a king of a large fruitful territory in the Americas.[329]

It is hard to believe that Locke's claim was true in his time. In any case, it is surely false on the global plane today. Billions are born into a world where all accessible resources are already owned by others. It is true that they can rent out their labor and then buy natural resources on the same terms as the affluent can. But their educational and employment opportunities are almost always so restricted that, no matter how hard they work, they can barely earn enough for their survival and certainly cannot secure anything like a proportionate share of the world's natural resources. The global poor get to share the burdens resulting from the degradation of our natural environment while having to watch helplessly as the affluent distribute the planet's abundant natural wealth amongst themselves. With average annual *per capita* income of about $85, corresponding to the purchasing power of $338 in the US,[330] the poorest fifth of humankind are today just about as badly off, economically, as human beings could be while still alive. It is, then, not true, what according to Locke and Nozick would need to be true, that all are better off under the existing appropriation and pollution rules than anyone would be with the Lockean Proviso. According to the second approach, the citizens and governments of the affluent states are therefore violating a negative duty of justice when they, in collaboration with the ruling elites of the poor countries, coercively exclude the poor from a proportional resource share.

8.2.3 The effects of a common and violent history

The third approach adds one condition to the five of radical inequality:

10 The social starting positions of the worse-off and the better-off have emerged from a single historical process that was pervaded by massive, grievous wrongs.

The present circumstances of the global poor are significantly shaped by a dramatic period of conquest and colonization, with severe oppression, enslavement, even genocide, through which the native institutions and cultures of four continents were destroyed or severely traumatized. This is not to say (or to deny) that affluent descendants of those who took part in these crimes bear some special restitutive responsibility toward impoverished descendants of those who were victims of these crimes. The thought is rather that we must not uphold extreme inequality in social starting positions when the allocation of these positions depends upon historical processes in which moral principles and legal rules were massively violated. A morally deeply tarnished history should not be allowed to result in *radical* inequality.

This third approach is independent of the others. For suppose we reject the other two approaches and affirm that radical inequality is morally acceptable when it comes about pursuant to rules of the game that are morally at least somewhat plausible and observed at least for the most part. The existing radical inequality is then still condemned by the third approach on the ground that the rules were in fact massively violated through countless horrible crimes whose momentous effects cannot be surgically neutralized decades and centuries later.[331]

Some friends of the present distribution claim that standards of living, in Africa and Europe for instance, would be approximately the same if Africa had never been colonized. Even if this claim were both clear and true, it would still be ineffective, because my argument applies to persons, not continents. If world history had transpired without colonization and enslavement, then there would perhaps now still be affluent people in Europe and poor ones in Africa, much as in the Venus scenario. But these would be persons and populations quite different from those now actually living there. So we cannot tell starving Africans that *they* would be starving and *we* would be affluent even if the crimes of colonialism had never occurred. Without these crimes there would not be the actually existing radical inequality which consists in *these* persons being affluent and *those* being extremely poor.

So the third approach, too, leads to the conclusion that the existing radical inequality is unjust, that coercively upholding it violates a negative duty, and that we have urgent moral reason to eradicate world poverty.

8.3 A moderate proposal

The reform proposal now to be sketched is meant to support my second thesis: that the status quo can be reformed in a way that all three approaches would recognize as a major step toward justice. But it is also needed to close gaps in my argument for the first thesis. The proposal should show that the existing radical inequality can be traced to the structure of our global economic order (condition **7**). And it should also show that condition **5** is met; for, according to all three approaches, the status quo is unjust only if we can improve the circumstances of the global poor without thereby becoming badly off ourselves.

I am formulating my reform proposal in line with the second approach, because the other two would support almost any reform that would improve the circumstances of the global poor. The second approach narrows the field by suggesting a more specific idea: those who make more extensive use of our planet's resources should compensate those who, involuntarily, use very little. This idea does not require that we conceive of global resources as the common property of humankind, to be shared equally. My proposal is far more modest by leaving each government in control of the natural resources in its territory. Modesty is important if the proposed institutional alternative is to gain the support necessary to implement it and is to be able to sustain itself in the world as we know it. I hope that the GRD satisfies these two desiderata by staying close to the global order now in place and by being evidently responsive to each of the three approaches.

In light of the vast extent of global poverty today, one may think that a massive GRD would be necessary to solve the problem. But I doubt this is so. Present radical inequality is the cumulative result of decades and centuries in which the more affluent societies and groups have used their advantages in capital and knowledge to expand these advantages ever further. This inequality demonstrates the power of long-term compounding more than powerful centrifugal tendencies of our global market system. It is, then, quite possible that, if radical inequality has once been eradicated, quite a small GRD may, in the context of a fair and open global market system, be sufficient continuously to balance those ordinary centrifugal tendencies of markets enough to forestall its reemergence. The great magnitude of the problem does suggest, however, that initially more may be needed so that it does not take too long before severe poverty is erased and an acceptable distributional profile is reached. To get a concrete sense of the magnitudes involved, let us consider an initial, maximal figure of 1 percent of aggregate global income, currently about $312 billion annually.[332] This corresponds to the income shortfall that separates the 2,801 million human beings living below the World Bank's $2/day (strictly: $2.15 PPP 1993) poverty line from this line.[333] Such an amount, if well targeted and effectively spent, would make a phenomenal difference to the poor even within a few years. On the other hand, the amount is rather small for the rest of us: close to the annual defense budget of just the US alone, two-thirds of the annual "peace dividend" (see n. 143), and about half the market value of the current annual crude oil production.[334]

Let us stay with the case of crude oil for a moment and examine the likely effects of a $2 per barrel GRD on crude oil extraction. This dividend would be owed by the countries in which oil is extracted, though most of this cost would be passed along, through higher world market prices, to the end-users of petroleum products. At $2 per barrel, over 18 percent of the high initial revenue target could be raised from crude oil alone – and comfortably so: at the expense of raising the price of petroleum products by about a nickel per gallon. It is thus clearly possible – without major changes to our global economic order – to eradicate world hunger within a few years by raising a sufficient revenue stream from a limited number of resources and pollutants. These should be selected carefully, with an eye to all collateral effects. This suggests the following desiderata. The GRD should, first, be easy to understand and to apply. It should, for instance, be based on resources and pollutants whose extraction or discharge is easy to monitor or estimate, in order to ensure that every society is paying its fair share and to assure everyone that this is so. Such transparency also helps fulfill a second desideratum of keeping overall collection costs low. The GRD should, third, have only a small impact on the price of goods consumed to satisfy basic needs. And it should, fourth, be focused on resource uses whose discouragement is especially important for conservation and environmental protection. In this last respect, the GRD reform can produce great ecological benefits that are hard to secure in a less concerted way because of familiar collective-action problems: each society has little incentive to restrain its consumption and pollution, because the opportunity cost of such restraint falls on it alone while the costs of depletion and pollution are spread worldwide and into the future.

The scheme for disbursing GRD funds is to be designed so as to make these funds maximally effective toward ensuring that all human beings can meet their own basic needs with dignity. Such design must draw upon the expertise of economists and international lawyers. Let me nonetheless make some provisional suggestions to give more concreteness to the proposed reform. Disbursement should be made pursuant to clear and straightforward general rules whose administration is cheap and transparent. Transparency is important to exclude political favoritism and the appearance thereof. It is important also for giving the government of any developing country clear and strong incentives toward eradicating domestic poverty. To optimize such incentive effects, the disbursement rules should reward progress: by allocating more funds to this country and/or by assigning more of its allocation directly to its government.

This incentive may not always prevail. In some poor countries, the rulers care more about keeping their subjects destitute, uneducated, docile, dependent, and hence exploitable. In such cases, it may still be possible to find other ways of improving the circumstances and opportunities of the domestic poor: by making cash payments directly to them or to their organizations or by funding development programs administered through UN agencies or effective non-governmental organizations. When, in extreme cases, GRD funds cannot be used effectively in a particular country, then there is no reason to spend them there rather than in those many other places where these funds can make a real difference in reducing poverty and disadvantage.

Even if the incentives provided by the GRD disbursement rules do not always prevail, they shift the political balance of forces in the right direction. A good government brings enhanced prosperity through GRD support and thereby generates more popular support which in turn tends to make it safer from coup attempts. A bad government finds the poor harder to oppress when they receive GRD funds through other channels and when all strata of the population have an interest in realizing GRD-accelerated economic improvement under a different government more committed to poverty eradication. With the GRD in place, reforms will be pursued more vigorously and in more countries, and will succeed more often and sooner, than would otherwise be the case. Combined with suitable disbursement rules, the GRD can stimulate a peaceful international competition in effective poverty eradication.

This rough and revisable sketch has shown, I hope, that the GRD proposal deserves serious examination as an alternative to conventional development assistance. While the latter has an aura of handouts and dependence, the GRD avoids any appearance of arrogant generosity. It merely incorporates into our global institutional order the moral claim of the poor to partake in the benefits from the use of planetary resources. It implements a moral right – and one that can be justified in multiple ways: namely also forward-looking, by reference to its effects, and backward-looking, by reference to the evolution of the present economic distribution.

Moreover, the GRD would also be vastly more efficient. The disbursement of conventional development assistance is governed by political considerations:[335] only 19 percent of the $56 billion in official development assistance (year 1999) goes to the 43 least developed countries.[336] And only 8.3 percent is spent on meeting basic needs – much less than the 20 percent the high-income countries promised in the "20 : 20 compact" made within the OECD.[337] All high-income countries together thus spend about $4.65 billion annually on meeting basic needs abroad – 0.02 percent of their combined GNPs, about $5.15 annually from each citizen of the developed world and $3.83 annually for each person in the poorest quintile. The GRD, by contrast, would initially raise 67 times as much exclusively toward meeting the basic needs of the global poor.

Since the GRD would cost more and return less in direct political benefits, many of the wealthier and more powerful states might be tempted to refuse compliance. Wouldn't the GRD scheme then require a global enforcement agency, something like a world government? In response, I agree that the GRD would have to be backed by sanctions. But sanctions could be decentralized. Once the agency facilitating the flow of GRD payments reports that a country has not met its obligations under the scheme, all other countries are required to impose duties on imports from, and perhaps also similar levies on exports to, this country to raise funds equivalent to its GRD obligations plus the cost of these enforcement measures. Such decentralized sanctions stand a very good chance of discouraging small-scale defections. Our world is now, and is likely to remain, highly interdependent economically. Most countries export and import between 10 and 50 percent of their gross domestic product. No country would profit from shutting down foreign trade for the sake of avoiding its GRD obligation. And each would have reasons to fulfill its GRD obligation voluntarily: to retain control over how the funds are raised, to avoid paying extra for enforcement measures, and to avoid the adverse publicity associated with non-compliance.

To be sure, such a scheme of decentralized sanctions could work only so long as both the US and the EU continue to comply and continue to participate in the sanction mechanism. I assume that both will do this, provided they can be brought to commit themselves to the GRD scheme in the first place. This prerequisite, which is decisive for the success of the proposal, is addressed in section 8.5. It should be clear, however, that a refusal by the US or the EU to participate in the eradication of world poverty would not affect the implications of the present section 8.3. The feasibility of the GRD suffices to show that extensive and severe poverty is avoidable at moderate cost (condition **5**), that the existing global order plays an important role in its persistence (condition **7**) and that we can take what all three approaches would recognize as a major step toward justice (second thesis).

8.4 The moral argument for the proposed reform

By showing that conditions **1–10** are met, I hope to have demonstrated that present global poverty manifests a grievous injustice that can and should be abolished through institutional reform – involving the GRD scheme, perhaps, or some superior alternative. To make this train of thought as transparent and criticizable as possible, I restate it now as an argument in six steps. The first two steps involve new formulations, so I comment on them briefly at the end.

(1) If a society or comparable social system, connected and regulated by a shared institutional order (condition **6**), displays radical inequality (conditions **1–5**), then this institutional order is *prima facie* unjust and requires justification. Here the burden of proof is on those who wish to defend this order and its coercive imposition as compatible with justice.

(2) Such a justification of an institutional order under which radical inequality persists would need to show either

- **(2a)** that condition **10** is not met, perhaps because the existing radical inequality came about fairly: through a historical process that transpired in accordance with morally plausible rules that were generally observed; or
- **(2b)** that condition **9** is not met, because the worse-off can adequately benefit from the use of the common natural resource base through access to a proportional share or through some at least equivalent substitute; or
- **(2c)** that condition **8** is not met, because the existing radical inequality can be traced to extra-social factors (such as genetic handicaps or natural disasters) which, as such, affect different persons differentially; or
- **(2d)** that condition **7** is not met, because any proposed alternative to the existing institutional order either
  - is impracticable, that is, cannot be stably maintained in the long run; or
  - cannot be instituted in a morally acceptable way even with good will by all concerned; or
  - would not substantially improve the circumstances of the worse-off; or
  - would have other morally serious disadvantages that offset any improvement in the circumstances of the worse-off.

(3) Humankind is connected and regulated by a shared global institutional order under which radical inequality persists.

(4) This global institutional order therefore requires justification <from **(1)** and **(3)**>.

(5) This global institutional order can be given no justification of forms **(2a)**, **(2b)**, or **(2c)**. A justification of form **(2d)** fails as well, because a reform involving introduction of a GRD provides an alternative that is practicable, can (with some good will by all concerned) be instituted in a morally acceptable way, would substantially improve the circumstances of the worse-off, and would not have disadvantages of comparable moral significance.

(6) The existing global order cannot be justified <from (**4**), (**2**), and (**5**)> and hence is unjust <from (**1**)>.

In presenting this argument, I have not attempted to satisfy the strictest demands of logical form, which would have required various qualifications and repetitions. I have merely tried to clarify the structure of the argument so as to make clear how it can be attacked.

One might attack the first step. But this moral premise is quite weak, applying only if the existing inequality occurs within a shared institutional order (condition **6**) *and* is radical, that is, involves truly extreme poverty and extreme differentials in standards of living (conditions **1**–**5**). Moreover, the first premise does not flatly exclude any institutional order under which radical inequality persists, but merely demands that it be justified. Since social institutions are created and upheld, perpetuated or reformed by human beings, this demand cannot plausibly be refused.

One might attack the second step. But this moral premise, too, is weak, in that it demands of the defender of the status quo only one of the four possible showings, (**2a**)–(**2d**), leaving him free to try each of the conceptions of economic justice outlined in section 8.2 even though he can hardly endorse all of them at once. Still, it remains open to argue that an institutional order reproducing radical inequality can be justified in a way that differs from the four, (**2a**)–(**2d**), I have described.

One might try to show that the existing global order does not meet one of the ten conditions. Depending on which condition is targeted, one would thereby deny the third premise or give a justification of forms (**2a**) or (**2b**), or (**2c**), or show that my reform proposal runs into one of the four problems listed under (**2d**).

The conclusion of the argument is reached only if all ten conditions are met. Existing global poverty then manifests a *core injustice*: a phenomenon that the dominant strands of Western normative political thought jointly – albeit for diverse reasons – classify as unjust and can jointly seek to eradicate. Insofar as advantaged and influential participants in the present international order grant the argument, we acknowledge our shared responsibility for its injustice. We are violating a negative duty of justice insofar as we contribute to (and fail to mitigate) the harms it reproduces and insofar as we resist suitable reforms.

8.5 Is the reform proposal realistic?

Even if the GRD proposal is practicable, and even if it could be implemented with the good will of all concerned, there remains the problem of generating this good will, especially on the part of the rich and mighty. Without the support of the US and the EU, massive global poverty and starvation will certainly not be eradicated in our lifetimes. How realistic is the hope of mobilizing such support? I have two answers to this question.

First, even if this hope is not realistic, it is still important to insist that present global poverty manifests a grievous injustice according to Western normative political thought. We are not merely distant witnesses of a problem unrelated to ourselves, with a weak, positive duty to help. Rather we are, both causally and morally, intimately involved in the fate of the poor by imposing upon them a global institutional order that regularly produces severe poverty and/or by effectively excluding them from a fair share of the value of exploited natural resources and/or by upholding a radical inequality that evolved through a historical process pervaded by horrendous crimes. We can realistically end our involvement in their severe poverty not by extricating ourselves from this involvement, but only by ending such poverty through economic reform. If feasible reforms are blocked by others, then we may in the end be unable to do more than mitigate some of the harms we also help produce. But even then a difference would remain, because our effort would fulfill not a duty to help the needy, but a duty to protect victims of any injustice to which we contribute. The latter duty is, other things being equal, much more stringent than the former, especially when we can fulfill it out of the benefits we derive from this injustice.

My second answer is that the hope may not be so unrealistic after all. My provisional optimism is based on two considerations. The first is that moral convictions can have real effects even in international politics – as even some political realists admit, albeit with regret. Sometimes these are the moral convictions of politicians. But more commonly politics is influenced by the moral convictions of citizens. One dramatic example of this is the abolitionist movement which, in the nineteenth century, pressured the British government into suppressing the slave trade.[338] A similar moral mobilization may be possible also for the sake of eradicating world poverty – provided the citizens of the more powerful states can be convinced of a moral conclusion that really can be soundly supported and a path can be shown that makes only modest demands on each of us.

The GRD proposal is morally compelling. It can be broadly anchored in the dominant strands of Western normative political thought outlined in section 8.2. And it also has the morally significant advantage of shifting consumption in ways that restrain global pollution and resource depletion for the benefit of future generations in particular. Because it can be backed by these four important and mutually independent moral rationales, the GRD proposal is well positioned to benefit from the fact that moral reasons can have effects in the world. If some help can be secured from economists, political scientists, and lawyers, then moral acceptance of the GRD may gradually emerge and become widespread in the developed West.

Eradicating world poverty through a scheme like the GRD also involves more realistic demands than a solution through private initiatives and conventional development aid. Continual mitigation of poverty leads to fatigue, aversion, even contempt. It requires the more affluent citizens and governments to rally to the cause again and again while knowing full well that most others similarly situated contribute nothing or very little, that their own contributions are legally optional, and that, no matter how much they give, they could for just a little more always save yet further children from sickness or starvation.

The inefficiency of conventional development aid is also sustained by the competitive situation among the governments of the donor countries, who feel morally entitled to decline to do more by pointing to their even less generous competitors. This explanation supports the optimistic assumption that the affluent societies would be prepared, in joint reciprocity, to commit themselves to more than what they tend to do each on its own. Analogous considerations apply to environmental protection and conservation, with respect to which the GRD also contributes to a collective solution. When many parties decide separately in this matter, then the best solution for all is not achieved, because each gets almost the full benefit of its pollution and wastefulness while the resulting harms are shared by all ("tragedy of the commons"). An additional point is that national development-aid and environmental-protection measures must be politically fought for or defended year after year, while acceptance of the GRD scheme would require only one – albeit rather more far-reaching – political decision.

The other optimistic consideration has to do with prudence. The times when we could afford to ignore what goes on in the developing countries are over for good. Their economic growth will have a great impact on our environment and their military and technological gains are accompanied by serious dangers, among which those associated with nuclear, biological, and chemical weapons and technologies are only the most obvious. The transnational imposition of externalities and risks will ever more become a two-way street as no state or group of states, however rich and mighty, will be able effectively to insulate itself from external influences: from military and terrorist attacks, illegal immigrants, epidemics and the drug trade, pollution and climate change, price fluctuations and scientific-technological and cultural innovations. It is, then, increasingly in our interest, too, that stable democratic institutions should emerge in the developing countries – institutions under which governmental power is effectively constrained through procedural rules and basic rights. So long as large segments of these peoples lack elementary education and have no assurance that they will be able to meet even their most basic needs, such democratic institutions are much less likely than explosive mixtures of religious and ideological fanaticism, violent opposition movements, death squads, and corrupt and politicized militaries. To expose ourselves to the occasional explosions of these mixtures would be increasingly dangerous and also more costly in the long run than the proposed GRD.

This prudential consideration has a moral side as well. A future that is pervaded by radical inequality and hence is unstable would endanger not only the security of ourselves and our progeny, but also the long-term survival of our society, values, and culture. Not only that: such a future would, quite generally, endanger the security of all other human beings and their descendants as well as the survival of their societies, values, and cultures. And so the interest in peace – in a future world in which different societies, values, and cultures can coexist and interact peacefully – is obviously also, and importantly, a moral interest.

Realizing our prudential and moral interest in a peaceful and ecologically sound future will – and here I go beyond my earlier modesty – require supranational institutions and organizations that limit the sovereignty rights of states more severely than is the current practice. The most powerful states could try to impose such limitations upon all the rest while exempting themselves. It is doubtful, however, that today's great powers will summon the political will to make this attempt before it is too late. And it is doubtful also whether they could succeed. For such an attempt would provoke the bitter resistance of many other states, which would simultaneously try very hard, through military buildup, to gain access to the club of great powers. For such a project, the "elites" in many developing countries could probably mobilize their populations quite easily, as the recent examples of India and Pakistan illustrate.

It might, then, make more sense for all to work toward supranational institutions and organizations that limit the sovereignty rights of all states equally. But this solution can work only if at least a large majority of the states participating in these institutions and organizations are stable democracies, which presupposes, in turn, that their citizens are assured that they can meet their basic needs and can attain a decent level of education and social position.

The current geopolitical development drifts toward a world in which militarily and technologically highly advanced states and groups, growing in number, pose an ever greater danger for an ever larger subset of humankind. Deflecting this development in a more reasonable direction realistically requires considerable support from those other 85 percent of humankind who want to reduce our economic advantage and achieve our high standard of living. Through the introduction of the GRD or some similar reform we can gain such support by showing concretely that our relations to the rest of the world are not solely devoted to cementing our economic hegemony and that the global poor will be able peacefully to achieve a considerable improvement in their circumstances. In this way and only in this way can we refute the conviction, understandably widespread in the poor countries, that we will not give a damn about their misery until they have the economic and military power to do us serious harm. And only in this way can we undermine the popular support that aggressive political movements of all kinds can derive from this conviction.

8.6 Conclusion

We are familiar, through charity appeals, with the assertion that it lies in our hands to save the lives of many or, by doing nothing, to let these people die. We are less familiar with the assertion examined here of a weightier responsibility: that most of us do not merely let people starve but also participate in starving them. It is not surprising that our initial reaction to this more unpleasant assertion is indignation, even hostility – that, rather than think it through or discuss it, we want to forget it or put it aside as plainly absurd.

I have tried to respond constructively to the assertion and to show its plausibility. I don't pretend to have proved it conclusively, but my argument should at least raise grave doubts about our commonsense prejudices, which we must in any case treat with suspicion on account of how strongly our self-interest is engaged in this matter. The great moral importance of reaching the correct judgment on this issue also counsels against lightly dismissing the assertion here defended. The essential data about the lives and deaths of the global poor are, after all, indisputable. In view of very considerable global interdependence, it is extremely unlikely that their poverty is due exclusively to local factors and that no feasible reform of the present global order could thus affect either that poverty or these local factors. No less incredible is the view that ours is the best of all possible global orders, that any modification of it could only aggravate poverty. So we should work together across disciplines to conceive a comprehensive solution to the problem of world poverty, and across borders for the political implementation of this solution.

Notes

General Introduction

1 The *Universal Declaration of Human Rights* was approved and proclaimed by the General Assembly of the UN on December 10, 1948, as resolution 217 A (III). All abbreviations and acronyms, such as UDHR and UN, are explicated in the index.

2 Throughout this book, the \$-sign refers to the US currency. The data used in this paragraph and the next are more fully presented and referenced in § 4.3. International poverty lines are stated in \$PPP (purchasing power parity), inflating the incomes of the poor to reflect the greater purchasing power of money in the developing world. In typical poor countries, the commonly used \$1/day and \$2/day poverty lines correspond to about $\$^1/_3$ and $\$^2/_3$ per person per day at market exchange rates. The 1,214 million people living below the lower of these lines on average live 30% below it: on about 23 cents per person per day.

3 Throughout this book, the word "billion" is used in the American sense as signifying 1,000 million. Accordingly, "trillion" stands for 1,000 billion or 1 million million.

4 Milanovic, "True World Income Distribution," p. 88, cf. p. 73. The figure of $^1/_4$ is approximate. The loss in real income for the bottom 5 percent of humankind was actually 23 percent over the period (ibid., p. 74 n. 19). Income inequality among persons worldwide rose "from a Gini of 62.5 in 1988 to 66.0 in 1993. This represents an increase of 0.6 Gini points per year. This is a very fast increase, faster than the increase experienced by the US and UK in the decade of the 1980s" (ibid., p. 88). This Gini is calculated by constructing a cumulative income graph that shows the

percentage of total income (y-axis) had by the bottom 1 percent, bottom 2 percent, etc., of the population (x-axis). The graph rises toward the right at an ever steeper rate. One connects the beginning and end points (0 and 100 percent) of the graph with a straight line. The Gini coefficient is the area between this straight line and the graph divided by the whole triangular area under the straight line. It is often, as in the quote here, stated as a percentage.

5 In this General Introduction, I am using "we," "us," "our" to refer to adult citizens of the US, EU, Canada, Australia, New Zealand – at least those who share the economic security and basic Western values of these countries. By focusing on our responsibilities with regard to world poverty, I am not suggesting that the responsibilities of the Japanese are importantly different, and certainly not that the "elites" in the developing world have no such responsibilities.

6 This is also reflected in patterns of charitable giving which, in the US, totals about $200 billion annually. Only 1.3 percent of this amount goes to organizations concerned with international affairs, a fraction of that to organizations working toward the fulfillment of basic needs abroad. Cf. *Giving USA 2001* for details.

7 See esp. Marx, "The German Ideology," pp. 172–3, 192–3. Cf. Cohen, *Karl Marx's Theory of History*.

8 This thought goes back at least to Malthus, *An Essay on the Principle of Population*, and came to renewed prominence in the 1970s through Hardin's much-cited "Living on a Lifeboat." Cf. also Hardin: *Living within Limits* and "Lifeboat Ethics: The Case against Helping the Poor."

9 Cf. e.g. Sen, "Population: Delusion and Reality."

10 Rorty, "Who are We?," pp. 14–15.

11 e.g. Alesina and Dollar, "Who Gives Foreign Aid to Whom and Why?"

12 UNDP, *Report 2001*, p. 190, and UNDP, *Report 2000*, p. 79.

13 Cf. text around n. 16, and Reddy and Pogge, "How *Not* to Count the Poor."

14 *Rome Declaration on World Food Security*.

15 Ibid., Annex II to the *Final Report of the World Food Summit*. The US also argued that the FAO was greatly exaggerating the contribution needed from the developed countries: "As part of the *U.S. Action Plan on Food Security*, USAID commissioned a separate study of the projected cost of meeting the World Food Summit target and a strategy for reaching this goal. The study, completed in mid 1998, focused on a potential framework for ODA investments and estimated that the target could be reached with additional global ODA of $2.6 billion annually, as compared to the FAO's estimate of $6 billion annually" (*U.S. Action Plan*, Appendix A). The US government thus is on record arguing that, contrary to the third idea, money *can* be used effectively to help reduce poverty. It just does not see this as an obligation or priority: the $2.6 billion in additional official development assistance it suggests amounts to less than $3 annually from each citizen of the developed countries.

16 The *UN Millennium Declaration* included this reinterpretation by resolving "to halve, by the year 2015, the proportion of the world's people whose income is less than one dollar a day and the proportion of people who suffer from hunger." FAO celebrates this inclusion and pretends not to notice the shift (www.fao.org/news/2001/010304-e.htm).
17 UNDP, *Report 1997*, p. 5, and UNDP, *Report 2001*, p. 22. Leaving China aside, the number of the undernourished has been rising.
18 Lipton, "The 2015 Poverty Targets," calculates that, if the trends of 1990–98 persist, poverty as defined by the $1 PPP a day poverty line will decline from 24.5 percent of the developing countries' population in 1996 to 23.2 percent in 2015 – reflecting a decline in China from 17% to 4.7% and an increase in the remainder of the developing world from 27% to 28.7%. If these projections come true, the number of human beings subsisting below the World Bank's lower poverty line will actually increase by over 21 percent: to 1,442.4 million in 2015, from 1,190.6 million in 1996 (World Bank, *Report 2000/2001*, p. 23).
19 This critique is exemplified in Singer, "Famine, Affluence and Morality," and Unger, *Living High and Letting Die.*
20 Cf. § 1.4. Merely failing to reduce severe poverty could still be a significant moral flaw in social institutions.
21 The leftist political coalition responsible for these policies was nonetheless soundly defeated in the last assembly elections, May 10, 2001, gaining only 40 seats out of 140.
22 In §§ 4.8 and 5.3, esp.
23 The global poor suffer, for instance, from the pollution produced in the developed countries over many decades – while they are, unlike us, excluded from the benefits. They suffer the effects of global warming caused by our emissions of greenhouse gases. They suffer the effects of the drug trade fueled by the huge demand for drugs in the US and EU and the effects of the war on drugs prosecuted by the US and EU governments. They are hurt by the depletion of natural resources which are scarcer and dearer than they would be if the affluent countries were prepared to moderate their consumption. They suffer from the AIDS epidemic, whose spread is assisted by affluent sex tourists, and from disease strains that have become resistant to ordinary drugs because of treatment practices in the developed countries – medical problems aggravated by patent rules that make effective drugs unaffordable to most patients in poor countries.
24 Cf. § 5.2.
25 *The Economist*, September 25, 1999, p. 89. The three cited studies – Hertel and Martin, UNCTAD, Finger and Schuler – are listed in the bibliography.
26 Wolf, "Broken Promises to the Poor."
27 After years of heavy pressure and 10-digit arrears, the US finally (Christmas 2000) won a reduction from 25 to 22 percent – even while its share of aggregate global income is 31 percent (World Bank, *Report 2002*,

p. 233). While pressing mightily for the reduction, the US government was also debating what to do with the annual budget surpluses in excess of $100 billion expected for the foreseeable future.

28 Cf. www.pro-un.org/year2000.htm

29 Cf. the authoritative investigations *Rwanda: The Preventable Genocide*, produced by the International Panel of Eminent Personalities commissioned by the Organization of African Unity, and *Report of the Independent Inquiry into the Actions of the United Nations during the 1994 Genocide in Rwanda*. See also Gourevitch, *We Wish to Inform You*.

30 Arms sold to the developing countries facilitate repression, fuel civil wars, and divert funds from meeting basic needs. In 2000, the rich countries spent about $4,650 million on development assistance for meeting basic needs abroad (text around n. 337) while also selling the developing countries an estimated $25,438 million in conventional weapons. This represents 69 percent of the entire international trade in conventional weapons, valued at $36,862 million. The main sellers of arms are the US, with over 50 percent of sales, then Russia, France, Germany, and the UK, with another 37 percent. See Congressional Research Service, *Conventional Arms Transfers to Developing Nations*.

31 Locke, "An Essay Concerning the True Original," § 95. See § 5.2 for a more detailed invocation of Locke.

32 Hume, *A Treatise on Human Nature*, p. 269 (book I, part IV, § VII).

33 Parfit, *Reasons and Persons*, p. 282.

Chapter 1 Human Flourishing and Universal Justice

34 One can get a sense of this variety by recalling the more influential contributions to our topic just within analytic philosophy of the past 20 years. Among these are the responses articulated in the following books: Annas, *The Morality of Happiness*; Elster, *Sour Grapes*; Frankfurt, *The Importance of What We Care About*; Galston, *Justice and the Human Good*; Gibbard, *Wise Choices, Apt Feelings*; Griffin, *Well-Being*; MacIntyre, *After Virtue*; Nagel, *Mortal Questions*; Nozick, *The Examined Life*; Nussbaum, *The Fragility of Goodness*; Parfit, *Reasons and Persons*; Raz, *The Morality of Freedom*; Rorty, *Contingency, Irony, and Solidarity*; Scanlon, *What We Owe to Each Other*; Slote, *Goods and Virtues* and *From Morality to Virtue*; Taylor, *Sources of the Self*; Tugendhat, *Vorlesungen über Ethik*; Williams, *Moral Luck*, *Ethics and the Limits of Philosophy*, *Shame and Necessity*, and *Making Sense of Humanity*; and Wollheim, *The Thread of Life*.

35 See Plato, *The Republic*, 357a–358d.

36 In fact, Plato's argument seeks to show that being just is good in both ways (*Republic*, 357c–358a) – is a component in its own right (*Republic*, Books 2–7, esp. 444d–e) and a means to other components, such as well-being, pleasure, esteem (*Republic*, Books 8–10, esp. 587e–588a, 612d–614b).

37 Kant is offering this example in his *Critique of Practical Reason*. See Kant, *Kants gesammelte Schriften*, vol. 5, p. 60.

38 Achievement, in turn, might be understood in different time frames: more narrowly, in terms of the ethical quality of a person's *deeds*, and/or more broadly, in terms of the ethical significance of her life's historical *impact* on the world.

39 We see an extreme instance of this phenomenon in act-utilitarian doctrine according to which the personal value of a human life is measured by the quantity of happiness it contains while its ethical value is measured by its impact on general happiness. When a utilitarian reflects on the value of a human life from within, its ethical value will predominate: What matters is that one's life should have the greatest possible positive impact on general happiness. To what extent one should seek one's own happiness is an empirical-instrumental question. One should seek one's own happiness whenever this is the best way of promoting general happiness – and otherwise one ought to promote general happiness, even at the expense of one's own. When a utilitarian reflects on the value of a human life from without, its personal value will predominate: what matters is that others be as happy as possible. To what extent one should also want them to be promoters of happiness is an empirical-instrumental question. One should promote the ethical value of human lives whenever this is the best way of promoting the personal value of human lives – and otherwise one ought to promote personal value, even at the expense of ethical value.

40 "Social order," "institutional scheme," and "regime" are also used.

41 The moral assessment of social institutions may thus involve more than a criterion of justice, as one may also want to consider, for example, how institutions affect other species of animals or how well they accord with God's will. My definition places such issues outside the discourse about justice, which can therefore contribute only one essential component of the moral assessment of social institutions.

42 See Aristotle, *Nicomachean Ethics*, 1100a10–31 (book 1, ch. 10).

43 For further discussion of this topic, see Meyer, "More Than They Have a Right To."

44 This point is analogous to one that arises when we seek to optimize some process of production. Even if it is true that each part of the process is designed in the best possible way given the way the other parts are designed, it may still be possible greatly to improve the entire process: by redesigning all parts together or, more importantly, by altering its very structure (including its division into parts).

45 The goal of free intercultural agreement on a universal criterion of justice does, however, involve the hope that most cultures can sustain reflection and discussion about matters of *justice* that transcend the confines of their own traditions and are sensitive to the outlooks prevalent in other cultures. §§ 1.3 and 1.5 indicate how cultures might fulfill this hope even without fulfilling the demand I reject in the text.

46 Here a person's most favored outcome is assigned the value 1 and her least favored outcome is assigned the value 0. The value of any other outcome Q is then that n ($0 \leq n \leq 1$) which makes the following true: the person is indifferent between Q with certainty, on the one hand, and a lottery pursuant to which her most favored outcome occurs with probability n and her least favored outcome with probability ($1 - n$), on the other hand.

47 This issue of fulfillment *versus* satisfaction confronts any account of human flourishing and thus is quite independent of my focus on such accounts within the context of developing a globally sharable criterion of justice for the moral assessment of institutional schemes.

48 Thus, your aspiration to be loved is *fulfilled* insofar as you truly are loved, and *satisfied* insofar as you live in the happy consciousness of being loved. Obviously, an aspiration may be fulfilled without being satisfied and also satisfied without being fulfilled: you may be loved while believing that you are not; or you may believe falsely that you are loved. The fulfillment of an aspiration may be a matter of degree insofar as its realization in the world may be more or less complete. The satisfaction of such an aspiration may then be a matter of degree twice over, for it also depends on the degrees of confidence with which a person ascribes particular degrees of fulfillment to the aspiration in question.

49 A person's first-order desires are those desires that are not about her own desires. Many of our desires fall into this category. But many do not, as when I desire to shed, to strengthen or to weaken, to indulge or to frustrate, to attend to or to neglect one of my present desires, for example, or when I desire to acquire a new one.

50 The latter demand is that social institutions should engender fitting pairs of values and options – should work so that persons have the options they value and value the options they have.

51 There must be tight limits, however, on how a society may sanction another when it judges the institutions of the latter to accord with the universal criterion but not with the former's own more ambitious criterion of justice. Agreement on a universal criterion would lose much of its point, if fulfillment of this criterion did not shield national regimes against coercive reform efforts from outside.

52 I do not here mean to rule out the possibility that some societies or other groups may think of the universal criterion as exhausting what justice requires. This criterion – though it should not be understood as exhaustive – should not be understood as nonexhaustive either. Both of these understandings would needlessly undermine its widespread acceptance and hence the plausibility of its claim to universality.

53 See § 1.2, second paragraph.

54 Paradigmatic for this answer is Rawls's broad list, which includes various basic liberties as well as income and wealth, powers and prerogatives of office, and social bases of self-respect. See Rawls, *A Theory of Justice*, esp. § 15, and "Social Unity and Primary Goods." Cf. Dworkin, "What is Equality? Part II," and Scanlon, "Preference and Urgency."

55 Capabilities are defined in terms of what a person can do or be. In contrast to the Rawlsian answer, this way of conceiving basic goods makes their measurement sensitive to differences in persons' specific needs and endowments. Thus Sen has us focus, for example, not on a person's income as such, but on her income relative to her specific nutritional and other needs. See Sen, *Commodities and Capabilities*, and also Nussbaum and Sen, eds., *The Quality of Life*, esp. Cohen's helpful essay "Equality of What?"

56 One might need to rethink this formulation if it can plausibly be maintained that even persons falling below the threshold in regard to one or more basic goods should be assigned standard of living 1 so long as they sufficiently exceed the threshold with regard to other basic goods.

57 The arithmetic mean is the sum of the measurements for the various affected persons divided by the number of persons, N. The geometric mean is the Nth root of the product of those measurements. Sum-ranking simply uses the sum of all measurements. Maximin takes the lowest measurements to be representative. Inequality is specified in various different ways. One straightforward measure is the quintile inequality ratio, the share of the top fifth divided by that of the bottom fifth of the relevant population. Another common measure of inequality is the Gini coefficient (cf. n. 4).

58 Each resident would face an annual risk of 0.0035 percent (= 10,000/285,000,000) on average. Compounded over an average lifespan of 77 years, the overall risk for each resident would be 0.27 percent.

59 According to the National Safety Council, traffic fatalities numbered 43,501 in 1998 and were down roughly 1 percent from that in 1999 and 2000 (www.nsc.org/library/rept2000.htm#road).

60 The risk each year is about 0.015 percent (= 43,000/285,000,000), but compounds to about 1.16 percent over a lifetime.

61 National Safety Council (www.nsc.org/library/rept2000.htm#road), adding that "about 3 in every 10 Americans will be involved in an alcohol-related traffic accident at some time in their lives."

62 This argument is presented more fully in § V.C of Pogge, "Three Problems." As I mention there, a full calculation would have to subtract, from the number of traffic deaths avoided (860 annually, in the text), not only those who will die prematurely by execution (100), but also any increase in the number of persons killed by drunk drivers desperately trying to evade capture. And the reform could have further positive and negative effects on the number of premature deaths as well. §§ V.A and V.B of the same essay discuss how similar reasoning may support other morally dubious reforms in the criminal-law domain, such as increased use of strict-liability statutes, rougher methods in the apprehension and treatment of suspects, and lower standards of evidence.

63 This point is more fully elaborated, with special attention to the institutional allocation of medical care, in Pogge, "Relational Conceptions of Justice."

64 This implicit attitude of social institutions is independent of the attitudes or intentions of the persons shaping and upholding these institutions. Only the former makes a difference to how just the institutions are – the latter make a difference only to how blameworthy persons are for their role in imposing them.

65 The case of smoking may exemplify a fluid transition between scenarios 2 and 6 insofar as private agents (cigarette companies) are legally permitted to try to render persons addicted to nicotine.

66 A core injustice is one identified by the core criterion, and thus an injustice recognized as such by all the more demanding conceptions of justice overlapping in this core criterion. I explore this notion from a somewhat different angle in ch. 8.

67 To illustrate: whether it is unjust for social institutions not to entitle indigent persons to treatment for a certain lung disease – and, if so, how unjust this is – may well depend on whether this disease is contracted through legally authorized pollution by others or self-caused through smoking in full awareness of its risks.

68 To be sure, the anonymity condition permits a criterion of justice to be sensitive to whether two different kinds of hardship are correlated (e.g. to count it as a greater injustice if the groups of those excluded from higher education and of those excluded from political participation overlap than if they are disjoint). But being black, female, or Jewish are not, as such, hardships. Sex, color, and religion are precisely the kinds of factors that the anonymity condition was meant to screen out.

69 The injustice would be even greater, if women were legally required to do most of the housework, or legally barred from many educational opportunities – but this is a matter of the first missed weighting dimension (scenarios 1 *versus* 3) extensively discussed at the beginning of this § 1.4.

70 Something similar can be said of the much vaguer approach advocated by Habermas through his Principle U. See esp. Habermas, *Moralbewusstsein*, pp. 75–6, and *Erläuterungen*, pp. 130–76.

71 For more detail, see Pogge, "Three Problems" and "Gleiche Freiheit für alle?"

72 Thus, for example, Habermas: "The concept of human rights is not of moral origin, but . . . *by nature* juridical." Human rights "belong, through their structure, to a scheme of positive and coercive law which supports justiciable individual right claims. Hence it belongs to the meaning of human rights that they demand for themselves the status of constitutional rights." Habermas, "Kants Idee des ewigen Friedens." The quotes are from p. 310 and p. 312, italics are in the original, the translation is mine. Though Alexy explicitly refers to human rights as moral rights, he holds an otherwise similar position which equates the institutionalization of human rights with their transformation into positive law. See Alexy, "Die Institutionalisierung der Menschenrechte im demokratischen Verfassungsstaat."

73 This proposal is elaborated in more detail in ch. 2 and in Pogge, "Human Rights and Human Responsibilities."
74 Such criticism has been voiced, for instance, by Singapore's patriarch Lee Kuan Yew and in Mary Ann Glendon, *Rights Talk*.
75 Grundgesetz, Article 2.2, in Press and Information Office of the Federal Government, *The Basic Law*, p. 14.
76 See esp. §§ 4.8, 4.9, 5.3, 6.2.
77 See chs 6–8 and Pogge, "Human Rights and Human Responsibilities."
78 Cf. n. 246.
79 Such measures would still function in the context of assessing social institutions and would thus presumably be probabilistic (*ex ante*) and focused on publicly ascertainable *access* to a quantitatively and qualitatively *adequate* share of certain goods. In these regards they would differ from measures of human flourishing that we employ in small-scale contexts, where we may be concerned to enrich the life of a friend, for example, or our own.

Chapter 2 How Should Human Rights be Conceived?

80 For more on the historical details, see esp. Tuck, *Natural Rights Theories*, and Tuck, "The 'Modern' Theory of Natural Law."
81 Hobbes, *Leviathan*, p. 190. As Tuck stresses in his later piece, such uses were exceedingly common in the period from Grotius to Kant.
82 One might make this condition somewhat stronger: a moral demand is unrestricted only if how wrong given violations of it are does not depend on the violators' particular epoch, culture, religion, moral tradition, or philosophy. Equal violations of it are equally wrong, irrespective of whether the violators are well-educated citizens of a developed 20th-century society, say, or members of a far more primitive 13th-century society. One must then add that, though equally wrong, they are not equally blameworthy; the perpetration of a massacre by typical German soldiers under Nazi rule is surely more blameworthy, more clearly beyond excuse, than that of an otherwise similar massacre by typical Mongol soldiers under Genghis Khan. I will not discuss these matters further here.
83 How expansively these five terms should be understood depends on the size and heterogeneity of the world we know. Today, a fairly expansive understanding is requisite. The time from the Renaissance to the French and American Revolutions can count as an epoch, but not the Thirty Years' War; Europe can count as a culture, but not Belgium; Christianity, and also atheism, can count as religions, but not Anglicanism; moral traditions might be utilitarianism, social contract theory, perfectionism and deontological ethics, but not the particular moral conceptions of Kant or Sidgwick; philosophies, finally, might include rationalism, empiricism, idealism, moral realism, intuitionism, but not particular variants of them. Without such an expansive understanding, sharability

would not amount to very much in the present world: a moral demand could count as sharable in all five dimensions without being really broadly accessible.

84 Mackie uses the phrase "what gives point to" to single out this most important sense of priority. See his "Can There Be a Right-Based Moral Theory?," Postscript. This moral or foundational priority must be distinguished from conceptual or definitional priority, which may run the other way. As Mackie suggests, the concept of a duty may well be clearer than that of a right and it may then make sense to define rights in terms of duties. Raz proposes such a definition: "'x has a right' if and only if x can have rights, and other things being equal, an aspect of x's well-being (his interest) is a sufficient reason for holding some other person(s) to be under a duty." See Raz, "On the Nature of Rights," p. 194.

85 This connection is explicated and defended in Feinberg, "The Nature and Value of Rights."

86 For this position, together with its corollary that babies have no rights, see Hart, "Are There Any Natural Rights?"

87 These and related points are made and defended more elaborately in Gewirth, "The Basis and Content of Human Rights."

88 For a more extensive discussion of the limitations of the rights idiom, see Pogge, "O'Neill on Rights and Duties."

89 Rawls, "Justice as Fairness: Political not Metaphysical."

90 This second component is compatible with the view that the weight agents ought to give to the human rights of others varies with their relation to them – that agents have stronger moral reasons to secure human rights in their own country, for example, than abroad – so long as this is not seen as due to a difference in the moral significance of these rights, impersonally considered. (I can consistently believe that the flourishing of all children is equally important and that I should show greater concern for the flourishing of my own children than for that of other children.)

91 The switch in idiom from "interests" to "needs" is meant merely to flag the idea that only the most important interests of human beings should be seen as giving rise to human rights. The switch is not supposed to prejudge any substantive questions about how human rights should be specified. Basic needs, just like interests, could still be conceived in a person-relative way (so that what a person's basic needs are depends in part on some of her personal characteristics such as gender or handicaps) or even in subjective terms (so that what a person's basic needs are depends in part on some of her goals, desires, or preferences).

92 I intend the word "object" here in a broad sense so as not to prejudge any substantive issues. The object of a right is whatever the right is a right to. Such objects might be freedoms-from, freedoms-to, as well as physical security or an adequate food supply.

93 I shall drop the parenthetic addition from now on; but see n. 100.

94 Arguably, this point was recognized by the Inter-American Court of Human Rights when it held Honduras responsible for crimes of

"disappearing" persons, without finding that government officials were involved – imputing these crimes to the government on the ground that it had failed to exercise due diligence to prevent and to respond to them (*Velasquez*; July 29, 1988; series C, number 4).

95 In the case of some human rights, (re)organizing a society so that all have secure access to its object will require that there be a legal right identical in content. It is hard to imagine a society under modern conditions whose members are secure in their property or have secure access to freedom of expression even while no legal right thereto exists. In other cases, an individual legal right of matching content may not be necessary. We can envision, for example, a society in which all have secure access to minimally adequate nutrition even without a legal right thereto. While a corresponding legal right may be necessary in some cases and unnecessary in others, any such legal right may be ineffective and is therefore insufficient for maintaining secure access to the object of the human right to which it corresponds. (I assume that there is no human right whose sole object is that there be some legal right on the books.)

96 This chapter is silent on cultural rights. See Pogge, "Group Rights and Ethnicity," for some thoughts on this issue.

97 This is the general picture presented in Hohfeld, *Fundamental Legal Conceptions*. This picture is used to explicate the notion of human rights in Wellman, "A New Conception of Human Rights." See also Wellman, *A Theory of Rights*.

98 Luban, "Just War and Human Rights," p. 209. A comprehensive maximalist account is developed in Shue, *Basic Rights* – or so I had thought. In a new afterword Shue cautions, however, that his position is less than fully maximalist. He holds that we are required to aid any persons whose rights have been violated – but not those whose rights are unfulfilled due to, say, natural causes (ibid., p. 159). He does not explain why he believes this distinction among positive duties to be morally significant.

99 By counting official denials and deprivations more heavily than otherwise equivalent private ones, I am abandoning a position I had once defended (in *Realizing Rawls*) – the position that social institutions should be assessed from a broadly consequentialist prospective-participant perspective (such as Rawls's original position). Prospective participants do not care whether the objects of their human rights are endangered by the government or by private agents. Hence they would, other things equal, allow the two kinds of risk an equal impact upon the moral assessment of social institutions. I now hold that the injustice of a society is significantly greater if, other things equal, insecure access to the objects of human rights is due to the risk of being denied X or deprived of X officially, i.e. due to the risk of human-rights violations. Even though a significant risk of being executed for my expressed political beliefs is no worse for me than an otherwise equal risk of being killed by an assassin

for the same reason, the former signifies a greater injustice in the relevant social order, a worse human-rights record on the part of the society in question. A fuller recantation of my earlier hypothetical-contract thinking is in Pogge, "Three Problems" and "Gleiche Freiheit für alle?" Cf. § 1.4 and the second paragraph of § 2.3.

100 Still, the institutional understanding leaves room for the possibility that, even in peacetime, we share responsibility for human-rights fulfillment abroad. (Such responsibility is a given for the interactional maximalist and impossible for the interactional minimalist.) We have such responsibility if we are influential and privileged participants in a transnational scheme of social institutions under which some persons are regularly, predictably, and avoidably denied secure access to the objects of their human rights. I believe that this empirical condition is satisfied and that we thus have a human-rights-based duty to work for reforms of our global institutional order that would reduce or eliminate the incidence of wars and of severe poverty, both of which tend to produce human-rights violations and insecure access on a massive scale. Cf. Pogge, "Human Rights and Human Responsibilities" and "An Egalitarian Law of Peoples."

101 The expression "utilitarianism of rights" was coined, with critical intent, in Nozick *Anarchy, State, and Utopia*, p. 28. Such a view, suggested by the sentence quoted from Luban (n. 98) relates the goal of maximizing rights fulfillment directly to agents. It takes a consequentialist approach in *ethics* and thus admits of the usual alternative specifications: A utilitarianism of rights might be of the ideal or real as well as of the act, rule, or motive variety. There are also other variants of consequentialism, such as Bentham's utilitarianism which is meant to apply to social institutions (such as a society's penal system). So there could be a utilitarianism of rights of the institutional sort. One way in which such a position would differ from what I advocate here is clarified by n. 99.

102 The degree of a person's responsibility for injustice must plausibly depend on the means at her disposal and perhaps also on how advantaged she is within the social order in question. The degree of a person's blameworthiness will depend on further factors as well, such as her education, experience, and circumstances.

103 Quoted by Gould, "The Moral State of Tahiti," p. 19.

104 Compare O'Neill, *Faces of Hunger*, p. 101. The topic of manifesto rights is further discussed in Pogge, "O'Neill on Rights and Duties," pp. 239–47.

Chapter 3 Loopholes in Moralities

105 The notion of a code is closely linked to the idea of codification, and it may therefore seem surprising that I speak of moral codes. After all, it is one distinctive feature of the moralities we are familiar with in the modern world that, unlike the law, they are *not* codified, nor officially adjudicated and enforced. We live, one might say, in a world without moral

codes. But then my talk of moral codes is a response to a theoretical need rather than to an empirical reality. We cannot engage in any meaningful analysis of the effects of moralities unless we can fix upon some rather determinate specimen to which this analysis can be, somewhat rigorously, applied. Talk of moral codes reflects, then, an idealization. I will ask you to consider hypothetical cases in which determinate moral codes are counterproductive. We may conclude upon reflection that adherents of such a code have reason to revise it. And this conclusion may have implications for ourselves, if our moral beliefs – though amorphous and diverse – are sufficiently similar in content and effects to the hypothetical moral code of the example.

106 I will skip the phrase "by the code's own lights" wherever possible. But it must be kept in mind that we are throughout dealing with counterproductivity, that is, with cases where moralities undermine their own effectiveness or, as it were, regret their own effects.

107 E.g. a tax deduction for charitable gifts provides an incentive to many taxpayers. But for some of these, the incentive may not tip the scales – they are more inclined than they would otherwise be, but still not inclined enough, to give. And others may not know about the tax deduction or may not realize how they can take advantage of it. Codes may then give incentives that do not affect conduct at all. As I will show, some such incentives are problematic nonetheless.

108 These two paradigm cases do not exhaust the realm of possibilities. A moral code may be socially prevalent in a small social system, may be held by a minority within a society (with the majority perhaps committed to some other code), may be held by an individual who is highly influential in a society (the President of the US), and so forth. In all these cases, the effects of the code are shaped by the life context in which it is operative.

109 I am here assuming that ideal adherents, having normal interests, care more about enhancing their own income than the government's and would also rather avoid enlistment. In the second example, serving in the military is morally required and legally voluntary.

110 See § 3.0, fifth paragraph.

111 Some preliminary thoughts on the latter question are presented in Pogge, "The Effects of Prevalent Moral Conceptions."

112 Similarly, in the academic world, university presidents and trustees have sometimes defended their decision to invest part of their institution's endowment in morally questionable ways by appealing to their fiduciary obligations toward the university and its members. They imply that an investment (e.g. in South African goldmines under apartheid or in certain arms export firms) can be ethically acceptable when it is made in behalf of the university even though it would not be ethical if it were made with personal funds.

113 It is important that the lawyer, too, is in compliance with what E requires (that the *aggregate* moral status of Option B is "permitted"). I am not interested here in the opportunity, which some ethical codes may

afford, of reducing one's own wrongdoing (one's share of responsibility for some transaction) by partly shifting it off to another.

114 More precisely, such an ethic – as sketched for example in Fried, "The Lawyer as Friend" – gives landlords an ideal compliance incentive to prefer B over A2 and an ideal reward incentive to prefer B over A1.

115 I am presenting here a moderate version of what Samuel Scheffler calls the "distributive objection" to associative duties or special responsibilities (Scheffler, *Boundaries and Allegiances*, pp. 56–64 and 83–95). In the more radical version Scheffler discusses, the objection poses a comprehensive challenge to special relationships insofar as these enable persons (Alice and Beth) to change the moral situation such that they ought to give priority to one another over outsiders (Carla). In my moderate version, the objection poses a partial challenge to special relationships: only insofar as these enable Alice and Beth to change the moral situation so as to reduce what each minimally owes Carla. Scheffler claims in effect that my moderate version collapses into the radical one, that I overlook that "part of what it is to have [special] responsibilities to one's associates is to be required, within limits, to give their interests priority over the interests of non-associates, in cases where the two conflict" (ibid., p. 87). I do not think I am overlooking this point. I can easily accept it because I do not believe that what persons minimally owe to another person is to give his or her interests equal consideration with everyone else's. Even *without* any special relationship, it is permissible for Alice to give priority to Beth's interests over Carla's in many ways, e.g. by helping Beth rather than Carla even when Carla's need is somewhat greater. *With* the special relationship, this permission may turn into an obligation. My moderate objection allows this and thus does not challenge special relationships as such. It only constrains their moral effects. If, in the *absence* of a special relationship with Beth, Alice must not do certain things to Carla (e.g. take one of Carla's kidneys without consent to save Beth's life), then Alice has the same negative duty also in the *presence* of a special relationship with Beth. If, in the *absence* of a special relationship with Beth, Alice must do certain things for Carla (e.g. give priority to saving Carla's eye over saving Beth's finger), then Alice has the same positive duty also in the *presence* of a special relationship with Beth. By imposing these constraints, my view differs from what is commonly believed about the moral effects of special relationships (see ibid., pp. 52–3). But by imposing *only* these constraints, my view still allows special relationships to have significant moral effects. This view thus is distinct from the more radical distributive objection Scheffler discusses – a genuine intermediate possibility. I am grateful to Scheffler for stimulating me to add this note of clarification here.

116 The phrase "for no good reason" alludes to the possibility of plausible counterclaims. If additional hiring of lawyers were morally important, and if the incentive of Case 1 were an effective way of promoting this important value, then there might be a good reason for the incentive.

117 You may feel that it was pretty clear, even before my argument, that a plausible ethic should not condone your father's conduct. But we will soon see (§§ 3.6 and 3.7) that the problem of loopholes requires a far deeper revision of E. Moreover, I have specifically chosen E for the purpose of giving a plausible illustration of a constraint that I believe should be imposed upon *any* moral conception. As will emerge, this constraint poses a radical challenge to other moral views that are commonly held.

118 Once national borders have been drawn in southern Africa, it will, with time, come to seem obvious that the white state may be organized democratically so that its government will have strong incentives vigorously to promote the interests of its citizens against the (however disadvantaged) people of neighboring states, who, after all, have their own (however ineffective) governments to take care of their interests.

119 Even if E and J are understood in this way, they could still be attacked for giving regrettable *concrete* incentives. But the complaint that they contain loopholes is now blocked, for ideal adherents of E and J would not implement either your father's idea or the homelands reform, if doing so were forbidden.

120 Though I have discussed how responsibility should be distributed between the team and its creator, I am not considering in this chapter how responsibility should be distributed within that team.

Chapter 4 Moral Universalism and Global Economic Justice

121 See text at n. 145.

122 See nn. 125–30 and accompanying text. The global poverty gap is about $44 billion annually for the World Bank's official international poverty line and $300 billion annually for its doubled poverty line. These figures correspond to 0.14 and 0.96 percent, respectively, of aggregate global income ($31,171 billion annually) and to 0.18 and 1.21 percent, respectively, of the combined gross national incomes of the high-income economies ($24,829 billion annually). See World Bank, *Report 2002*, p. 233, reporting data for the year 2000.

123 April 11, 1919. The proposal received a majority in the relevant committee (11 of the 17 members present), but Woodrow Wilson, as chair, ruled that this particular amendment needed unanimous support to pass. See Naoko Shimazu, *Japan, Race and Equality*, p. 30.

124 This appeal to special ties and "priority for compatriots" is further discussed in chs 3 and 5. The appeal is usually made in behalf of societies that could easily build just and thriving national communities even in a more egalitarian global economic order. The difference would be that the remaining majority of humankind might then enjoy the same luxury.

125 See www.worldbank.org/research/povmonitor/, which is periodically updated. The poverty line is explained in World Bank, *Report 2000/2001*, pp. 17 and 23.
126 I say "roughly" because the two equivalences cannot, strictly speaking, be combined by transitivity. The reason is that they are based on different goods-baskets. One goods-basket was used to determine what amount of a foreign currency had, in 1993, the same purchasing power as $393 then had in the US. Another goods-basket (defining the US consumer price index) was used to determine what amount of $s have, in 2001, the same purchasing power as $393 had in the US in 1993.
127 Chen and Ravallion, "How Did the World's Poorest Fare in the 1990s?," tables 2 and 4, dividing the poverty gap index by the headcount index.
128 Thus the World Bank equates India's *per capita* gross national income of $460 to $2,390 PPP, China's $840 to $3,940 PPP, Nigeria's $260 to $790 PPP, Pakistan's $470 to $1,960 PPP, Bangladesh's $380 to $1,650 PPP, Ethiopia's $100 to $660 PPP, Vietnam's $390 to $2,030 PPP, and so on (World Bank, *Report 2002*, pp. 232–3). These countries are listed here by the number of poor people they contain.
129 Chen and Ravallion, "How Did the World's Poorest Fare in the 1990s?," table 3. The figure given is 2,801.03 million for 1998.
130 Ibid., tables 3 and 4, again dividing the poverty gap index by the headcount index.
131 These four figures are from UNDP, *Report 2001*, pp. 22 and 9.
132 UNDP, *Report 1999*, p. 22.
133 Both figures are from UNDP, *Report 1998*, p. 49.
134 FAO, *The State of Food Insecurity in the World 1999*, p. 11.
135 World Bank, *Report 1999/2000*, p. 62. According to the International Labor Organization "some 250 million children between the ages of 5 and 14 are working in developing countries – 120 million full time, 130 million part time" (www.ilo.org/public/english/standards/ipec/simpoc/stats/4stt.htm).
136 In 2000, there were 55.694 million human deaths. The main causes highly correlated with poverty were (with death tolls in thousands): diarrhea (2,124) and malnutrition (445), perinatal (2,439) and maternal conditions (495), childhood diseases (1,385 – mainly measles), tuberculosis (1,660), malaria (1,080), meningitis (156), hepatitis (128), tropical diseases (124), respiratory infections (3,941 – mainly pneumonia), HIV/AIDS (2,943) and sexually transmitted diseases (217) (WHO, *The World Health Report 2001*, annex table 2). Cf. also FAO, *The State of Food Insecurity in the World 1999*, UNICEF, *The State of the World's Children 2002*, and USDA, *U.S. Action Plan on Food Security*, p. III: "Worldwide 34,000 children under age five die daily from hunger and preventable diseases."
137 The Vietnam War Memorial in Washington, designed by Maya Ying Lin, is a black granite wall, 439½ feet long, on which the names of 58,226 fallen US soldiers are engraved.

138 World Bank, *Report 2002*, p. 233.

139 Ibid., reflecting aggregate global income (sum of all gross national incomes) of $31,171 billion annually and a world population of 6,054 million (year 2000). Each quintile thus contains 1,211 million human beings.

140 Cf. also the figures provided in n. 122. Curiously, the World Bank does not publish data about the *per capita* or the collective income of the global poor, about their share of aggregate global income, or about the amount of extra income needed for all of them to reach the relevant poverty line.

141 UNDP, *Report 1999*, p. 3. "The additional cost of achieving and maintaining universal access to basic education for all, basic health care for all, reproductive health care for all women, adequate food for all and safe water and sanitation for all is . . . less than 4% of the combined wealth of the 225 richest people in the world" (UNDP, *Report 1998*, p. 30).

142 The number of people below the doubled international poverty line (cf. n. 129) has increased by 9.9 percent – or 20.7 percent if the special case of China is excluded (World Bank, *Report 2000/2001*, p. 23). Global population growth during the same period (1987–98) was about 18 percent (www.census.gov/ipc/www/worldpop.html).

143 Thanks to the end of the Cold War, the high-income economies were able to reduce their military expenditures from 4.1 percent of their combined GDPs in 1985 to 2.2 percent in 1998 (UNDP, *Report 1998*, p. 197; UNDP, *Report 2000*, p. 217). Their annual "peace dividend" currently amounts to over $450 billion (1.9 percent of their combined GDPs of currently $23,982 billion – UNDP, *Report 2001*, p. 181). In the same period, the same countries chose to reduce their combined net official development assistance from 0.34 percent of their combined GNPs to 0.24 percent (ibid., p. 190, giving details for each affluent country). Cf. text at nn. 336–7. Preliminary figures for the year 2000 indicate that the rich countries have further reduced their ODA to 0.22 percent of their combined GNPs (www1.oecd.org/media/release/ODA_april01.pdf).

144 The 1996 *Rome Declaration on World Food Security* described "more than 800 million people" as undernourished. This number has officially developed as follows: "nearly 800 million" (UNDP, *Report 1995*, p. 16, and UNDP, *Report 1996*, p. 20), "some 840 million" (UNDP, *Report 1997*, p. 5), "841 million" (UNDP, *Report 1998*, p. 49), "about 840 million" (UNDP, *Report 1999*, p. 22), "about 790 million" (UNDP, *Report 2000*, p. 8), "826 million" (UNDP, *Report 2001*, p. 22). The World Bank's Food Price Index fell from 124 in 1985 to 108 in 1996 to 84.5 in 2000 (statistics from "Global Commodity Markets" published by the World Bank's Development Prospects Group).

145 UNDP, *Report 1999*, p. 3. These ratios are based on market exchange rates, not purchasing power parities. This is appropriate when one is focusing, as I am throughout, not on income inequality as such, but on the avoidability of poverty. The global quintile income inequality ratio is much greater, if one compares individuals (or household averages)

rather than country averages. One would then, in the top quintile, replace the poorest citizens of rich countries with richer persons in poorer countries and analogously, in the bottom quintile, replace the wealthiest citizens of poor countries with poorer citizens in less-poor countries. So calculated, the global quintile income inequality ratio rose from 78 in 1988 to 113 in 1993, indicating an average annual growth gap of 7.7 percent (personal communication from Branko Milanovic, World Bank). This trend has continued. Today, the top quintile of human beings have around 90 percent of global income and the bottom quintile about one-third of 1 percent (see text following n. 139), which puts the global quintile income inequality ratio at about 270.

146 The figures just cited indicate an average annual growth gap of 1.66 percent for the colonial era (1820–1960), 2.34 percent for the period 1960–90, and 3.04 percent for the period 1990–97.

147 UNDP, *Report 2001*, p. 183. Outside Latin America, most national quintile income inequality ratios are between 4 and 10, e.g. Austria 3.2; Japan 3.4; Germany 4.7; Bangladesh 4.9; Spain 5.4; France 5.6; India 5.7; Switzerland 5.8; United Kingdom 6.5; Australia 7.0; China 8.0; USA 9.0; Malaysia 12.4; Nigeria 12.8; South Africa 22.6 (ibid., pp. 182–4).

148 $7,320 versus $7,350 (World Bank, *Report 2002*, pp. 232–3).

149 North Korea comes to mind, China around 1960, and the Soviet Union around 1930. But none of these cases displays the extreme income inequality of Sub-Subbrazil.

150 In this general statement, anti-universalism is entirely consistent with the thesis that the two minimal requirements (conjunctively or disjunctively) apply to the present global economic order. I address such anti-universalism, then, not because it threatens this thesis, but because it threatens the way I support this thesis here.

151 See esp. Miller, "Justice and Global Inequality," "National Self-Determination and Global Justice," and his forthcoming "The Ethics of Assistance: Morality, Affluence and the Distant Needy," which he has kindly allowed me to read.

152 Miller, "Two Ways to Think about Justice," p. 20.

153 Ibid., p. 16.

154 Ibid., p. 6.

155 Ibid., pp. 12–13.

156 The word "monism" is introduced in Murphy, "Institutions and the Demands of Justice." According to his usage, monism denies that there is a plurality of different contexts, or domains of value, each with its own fundamental moral principle(s). The fundamental principles of monistic moral conceptions thus are not contextually limited in range. Such a conception could nonetheless feature a plurality of fundamental moral principles and thus need not be monistic in the more usual sense.

157 Ibid., p. 280; Cohen, "Where the Action Is," pp. 22–3.

158 For an elaboration of these reasons, see Pogge, "On the Site of Distributive Justice." In accordance with his method of avoidance, Rawls would

probably prefer to make the weaker claim: to have shown that the moral principles appropriate to the basic structure *may* not be appropriate to other contexts or, generally, that different moral principles *may* be appropriate to different "domains of value." See the cautious formulations he employs in his discussion of a "model case of an overlapping consensus" in Rawls, *Political Liberalism*, pp. 169–71.

159 Rawls, *The Law of Peoples*, pp. 116–18. This argument exemplifies the strategy of justifying inequality by appeal to group autonomy.

160 See Pogge, *Realizing Rawls*, pp. 252–3, cf. "An Egalitarian Law of Peoples," pp. 211–13.

161 Rawls, *A Theory of Justice*, pp. 401, 7.

162 Ibid., pp. 90–1.

163 With regard to his own fellow citizens, Rawls writes: "It is inevitable and often desirable that citizens have different views as to the most appropriate political conception; for the public political culture is bound to contain different fundamental ideas that can be developed in different ways. An orderly contest between them over time is a reliable way to find which one, if any, is most reasonable." Rawls, *Political Liberalism*, p. 227, see also pp. 164 and 241.

164 Rawls, *The Law of Peoples*, pp. 67–8.

165 Ibid., p. 37.

166 This objection to Rawls's account is presented more fully in Pogge, "Rawls on International Justice."

167 See text at n. 124 for the appeal to special ties, text at n. 159 for the appeal to group autonomy, and the discussion of "decent peoples" in Rawls for the appeal to cultural diversity. This last appeal comes in two variants. Cultural diversity is adduced to justify that we may suspend our moral standards in dealing with foreigners who do not share our commitment to these standards (see Pogge, *Realizing Rawls*, pp. 269–70). But why may we then not likewise suspend these standards in dealing with compatriots who do not share this commitment? Cultural diversity is also adduced to argue that, given non-liberal cultures abroad, we may not reform the global economic order in light of liberal notions of fairness and equality of opportunity. But why may we then, despite the presence of non-liberal cultures within the US, realize such liberal notions in the national economic order?

168 Rawls offers a version of this view, suggesting that the causes of international inequality are purely domestic: "the causes of the wealth of a people and the forms it takes lie in their political culture and in the religious, philosophical, and moral traditions that support the basic structure of their political and social institutions, as well as in the industriousness and cooperative talents of its members, all supported by their political virtues. . . . Crucial also is the country's population policy" (Rawls, *The Law of Peoples*, p. 108). If a society does not want to be poor, it can curb its population growth or industrialize (ibid., pp. 117–18) and, in any case, "if it is not satisfied, it can continue to increase savings,

or, if this is not feasible, borrow from other members of the Society of Peoples" (ibid., p. 114). With the right culture and policies, even resource-poor countries like Japan can do very well. With the wrong culture and policies, resource-rich countries like Argentina may do very poorly (ibid., p. 108). Every people is master of its own fate – except only perhaps the Arctic Eskimos (ibid., p. 108 n. 34).

169 The spirit of many nationalist explanations reverting to history and culture is captured in Walzer's remark that "it is not the sign for some collective derangement or radical incapacity for a political community to produce an authoritarian regime. Indeed, the history, culture, and religion of the community may be such that authoritarian regimes come, as it were, naturally, reflecting a widely shared world view or way of life" (Walzer, "The Moral Standing of States," pp. 224–5). Detailed accounts are provided in Landes, *The Wealth and Poverty of Nations*, and in the essays collected in Harrison and Huntington: *Culture Matters*. Nationalist explanations reverting to societies' natural environments are exemplified in Diamond, *Guns, Germs, and Steel*.

170 Other aspects, though less significant, are considerably more obvious and, perhaps for this reason, currently under attack. One such obvious aspect is diplomatic immunity – recently invoked by General Augusto Pinochet – which shields crimes committed by high officials from prosecution in other countries. Another such obvious aspect is corporate bribery of foreign officials, which most developed countries have permitted and encouraged until recently. The non-governmental organization Transparency International (TI) has worked hard to publicize this problem, and its work has contributed to the 1997 *Convention on Combating Bribery of Foreign Officials in International Business Transactions* (cf. n. 243). Even if this *Convention* were to stamp out international bribery completely, the deep entrenchment of corruption in many ex-colonies would still be traceable (by way of a historical explanation) to the extensive bribery they were subjected to, with official encouragement from the affluent states, during their formative years.

171 See § 5.3, second paragraph.

172 As explicated in Hohfeld, *Fundamental Legal Conceptions*, a power involves the legally recognized authority to alter the distribution of first-order liberties, claims, and duties. Having *a* power or power*s* in this sense is distinct from having power (i.e. control over physical force and/or means of coercion).

173 For some background, see "Going on down," *The Economist*, June 8, 1996, pp. 46–8. A later update reports: "Oil revenues [are] paid directly to the government at the highest level. . . . The head of state has supreme power and control of all the cash. He depends on nobody and nothing but oil. Patronage and corruption spread downwards from the top" (*The Economist*, December 12, 1998, p. 19). Despite its huge oil revenues, Nigeria's real *per capita* GDP has declined by 22 percent between 1977 and 1998 (UNDP, *Report 2000*, p. 185).

174 In October 2003, Nigeria received a score of 1.4 out of 10 on the Corruption Perception Index, second from the bottom (www.transparency.org/cpi/2003/cpi2003.en.html).

175 For the 1975–99 period, these countries had long-term average annual rates of change in real GDP *per capita* as follows: Nigeria −0.8 percent, Congo/Zaire −4.7* percent, Kenya 0.4 percent, Angola −2.1* percent, Mozambique 1.3* percent, Brazil 0.8 percent, Venezuela −1.0 percent, Saudi Arabia −2.2 percent, United Arab Emirates −3.7* percent, Oman 2.8* percent, Kuwait −1.5* percent, Bahrain −0.5* percent, Brunei −2.1* percent, Indonesia 4.6 percent, the Philippines 0.1 percent (UNDP, *Report 2001*, pp. 178–81; stars indicate that a somewhat different period was used due to insufficient data). As a group, the resource-rich developing countries thus fell far below the 2.2 percent annual rate in real *per capita* growth of the high-income economies – even while the developing countries on the whole kept pace (with 2.3 percent) thanks to rapid growth in China and the rest of East and Southeast Asia (ibid., p. 181).

176 See n. 262 and surrounding text.

177 I add this caution because coups, civil wars, and oppression may be encouraged by the prospect of mere possession of resources, even without the power to confer internationally valid ownership rights. As I have learned from Josiah Ober, this is elegantly observed already in Thucydides, *The History of the Peloponnesian War*, book 1, ch. 2.

178 Many poor countries are weighed down by large debt service obligations that their unelected rulers incurred for unproductive purposes (including, most typically, purchases of weapons needed for internal repression). In Nigeria, for instance, the military rulers did not only steal and waste the oil revenues of several decades, but also left behind a national debt of $30 billion or 78.8 percent of GNP. Debt/GNP ratios for some other countries are as follows: Congo/Zaire 232 percent, Kenya 61.5 percent, Angola 297.1 percent, Mozambique 223.0 percent, Brazil 30.6 percent, Venezuela 39.6 percent, Indonesia 176.5 percent, the Philippines 70.1 percent (UNDP, *Report 2000*, pp. 219–21; for Congo/Zaire, the figure is from UNDP, *Report 1999*, p. 195). When the burden of debt service becomes too oppressive, the high-income countries occasionally grant some debt relief, thereby protecting their own banks from losses and, as a side effect, encouraging further lending to corrupt authoritarian rulers.

179 Ch. 6 outlines a reform specifically of the international resource and borrowing privileges, while chs 7 and 8 offer more general discussions of appropriate global institutional reforms.

180 Singer ("Famine, Affluence and Morality") has famously built his case for demanding obligations on an analogy with the situation of a healthy adult chancing upon a drowning infant whom he alone can rescue from a shallow pond. Many others have followed his lead, discussing the question on the basis of the tacit assumption that we are not contributing to the distress we are able to alleviate.

Chapter 5 The Bounds of Nationalism

181 Priority for one's race and its members has fallen out of favor after being taken to extremes in colonialism, slavery, and Nazi Germany. But it is also beginning to gain new respectability: a great deal of prestige has lately come to be attached to commitments to one's "ethnicity," which is more complex than race by involving a certain commonality of culture over and above commonality of descent. And giving priority on the basis of shared purely biological features (such as race and gender) has also become acceptable, provided the group in question is an underprivileged minority within the relevant society. (There are subtle variations in emphasis: some say that blacks should help *blacks*, others that *blacks* should help blacks.)

182 Raz, *Practical Reason and Norms*, ch. 1.2.

183 All these phenomena of compliance redefined are nicely illustrated in modern basketball and, especially, soccer.

184 They may take this view with regret: "Too bad that this is what the sport has come to, but, seeing that others behave in this way, we can hardly afford to forgo these options." I will say more about this defense by appeal to a "sucker exemption" at the end of this § 5.1.

185 Note that it is not the parents' opposition to affirmative action that makes their reasoning offensive. Citizens may reasonably believe that a level playing field does not require, or even rules out, affirmative action. What is offensive is that their political stance is based not on what they conscientiously believe to be right and fair to all, but on what they think will benefit their own children (as brought out by their thought that they would strongly support affirmative action if their own children stood to gain therefrom). The example illustrates, then, a disposition to slant the social order by tailoring its basic rules. The mother of the previous example, by contrast, slanted the social order by corrupting the administration of its rules. In public life as in sports, a level playing field requires both: that the rules be fair and that they be impartially administered.

186 This general idea has truly become global, as abuse of political authority and power to benefit one's friends and family has begun to provoke great moral resentment and outrage in numerous developing countries of Asia, Latin America, and (to a lesser extent) Africa.

187 By accepting this understanding of human rights as outer bounds on institutional schemes, one is not committed to the *UDHR*'s substantive conception, set forth in the preceding articles, of what these outer bounds are.

188 Ambassador David A. Colson, Deputy Assistant Secretary of State for Oceans, in testimony before the Subcommittee on Oceanography of the Merchant Marine and Fisheries Committee of the US House of Representatives (April 26, 1994).

189 *Agreement Relating to the Implementation of Part XI of the United Nations Convention on the Law of the Sea of 10 December 1982*. Its Article 2(1)

says: "In the event of an inconsistency between this agreement and Part XI, the provisions of this agreement shall prevail."

190 USDS, *US Commentary on the Law of the Sea Convention including the 1994 Amendments*, 3. "The Agreement fully meets the objections of the United States and other industrialized states to Part XI" (ibid., p. 2). These objections were that: "it established a structure for administering the seabed mining regime that does not accord the industrialized States influence in the regime commensurate with their interests; it incorporated economic principles inconsistent with free market philosophy; and its specific provisions created numerous problems from an economic and commercial policy perspective that would have impeded access by the US and other industrialized countries to the resources of the deep seabed beyond national jurisdiction" (ibid., pp. 2–3). Cf. www.state.gov/www/global/oes/oceans/fs_oceans_los.html

191 "The provisions of Annex III, article 5, of the Convention shall not apply." § 5(2) of the Annex to the *Agreement.*

192 § 7(1) of the Annex to the *Agreement* limits the sharing of profits to "economic assistance" to "developing countries which suffer serious adverse effects on their export earnings or economies resulting from a reduction in the price of an affected mineral or in the volume of exports of that mineral, to the extent that such reduction is caused by [seabed mining]." § 8(3) halves the application fee for exploration and exploitation of sites to $250,000 and § 8(2) eliminates the $1,000,000 annual production fee as well as the profit-related financial contributions (all of which were mandated in the *Convention*'s Annex III, Article 13).

193 Colson, testimony (n. 188).

194 Germany and Great Britain were especially willing to go along with such a move.

195 We can easily imagine Clinton saying, in analogy to our fictional parents, that he would of course have strongly favored the sharing of technologies and economic benefits, if he had been president of one of the poorer states. Few would have found such a remark morally offensive.

196 At current metals prices, seabed mining is not expected to become commercially viable for another 20 years or so.

197 For an explication and defense of the view that Article 28 requires our *global* institutional order, as well, to satisfy the outer bounds imposed by basic human rights, see Pogge, "Human Rights and Human Responsibilities." Chs 6–8 will illustrate how the global level of human-rights fulfillment is causally dependent on the structure of international institutions.

198 You may respond that any funds Part XI of the *Convention* might have raised for the least developed countries would have ended up in the pockets of their corrupt rulers and bureaucrats. This is indeed where much "development aid" ends up – because our politicians and bureaucrats need favors from them, not from the poor. But surely, the choice of throwing money at corrupt Third World elites *versus* ignoring world

poverty does not exhaust the available options. Clinton might well have pressed for terms that ensure that the funds raised are spent on effective poverty eradication.

199 For a more detailed elaboration of this argument, see ch. 3.

200 Note that this initiative is, in one sense, more plausible than Clinton's. One can argue that, since public benefits are generated at the expense of those who pay taxes, they alone should be eligible for them. Clinton cannot make a parallel argument, because ocean floor resources are not generated at anyone's expense. Of course, such resources will be harvested at the expense of mining firms. But this merely shows that the poor can claim a fair share not of the extracted resources, but only of the resources *in situ*. The value of these undeveloped resources could easily be determined through auctions in which competing firms would bid for the right to mine specific resources in specified regions of the ocean floor.

201 Hume, *An Enquiry Concerning the Principles of Morals*, pp. 25–6 (§ 3, part 1). Both Hume and Rawls stress rough equality of powers in the context of seeking to *explain*, not to justify, the exclusion of the very weak. See Rawls, *A Theory of Justice*, pp. 109–10.

202 The original part XI of the 1982 *UN Convention on the Law of the Sea* may be seen as a small initiative of this kind. Some more substantial reforms toward reducing the problems of undemocratic government, outsized national debts, and domestic poverty and inequality in the poorer countries are outlined in chs 6–8.

203 This huge discrepancy exists in the domain of general theory as well as in that of more concrete or "applied" work. Compare the amount of theorizing about domestic with that about international justice – or the moral scrutiny lavished on national affirmative-action legislation with that expended on the far more consequential ground rules structuring the world economy.

204 I concede that such conduct usually *is* morally worse if the victim is one's mother. But this may be not because one ought to be more concerned to avoid harming family members than to avoid harming strangers, but because the harm is so much greater: the son is not merely inflicting physical pain without provocation; he is also showing ingratitude toward the person who raised him, deeply hurting her love and trust, and/or the like. Sam Scheffler holds by contrast that, according to ordinary morality, negative duties to strangers are more easily overridden by positive duties or by considerations of cost to the agent than negative duties to associates and family members are. See Scheffler, *Boundaries and Allegiances*, pp. 52–3.

205 Goodin, "What is So Special about Our Fellow Countrymen?" The list is at pp. 668–9, the quote is from p. 673.

206 My formulation of the two provisos is deliberately vague as there is of course no agreement on how they should be specified exactly. Nevertheless, the fact remains that a weakening of negative duties through a

special relationship such as compatriotism would be found acceptable in modern Western moral thinking only if it satisfied two substantial provisos of the general form I have sketched.

207 I hope I have made clear enough that this is not presented as a strict, or lexical, hierarchy. It is generally acknowledged that a higher moral reason can be outweighed by a lower, if more is at stake in the latter. Public reaction to the continuing massacres of the 20th century shows, however, that the "exchange rates" are extreme. Sexual harassment in a domestic corporation engenders a much more powerful response than a genocidal massacre abroad. It should also be clear that this hierarchy does not cover the whole domain of moral reasons. It leaves out reasons to protect persons from harms that do not involve wrongdoing (e.g. natural harms) as well as reasons to benefit others. I would think that these are on a par with moral reasons to protect others from third-party wrongs ((2a)–(2z)), but am content to leave this question open here.

208 In our efforts to stop wrongs in which our society, and therefore we, are materially involved, we must, then, generally give priority to greater wrongs inflicted on foreigners over lesser wrongs inflicted on compatriots – "generally," because such decisions will also have to take account of the degree of our involvement and of the costs and prospects of our rectification efforts.

209 Many consider it perfectly alright for donors to favor even relatively trivial or well-supplied domestic causes – one's alma mater, the local park or museum, one's congregation – over relatively cheap life-saving efforts in the Third World: it is alright to favor the causes one personally cares about and good to "give back" to one's community whose improvement benefits one's own family as well.

210 They have argued that we should focus our beneficence on the global poor because the moral significance of a harm's position in the (2a)–(2z) hierarchy is less than ordinary moral thinking supposes and/or because the position of the global poor at the bottom of the list is overcome by the much lower cost/benefit ratio involved in helping them. For the price of enabling one poor local youngster to attend summer camp, we can save many foreign children's lives by giving the money to UNICEF for oral rehydration therapy. Representative examples of such lines of argument are Singer, "Famine, Affluence and Morality"; Rachels, "Killing and Starving to Death"; Kagan, *The Limits of Morality*; Unger, *Living High and Letting Die*. Two notable exceptions are O'Neill, "Lifeboat Earth," and Nagel, "Poverty and Food." Both emphasize our active involvement in the production of poverty. See also Pogge, *Realizing Rawls*, pp. 32–6 and 276–80.

211 Rawls, *A Theory of Justice*, p. 98.

212 Ibid., p. 94. Natural duties to mutual aid and to mutual respect are there categorized as positive, and natural duties not to injure and not to harm the innocent as negative. Rawls does not make clear how he understands the negative/positive distinction. This does not matter, because I am

concerned only with what he implies: that our natural duty of justice has the lesser weight of a positive duty.

213 Ibid., p. 99; a parallel passage is on pp. 293–4. See also p. 216: "as far as circumstances permit, we have a natural duty to remove any injustices, beginning with the most grievous as identified by the extent of the deviation from perfect justice."

214 This loss may come from there being slightly less money available for administering our institutional order and from there being a slightly greater risk of damage to mutual trust from discovered noncompliance. I am assuming, quite in the spirit of Rawls, that the duty of justice is an interpersonal responsibility, a duty owed solely to other persons.

215 Rawls has extensively discussed the problem of stability and tried to solve it by envisioning the citizens of his well-ordered society as having a sense of justice that is effective and normally overriding. See e.g. Rawls, *Political Liberalism*, pp. 141–2. The puzzle is how citizens' strong moral desire to comply can derive from their allegiance to a moral conception that recognizes only a weak moral reason to do so.

216 In both cases, it is widely acknowledged that a positive duty can still win out when much more is at stake (cf. n. 207): one may usually break a promise, violate a just property regime, or injure an innocent when doing so is necessary to save a human life, for example.

217 Kant bases such imposition on the enforceable imperative: "Act outwardly so that the free employment of your will [*Willkür*] can coexist with the freedom of everyone according to a universal law." Kant, *Metaphysik der Sitten*, in *Kants gesammelte Schriften*, vol. 6, p. 231.

218 This line of argument does not justify a negative duty to comply with *all* existing just institutions. Success at exceeding the speed limit, or at breaching many social conventions and rules of etiquette, usually does not depend on others being constrained to comply. One may think that this line of argument also fails when a noncomplying agent can claim to be in compliance with non-existing just institutions. He takes more freedom or resources than he is permitted to take under the existing just order, but does so in accordance with an equally just, albeit nonexisting, scheme whose rules everyone could be free to follow. Seeing that we could realize a just order by complying with the scheme he favors, why should he have a negative duty to comply with ours? I cannot answer this objection fully here. But the response must begin with the realization that it is generally not possible for each to take what he would be entitled to under the just order of his choice, irrespective of what order others are observing – whereas it is possible for each to take what he is entitled to under the one existing just order.

219 The Kantian strategy avoids the claim, suggested by Rawls, that a duty to comply with institutions can be derived from the mere fact that the institutions are just and (purport to) apply to us. This claim is convincingly criticized in Simmons, *Moral Principles and Political Obligation*, pp. 147–56. My sketch of how to justify a *negative* natural duty of

justice fits with, and can be enriched by, the response to Simmons given in Waldron, "Special Ties and Natural Duties."

220 I use "legitimacy" here in the sociological sense specified by Max Weber. It is of the essence of justice that a majority's consent cannot lend *moral* legitimacy to the mistreatment of a minority. The Nazi case exemplifies harms inflicted by state officials, but essentially the same conclusion holds when the state merely legally sanctions undue harms and protects and aids those who inflict them, as when slavery was legally authorized in the US and slaveholder rights were enforced by state officials, who helped put down revolts and capture fugitive slaves.

221 This conclusion squares well with common convictions, for example, that one has a stronger reason to oppose rules that exclude blacks or women from a club so long as one is oneself a member of it, even if the very same persons are excluded from other clubs whose rules one could oppose as effectively.

222 Oskar Schindler, as depicted in Steven Spielberg's *Schindler's List*, compensated for his contributions to the economy of Nazi Germany by protecting some of its victims.

223 The difference principle requires that "social and economic inequalities . . . are to be to the greatest benefit of the least advantaged members of society" (Rawls, *Political Liberalism*, p. 6). A global difference principle is rejected by Rawls himself (Rawls, *The Law of Peoples*, pp. 116–18), though others have argued that his theory commits him to accepting it. See Scanlon, "Rawls' Theory of Justice," p. 202; Barry, *The Liberal Theory of Justice*, pp. 128–33; Beitz, *Political Theory and International Relations*, pp. 149–76; and Pogge, *Realizing Rawls*, ch. 6.

224 The assumption seems particularly dubious when the injustice in question appears to have the character of an omission. One may agree that a legal order in which inter-spousal violence is not prohibited or not effectively deterred is unjust and nevertheless deny that those who impose such a legal order are harming women unduly (rather than merely failing to protect them from their husbands' wrongdoing).

225 Locke, "An Essay Concerning the True Original," § 27 and § 33. Locke imposes two further constraints on unilateral appropriations, which need not concern us here: one may take possession of any natural resource only by "mixing one's labor" with it (ibid., § 27) and only insofar as nothing will spoil in one's possession (ibid., § 31). We can also leave aside how the freedom of unilateral appropriation, and the constraints upon this freedom, can be derived from Locke's fundamental "Law of Nature" (ibid., § 6).

226 The Lockean provisos are not subject to majority rule – undue harms inflicted on a few cannot be justified by the fact that the many want to inflict them (cf. n. 220). It is rather the other way around: majority rule is itself an institution whose moral legitimacy depends on everyone's rational consent. Locke argues that majority rule satisfies this condition, while autocracy does not (ibid., § 93, § 137; see § 20, §§ 90–6).

227 Ibid., § 50.
228 Ibid., § 36.
229 Ibid., § 41, see § 37.
230 On the other hand, one might also object that Locke's baseline is not restrictive enough in another respect: it could be irrational to consent to social institutions under which everyone gains a little relative to the state of nature if there are feasible alternative institutions under which everyone gains more. Locke overlooks this point.
231 Ibid., § 73, § 121.
232 But see Rawls, *A Theory of Justice*, p. 145, making the surprising and unnecessary claim that "the general form of the slaveholder's argument is correct."
233 Brazil affords a suitable comparison: Its PPP gross national income *per capita* is close to that of the world at large (World Bank, *Report 2002*, pp. 232–3). For a country this wealthy in aggregate, it has a high incidence of severe poverty (ibid., p. 234). And its income inequality is among the highest in the world (ibid.), albeit still much lower than that of the world at large.
234 It is sometimes said that such poverty is not avoidable, that high inequality is the price for rapid economic growth which, over time, benefits all. But the available data tell a different story: The high-inequality countries (mainly in Latin America and Africa) have consistently shown very slow, or even negative growth in *per capita* GNP, while the developing countries with rapid economic growth (mainly in East Asia) have quintile income inequality ratios below 10 : 1, similar to those in many developed countries (UNDP, *Report 2001*, pp. 178–85). This should not be surprising: when inequalities are very large, those born among the poor often suffer nutritional, medical, or educational deficits or disadvantages that prevent them from effectively competing for the more important positions. More or less by default, these positions then go to persons born among the wealthy and thus attract less talent and effort than they would with a more open competition.
235 Rawls, if he held his theory of justice to be applicable to Brazil's social order at all, would be an exception, assigning to the Brazilian elite a merely positive duty to further just arrangements.
236 See § 4.3.3, esp. n. 145, where I estimate the current global quintile income inequality ratio to be about 270.
237 An analogous point plays a major role in debates about the significance of genetic vis-à-vis environmental factors: Factors that are quite unimportant for explaining the observed *variation* of a trait (e.g. height, IQ) in some population may be very important for explaining this trait's *overall level* (frequency) in the same population. Suppose that, in some province, the observed variation in female adult height (54–60 inches) is almost entirely due to hereditary factors. It is still quite possible that the height differentials among these woman are minor compared to how much taller they all would be (67–74 inches) if it had not been the case

that, when they were growing up, food was scarce and boys were preferred over girls in its distribution. Or suppose that we can predict quite accurately, on the basis of genetic information, who will get cancer and who will not. This would not show that the overall incidence of cancer is determined by the human gene pool. For it is still quite possible that, in a healthier environment, cancer would hardly occur at all.

238 This point, illustrated by my analysis of the international resource and borrowing privileges in § 4.9, is frequently overlooked. Rawls, for instance, attributes the human rights problems in the typical poor country exclusively to local factors: "the problem is commonly the nature of the public political culture and the religious and philosophical traditions that underlie its institutions. The great social evils in poorer societies are likely to be oppressive government and corrupt elites" (Rawls, "The Law of Peoples," p. 77). This superficial explanation is not so much false as incomplete. As soon as one asks, as Rawls does not, *why* so many of these countries have oppressive governments and corrupt elites, one will unavoidably hit upon global factors – such as the ones discussed in my two examples. Local elites can afford to be oppressive and corrupt, because, with foreign loans and military aid, they can stay in power even without popular support. And they are so often oppressive and corrupt, because it is, in light of the prevailing extreme international inequalities, far more lucrative for them to cater to the interests of foreign governments and firms rather than to those of their impoverished compatriots. Examples abound. There are, in the poor countries, plenty of governments that came to power and/or stay in power only thanks to foreign support. And there are plenty of politicians and bureaucrats who, induced or even bribed by foreigners, work against the interests of their people: *for* the development of a tourist-friendly sex industry (whose forced exploitation of children and women they tolerate and profit from), *for* the importation of unneeded, obsolete, or overpriced products at public expense, *for* the permission to import hazardous products, wastes, or productive facilities, *against* laws protecting employees or the environment, etc. It is perfectly unrealistic to believe that the corruption and oppression in the poor countries, which Rawls rightly deplores, can be abolished without a significant reduction in international inequality.

239 Ibid., p. 56.

240 Ibid., p. 77.

241 See e.g. Amnesty International, *Human Rights and U.S. Security Assistance.*

242 This proposal is elaborated in § 6.4.

243 The post-Watergate Congress of the US pioneered reform with its 1977 *Foreign Corrupt Practices Act* after the Lockheed Corporation was found to have paid – not a modest sum to some minor Third World official, but rather – a $2 million bribe to Prime Minister Kakuei Tanaka of powerful and democratic Japan. It took another 20 years for the other

rich countries, pressured by the US and Transparency International, to follow suit with the OECD *Convention on Combating Bribery of Foreign Officials in International Business Transactions*, which requires signatory states to criminalize the bribery of foreign officials. This convention took effect in February 1999 and as of November 2001 has been ratified by 34 states (www.oecd.org/FR/document/0,,FR-document-0-nodirectorate-no-6-16767-0,00.html). So, the reform proposed in the text is achieved: Most rich states now have laws that forbid corporations to bribe foreign officials. "But big multi-nationals continue to sidestep them with ease" (*The Economist*, March 2, 2002, pp. 63–5).

244 See n. 262 and surrounding text.

245 Cf. ch. 8 for a detailed proposal.

246 How much should we contribute to such reform and protection efforts? I would think: as much as would be necessary to eradicate the harms if others similarly placed made analogous contributions (regardless of what they actually contribute). Thus, if 1 percent of the collective income of the citizens of the high-income countries were sufficient to eradicate world poverty within a few years (§ 4.3.2), then we citizens of these countries should prevail upon our governments to contribute 1 percent of our national income or else should contribute individually about 1 percent of our incomes, if we can, or make some equivalent non-monetary contribution. The idea that those who, together, ought to eliminate some scalar harm should each do as much as would be necessary to eliminate the harm if the others also did their fair share is suggested in Parfit, *Reasons and Persons*, p. 31 ("collective consequentialism") and greatly elaborated in Murphy, *Moral Demands*.

247 See Bok, "Acting without Choosing."

248 But not unprecedented: many highly independent and progressive thinkers of the past saw nothing wrong with what we now regard as paradigm instances of severe injustice (e.g. slavery and the oppression of women).

Chapter 6 Achieving Democracy

249 To complement this brief account, let me mention some important works on large-scale modern democracy: Schumpeter, *Capitalism, Socialism, and Democracy*; Dahl, *A Preface to Democratic Theory*; Bobbio, *The Future of Democracy*; Lefort, *Democracy and Political Theory*; Elster and Slagstad, eds., *Constitutionalism and Democracy*; Dahl, *Democracy and its Critics*; Beitz, *Political Equality*; Held, *Models of Democracy*; Copp et al., eds., *The Idea of Democracy*; Rawls, *Political Liberalism*; Guinier, *The Tyranny of the Majority*; Habermas, *Between Facts and Norms*; Christiano, *The Rule of the Many*; Gutmann and Thompson, *Democracy and Disagreement*; Manin, *Principles of Representative Government*; Elster, ed., *Deliberative Democracy*; Rosenblum, ed., *Obligations of Citizenship*.

250 This literature is vast and still growing very rapidly. Here, and in n. 253, I can list only a few representative samples: Herz, ed., *From Dictatorship to Democracy*; Huntington, *The Third Wave*; Ackerman, *The Future of Liberal Revolution*; Linz and Stepan, *Problems of Democratic Transition and Consolidation*; Diamond, *Developing Democracy.*

251 Some representative examples are Wallerstein, *The Capitalist World Economy*, *The Politics of the World-Economy*, *After Liberalism*, *The Essential Wallerstein*; Falk, *The End of World Order*; Roberto Unger, *Democracy Realized.*

252 Regarding this goal, see esp. Höffe, *Demokratie im Zeitalter der Globalisierung*.

253 Important instances of such work include Weschler, *A Miracle, a Universe*; Kritz, ed., *Transitional Justice*; Nino, *Radical Evil on Trial*; Malamud-Goti, *Game without End*; Pablo de Greiff, "Trial and Punishment"; Minow, *Between Vengeance and Forgiveness*; Crocker, "Reckoning with Past Wrongs"; Hesse and Post, eds.: *Human Rights in Political Transitions*; Rotberg and Thompson, eds., *Truth v. Justice*; Teitel, *Transitional Justice*; Hayner, *Unspeakable Truths.*

254 See Parfit, *Reasons and Persons*, § 2.

255 See ibid., § 36.

256 Farer, "The United States as Guarantor" and "A Paradigm of Legitimate Intervention"; Hoffmann, "Delusions of World Order" and *The Ethics and Politics of Humanitarian Intervention.*

257 When a democratically legitimate government has been unconstitutionally replaced by an authoritarian junta, for example, some governments may not want to judge the change unconstitutional because they view the new government as "friendlier" and perhaps even had a hand in bringing it to power. Other governments may come under pressure from more powerful states to refrain from such a judgment – pressure they find it hard to resist when doing so would adversely affect their own interests.

258 Rulers would be greatly weakened by being officially found unconstitutional by the Democracy Panel. This would undermine their reputation and standing at home and abroad, denying them not only the borrowing privilege (and perhaps the resource privilege – cf. § 6.4), but also many of the benefits of normal international diplomatic, fiscal, financial, and trade cooperation.

259 One way to cope would be for this government to offer future resource exports as collateral for its debts. Potential authoritarian successors could then renege on these debts only by halting such resource exports altogether.

260 As evidence that something like this can happen, consider the 1997 OECD *Convention on Combating Bribery of Foreign Officials in International Business Transactions*, which ended a long-standing practice under which most developed states (though not the US after 1977) permitted their companies to bribe foreign officials and even to deduct such bribes from their taxable revenues. Public pressure, generated and amplified by Transparency International, played a vital role in building momentum

for this *Convention*, which thus sets a hopeful precedent (cf. n. 243). Still, one should not overlook that while the suppression of bribery may well be in the *collective* self-interest of the developed states and their corporations, the Democracy Panel and the Democracy Fund are not.

261 This name alludes to a period in Dutch history which began with the discovery of huge natural gas reserves in 1959 which, by the 1970s, produced revenues and import savings of about $5 billion–$6 billion annually. Despite this windfall (enhanced by the "oil-shock" increases in energy prices), the Dutch economy suffered stagnation, high unemployment, and finally recession – doing considerably worse than its peers throughout the 1970s and early 1980s.

262 Lam and Wantchekon, "Dictatorships as a Political Dutch Disease," pp. 35–6. In a later paper, Wantchekon presents data to show that "a one percent increase in resource dependence as measured by the ratio of primary exports to GDP leads to nearly 8 percent increase in the probability of authoritarianism" (Wantchekon, "Why do Resource Dependent Countries Have Authoritarian Governments?" p. 2). Similar findings are presented in Ross, "Does Resource Wealth Cause Authoritarian Rule?" Cf. also Collier and Hoeffler, "On Economic Causes of Civil War" and, for earlier work on the Dutch Disease, Sachs and Warner, "Natural Resource Abundance and Economic Growth."

263 The value of immovable public property abroad is rarely significant, and I will therefore ignore such property which, in any case, poses problems similar to those posed by movable goods.

264 We should remember this point whenever we hear it said that natural resources are no longer an important part of the global economy. Once we understand why this is true (relating the dollar value of resource sales to that of aggregate global income or aggregate international trade), we also understand why it is, in a deeper sense, false. Natural resources are of small significance only *modulo current price vectors*, which are heavily influenced by the international resource privilege and often also by the extreme global income inequality it helps cause. (Kenneth Arrow has kindly pointed out that consumption of some natural resources bears a roughly linear relation to household income so that aggregate demand is not much affected by variations in income inequality.) So the small fraction of their national incomes that rich countries spend on imported natural resources does not reflect the extent to which their economic prosperity depends on these resources – just as the small fraction of my income spent on water does not reflect the extent of my dependence on it. If we appraise depletable natural resources by their use value for all human beings, present and future, we must judge them grossly undervalued by current market prices. This undervaluation reflects a negative externality that the corrupt elites of resource-rich developing countries and the heavy consumers of resources together manage to impose upon the populations of those developing countries as well as on future generations, for whom such resources will be considerably less plentiful and more expensive.

265 This reflection begins to show how standard broadly Marxist accounts of global inequality have become inadequate to the real world. Thanks to high-tech production methods, the corporations of the developed world are becoming much less dependent on appropriating the cheap labor power of poor populations (which is not to deny that they do so, and do so profitably). Thanks to the enormous concentration of global buying power in the high-income economies, the corporations of the developed world are becoming much less dependent on opening the developing world's markets for their products, services, and lending (though they and their governments are working quite hard to achieve such "penetration" while protecting their own markets against "unfairly cheap" imports from the developing countries). The dependence of the developed world on the developing countries has shifted to their natural resources, crude oil first and foremost. This trend entails a shift in its interest in their people: The developed world need not be concerned about their being healthy enough to reproduce their labor power or affluent enough to buy its products. The fewer and the poorer they are, the less they will interfere with foreign appropriation of their resources.

266 The developed countries also enjoy more lucrative business opportunities as a third dubious benefit. Authoritarian rulers, made more frequent by the international resource privilege, are more likely to send the proceeds from resource sales right back to the affluent countries, to pay for high-margin weaponry and military advisers, advanced luxury products, real estate, and financial investments. Democratically responsive supplier governments, by contrast, tend to spend more of their resource revenues domestically (stimulating the country's economy) and tend to get better value for what they spend on imports.

Chapter 7 Cosmopolitanism and Sovereignty

267 The differences between these two concepts are not essential to the present discussion.

268 There is some debate about the extent to which we should give weight to the interests of future persons and also to those of past ones (whose deaths are still recent). I leave this issue aside because it is at right angles to the debate between cosmopolitanism and its alternatives.

269 One argument for a world state is advanced in Nielsen, "World Government, Security, and Global Justice." See also Höffe, *Demokratie im Zeitalter der Globalisierung*, discussing more modest political reforms.

270 I have in mind here a rather minimal conception of human rights, one that rules out truly severe abuses, deprivations, and inequalities while still being compatible with a wide range of political, moral, and religious cultures. The recent development of, and progress within, both governmental and nongovernmental international organizations supports the hope, I believe, that such a conception might, in our world, become the

object of a worldwide overlapping consensus. See ch. 1 and Pogge, "Human Rights and Human Responsibilities."

271 Interactional cosmopolitanism has been defended in numerous works. A paradigmatic statement is offered in Luban's essay "Just War and Human Rights," p. 209: "A human right, then, will be a right whose beneficiaries are all humans and whose obligors are all humans in a position to effect the right." Substantially similar moral positions are advanced in Singer, "Famine, Affluence and Morality"; Rachels, "Killing and Starving to Death"; Kagan, *The Limits of Morality*; Peter Unger, *Living High and Letting Die*. Nozick's *Anarchy, State, and Utopia* – however surprising the rights he singles out as fundamental – is also an instance of interactional cosmopolitanism. For institutional cosmopolitanism, see O'Neill, "Lifeboat Earth"; Nagel, "Poverty and Food"; Beitz, *Political Theory and International Relations*, part 3; Beitz, "Cosmopolitan Ideals and National Sentiment"; and Pogge, *Realizing Rawls*, part 3. Shue's influential book *Basic Rights* seems to me to waver between both variants of moral cosmopolitanism, leaving unclear whether Shue means the weight of our duties to protect and to aid the deprived to depend on whether we are or are not involved in (imposing upon them the social institutions that produce) their deprivation. Cf. n. 98.

272 This is done, for example, by Rawls, who asserts both a natural duty to uphold just social institutions as well as various other natural duties that do not presuppose shared social institutions, such as duties to avoid injury and cruelty, duties to render mutual aid, and a duty to bring about just social institutions where none presently exist. See Rawls, *A Theory of Justice*, pp. 98–9 and 293–4.

273 These two limitations are compatible with the belief that we have a duty to *create* a comprehensive institutional order. Thus Kant believed that any persons and groups who cannot avoid affecting one another ought to enter into a juridical condition. See *Kant's Political Writings*, pp. 73, 98n., 137 (*Kants Gesammelte Schriften*, vol. 8, pp. 289 and 349n.; vol. 6, p. 312).

274 The distinction between the established and the engendered effects of social institutions as well as the question of its moral significance are extensively discussed in Pogge, *Realizing Rawls*, §§ 2–4. The rejection of purely recipient-oriented modes of assessment (such as that enshrined in Rawls's original position) is of more recent vintage: "Three Problems" and "Gleiche Freiheit für alle?"

275 This notion is defined in probabilistic terms, perhaps by taking account of various personal characteristics. Thus it is quite possible that the human right to physical security is today fulfilled in the US for middle-aged whites or suburbanites but not for black youths or inner-city residents.

276 The explanatory move urged in this fictitious interjection is common among social theorists and philosophers. It is more fully criticized in §§ 4.8, 4.9, and 5.3.

277 Walzer, *Spheres of Justice*, p. 31.
278 Nozick, *Anarchy, State, and Utopia*, p. 149.
279 See ch. 2 and Pogge, "Human Rights and Human Responsibilities."
280 This means that A has no supervisor with authority to give directives with regard to A's exercise of authority over B. Unsupervised authority in this sense is compatible with judicial review.
281 It is quite possible, and not without historical justification, to define sovereignty the way I have defined absolute sovereignty. So defined, sovereignty would not survive division (when abroad, B would thus presumably lack a sovereign), and the expression "distribution of sovereignty" would be an oxymoron.
282 The central organs of the EU constitute a promising exception to this generalization. See Pogge, "Creating Supra-National Institutions Democratically," for further discussion.
283 This includes the sentiments of patriotism, if such there must be. Beitz points out two respects in which patriotic allegiance to political units may be desirable. It supports a sense of shared loyalty ("Cosmopolitan Ideals and National Sentiment," p. 599). And it allows one to see oneself as a significant contributor to a common cultural project: "Just as we can see ourselves as striving to realize in our own lives various forms of individual perfection, so we can see our countries as striving for various forms of social and communal perfection" (ibid., p. 600). Neither of these considerations entails that Britain, say, must be the sole object of your patriotic allegiance, rather than some combination of Glasgow, Scotland, Britain, Europe, humankind, and perhaps even such geographically dispersed units as the Anglican Church, the World Trade Union Movement, PEN, or Amnesty International.
284 Many individuals might, of course, identify more with one of their citizenships than with the others. But in a multilayered order such prominent identifications would be less frequent and, most important, would not converge: Even if some residents of Glasgow would see themselves as primarily British, others would identify more with Europe, with Scotland, with Glasgow, or with humankind at large.
285 This dogma – prefigured in Thomas Aquinas, Dante Alighieri, Marsilius of Padua, and Jean Bodin – is most fully stated by Hobbes in chs 14, 26, and 29 of *Leviathan*, who also introduces the idea of obligations *in foro interno*. For Kant's statements of it, see *Kant's Political Writings*, pp. 75, 81, 144–5 (*Kants gesammelte Schriften*, vol. 8, pp. 291–2 and 299; vol. 6, p. 319). The dogma maintained its hold well into the 20th century, when it declined with the Austinian conception of jurisprudence. See Austin, *The Province of Jurisprudence Determined*; Marshall, *Parliamentary Sovereignty and the Commonwealth*, part 1; Benn and Peters, *Social Principles and the Democratic State*, chs 3 and 12; and Hart, *The Concept of Law*.
286 Walzer, *Spheres of Justice*, p. 39.

287 Ibid.
288 Ibid., pp. 38–9.
289 Ibid., p. 39.
290 Ibid.
291 Ibid., pp. 38–9.
292 See § 4.3.1.
293 Such a reform is proposed in ch. 8. See also Beitz, *Political Theory*, pp. 136–43, and Barry, "Humanity and Justice in Global Perspective."
294 The qualification "legitimately" is necessary to rule out claims such as this: "I should be allowed a vote on the permissibility of homosexuality in all parts of the world, because the knowledge that homosexual acts are performed anywhere causes me great distress." I cannot enter a discussion of this proviso here, except to say that the arguments relevant to its specification are by and large analogous to the standard arguments relevant to the specification of Mill's no-harm principle: "the sole end for which mankind are warranted, individually or collectively, in interfering with the liberty of action of any of their number is self-protection" (Mill, *On Liberty*, p. 9).
295 I understand *opportunity* as being impaired only by (social) *disadvantages*, such as exclusion from the franchise, not by (natural) *handicaps*, such as a speech impediment. This is plausible only on a narrow construal of "handicap": insofar as natural causes reduce a person's chances only on account of cooperating social causes, this person counts as disadvantaged rather than as handicapped. Thus, being black and being female are genetic features, but they reduce a person's chances to influence political decisions only in certain social settings: in a racist/sexist culture. Here blacks and women count as disadvantaged by such a setting rather than handicapped by their race or gender. By contrast, those whose lesser ability to participate in public debate is due to their low intelligence are not disadvantaged but handicapped. Provided they had access to an adequate education, they do not count as having a less-than-equal opportunity.
296 The postulated human right is not a group right. Of course, the inhabitants of a town may appeal to this right to show that it was wrong for the national government, say, to impose some political decision that affects only them. In such a case, the townspeople form a group of those having a grievance. But they do not have a grievance *as a group*. Rather, *each* of them has such a grievance of not having been given her due political weight – just the grievance she would have had, had the decision been made by other townspeople with her excluded.
297 In the past dozen years, this thought has been much discussed in Europe under the subsidiarity label.
298 On what follows, see Höffe, *Demokratie im Zeitalter der Globalisierung*.
299 See § 5.1 for an illustration regarding the development of rules for the use of seabed resources.

300 This argument withstands the communitarian claim that we must renounce supranational democratic processes for the sake of safeguarding national self-determination. Such renunciation may indeed enhance the national autonomy of the privileged populations of the developed countries. But their gains in autonomy come at the expense of poorer populations who, despite their legal independence, have virtually no control over the most basic parameters that shape their lives. In fact, many of them are unable to influence even their own internationally powerless governments, which often face much stronger incentives to cater to foreign interests rather than to those of their constituents.

301 The contiguity condition needs some relaxing to allow territories consisting of a small number of internally contiguous areas whose access to one another is not controlled by other political units. The US would satisfy this relaxed condition through secure access among Puerto Rico, Alaska, Hawaii, and the remaining 48 contiguous states.

302 I won't try to be precise about "reasonable shape." The idea is to rule out territories whose borders are extremely long (relative to the square root of their area) or divide towns, integrated networks of economic activity, or the like. Perhaps newly incorporating areas should have some minimal number of inhabitants. But I think the threshold could be quite low. If a tiny border village wants to belong to the neighboring province, why should it not be allowed to switch?

303 What if minority groups are geographically dispersed, like the Serbs in Croatia? In such cases, there is no attractive way of accommodating those opposed to the formation of the new political unit. The second proposed principle would let the preference of the majority within the relevant territory prevail nonetheless. This is defensible, I think, so long as human rights are fulfilled. In such cases, when legitimate preferences are opposed and some must be frustrated, it seems reasonable to let the majority prevail.

304 See § 3.5 and Buchanan, *Secession*, pp. 114–25.

305 *This* topic is extensively discussed by Buchanan. He takes the current states system for granted and realistically adjusts his theory of secession to it. Departing from this system, I see yet one more reason for a multilayered global order in the fact that it would allow implementation of a morally more appealing theory of secession. A more sustained argument for the moral appeal of this theory in terms of democratic self-government is provided in Philpott, "In Defense of Self-Determination." See also Wellman, "A Defense of Secession," and the early, pioneering contribution by Beran, *The Consent Theory of Political Obligation*.

306 For example, as European states continue to transfer important governmental functions to international organizations such as the EU and to subnational political units, the conflict over whether there should be one or two states in the present territory of Belgium will become ever less important – for the two cultural groups as well as for any third parties.

307 Obviously, this illustration is not meant to reflect the actual situation on the Indian subcontinent.

308 While the precise definitions of "nation" and "nationality" are not essential to this discussion, I do assume that nationality is not defined entirely in voluntaristic terms (e.g. "a nation is a group of persons all of whom desire to constitute one political unit of which they are the only members"), in which case (a) would become trivial and (b) empty. The definition may still contain significant voluntaristic elements, as in Renan's proposal: "A nation is a grand solidarity constituted by the sentiment of sacrifices which one has made and those one is disposed to make again. It supposes a past" (quoted in Barry, "Self-Government Revisited," p. 136). So long as some nonvoluntaristic element is present, at least one of the two claims can get off the ground. Those who want to belong together as one political unit may be prevented from doing so when they lack an appropriate history of solidarity and sacrifices.

309 Margalit and Raz, "National Self-Determination," p. 456.

310 However, one should ask how this claim squares with, say, the history of the US in the 19th century. Those who enjoyed the rights of citizenship were highly heterogeneous in descent and upbringing and became fellow citizens through voluntary immigration. I do not believe these facts significantly reduced the level of solidarity and mutual trust they enjoyed, compared to the levels enjoyed in the major European states of that period. A careful study of this case might well show that people *can* be bound together by a common decision to follow the call of a certain constitution and ideology as well as the promise of opportunities and adventure. If so, this would suggest that the *will* to make a political life together is possible without unchosen commonalities and sufficient for solidarity and mutual trust. This result would hardly be surprising, seeing how easily the closest friendships we form can do without commonalities in facial features, native language, cultural background, and religious convictions.

311 Margalit and Raz, "National Self-Determination," pp. 443 and 456.

312 For an example, see Barry, "Do Countries Have Moral Obligations?," pp. 27–44.

313 Rawls makes this point: "we want to account for the social values, for the intrinsic good of institutional, community, and associative activities, by a conception of justice that in its theoretical basis is individualistic. For reasons of clarity among others, we do not want to . . . suppose that society is an organic whole with a life of its own distinct from and superior to that of all its members in their relations with one another" (*A Theory of Justice*, pp. 233–4).

314 Walzer, *Just and Unjust Wars*, p. 53. See also Walzer, "The Moral Standing of States," p. 219.

315 Walzer suggests this tack: "citizens of a sovereign state have a right, insofar as they are to be ravaged and coerced at all, to suffer only at one another's hands" (*Just and Unjust Wars*, p. 86).

Chapter 8 Eradicating Systemic Poverty: Brief for a Global Resources Dividend

316 Pogge,"An Egalitarian Law of Peoples," "Eine globale Rohstoffdividende," and "A Global Resources Dividend."
317 Reichel, "Internationaler Handel," Kesselring, "Weltarmut und Ressourcen-Zugang," Crisp and Jamieson, "Egalitarianism and a Global Resources Tax."
318 Kreide, "Armut, Gerechtigkeit und Demokratie," and Mandle, "Globalization and Justice."
319 For details, see § 4.3.1.
320 Extending Nagel, "Poverty and Food."
321 Suggested in O'Neill, "Lifeboat Earth"; Nagel, "Poverty and Food"; and Pogge, *Realizing Rawls*, § 24.
322 See §§ 4.8 and 5.3.
323 Arms sold to the developing countries facilitate repression, fuel civil wars, and divert funds from meeting basic needs. In 2000, the rich countries spent about $4,650 million on development assistance for meeting basic needs abroad (text around n. 337) while also selling the developing countries an estimated $25,438 million in conventional weapons. This represents 69 percent of the entire international trade in conventional weapons (valued at $36,862 million). The main sellers of arms are the US, with over 50 percent of sales, then Russia, France, Germany, and the UK, with another 37 percent. See Congressional Research Service, *Conventional Arms Transfers to Developing Nations.*
324 See §§ 6.3. and 6.4.
325 See § 4.3.3.
326 See also Nozick, *Anarchy, State, and Utopia*, ch. 4.
327 Locke, "An Essay Concerning the True Original," § 27 and § 33.
328 Ibid., § 36.
329 Ibid., § 41 and § 37.
330 See § 4.3.1.
331 See Nozick, *Anarchy, State, and Utopia*, p. 231.
332 Aggregate global income was $31,171 billion in the year 2000.
333 See n. 122. The poverty gap relative to the World Bank's better-known $1/day (strictly: $1.08 PPP 1993) poverty line is only $44 billion annually. But this line is too low to define an acceptable goal in a world as affluent in aggregate as ours. Even the higher poverty line allows a family of four to buy only as much each month as can be bought with $322 in the US. And bringing all human beings up to the higher poverty line would still leave the average person in the high-income economies with over 100 times more money and 28 times more purchasing power (cf. nn. 122, 129, 138, and surrounding texts).
334 Crude oil production is currently about 77 million barrels daily or about 28 billion barrels annually. At a typical price of $25 per barrel, this

comes to $700 billion annually though prices are higher or lower at times.

335 Alesina and Dollar, "Who Gives Foreign Aid to Whom and Why?"

336 UNDP, *Report 2001*, p. 190. Cf. n. 143.

337 UNDP, *Report 2000*, p. 79.

338 Drescher, *Capitalism and Antislavery*.

Bibliography

Ackerman, Bruce. *The Future of Liberal Revolution.* New Haven: Yale University Press, 1992.

Agreement Relating to the Implementation of Part XI of the United Nations Convention on the Law of the Sea of 10 December 1982. www.un.org/Depts/los/convention_agreements/texts/unclos/closindx.htm

Aiken, Will and Hugh LaFolette, eds. *World Hunger and Morality.* Upper Saddle River, NJ: Prentice-Hall, 1996.

Alesina, Alberto and David Dollar. *"Who Gives Foreign Aid to Whom and Why?"* Journal of Economic Growth 5 (2000), 33–64 (http://papers.nber.org/papers/w6612).

Alexy, Robert. "Die Institutionalisierung der Menschenrechte im demokratischen Verfassungsstaat." In *Die Philosophie der Menschenrechte.* Edited by S. Gosepath and G. Lohmann. Frankfurt: Suhrkamp, 1998.

Amnesty International. *Human Rights and U.S. Security Assistance.* Boston: AIUSA Publications, 1996.

Annas, Julia. *The Morality of Happiness.* Oxford: Oxford University Press, 1993.

Aristotle. *Nicomachean Ethics.* Translated by T. Irwin. Indianapolis: Hackett, 1985.

Austin, John. *The Province of Jurisprudence Determined.* [1832] London: Weidenfeld and Nicolson, 1955.

Barry, Brian. *The Liberal Theory of Justice.* Oxford: Clarendon Press, 1972.

——. "Do Countries Have Moral Obligations?" In *The Tanner Lectures on Human Value II.* Edited by S. M. McMurrin. Salt Lake City: University of Utah Press, 1981.

——. "Humanity and Justice in Global Perspective." In *Ethics, Economics, and the Law*. Edited by J. R. Pennock and J. W. Chapman. New York: New York University Press, 1982.

——. "Self-Government Revisited." In *The Nature of Political Theory*. Edited by David Miller and Larry Siedentop. Oxford: Clarendon Press, 1983.

——. *Theories of Justice*. Berkeley: University of California Press, 1989.

Beitz, Charles. *Political Theory and International Relations*. Princeton: Princeton University Press, 1979.

——. "Cosmopolitan Ideals and National Sentiment." *Journal of Philosophy* 80 (1983): 591–600.

——. *Political Equality*. Princeton: Princeton University Press, 1989.

Benn, S. I. and R. S. Peters. *Social Principles and the Democratic State*. London: Allen and Unwin, 1959.

Bentham, Jeremy. *An Introduction to the Principles of Morals and Legislation.* [1789] Edited by J. H. Burns and H. L. A. Hart. London: Methuen, 1982.

Beran, Harry. *The Consent Theory of Political Obligation*. London: Croom Helm Publishers, 1987.

Bobbio, Norberto. *The Future of Democracy*. Minneapolis: University of Minnesota Press, 1984.

Bok, Hilary. "Acting without Choosing." *NOÛS* 30 (1996): 174–96.

Buchanan, Allen. *Secession*. Boulder: Westview Press, 1991.

Cavallero, Eric. "Sovereignty and Global Justice." Doctoral dissertation, Yale University Philosophy Department, 2002.

Chen, Shaohua and Martin Ravallion. "How Did the World's Poorest Fare in the 1990s?" Working paper, August 2000. www.worldbank.org/research/povmonitor/pdfs/methodology.pdf

Christiano, Thomas. *The Rule of the Many: Fundamental Issues in Democratic Theory*. Boulder: Westview Press, 1996.

Cohen, Gerald A. *Karl Marx's Theory of History: A Defence*. Oxford: Oxford University Press 1978.

——. "Equality of What? On Welfare, Goods, and Capabilities." In *The Quality of Life*. Edited by Martha Nussbaum and Amartya K. Sen. Oxford: Oxford University Press, 1993.

——. "Where the Action Is: On the Site of Distributive Justice." *Philosophy and Public Affairs* 26 (1997): 3–30.

Collier, Paul and Anke Hoeffler. "On Economic Causes of Civil War." *Oxford Economic Papers* 50 (1998): 563–73.

Congressional Research Service. *Conventional Arms Transfers to Developing Nations, 1993–2000*. Washington, DC: Library of Congress, 2001. http://usinfo.state.gov/topical/pol/arms/stories/01082201.htm

Copp, David et al., eds. *The Idea of Democracy*. Cambridge: Cambridge University Press, 1993.

Crisp, Roger and Dale Jamieson. "Egalitarianism and a Global Resources Tax: Pogge on Rawls." In *The Idea of a Political Liberalism: Essays on*

Rawls. Edited by Victoria Davion and Clark Wolf. Lanham, MD: Rowman and Littlefield, 2000.

Crocker, David A. "Reckoning with Past Wrongs: A Normative Framework." *Ethics and International Affairs* 13 (1999): 43–64.

Crocker, David A. and Toby Linden, eds. *Ethics of Consumption: The Good Life, Justice, and Global Stewardship*. Lanham, MD: Rowman and Littlefield, 1998.

Dahl, Robert. *A Preface to Democratic Theory*. Chicago: University of Chicago Press, 1956.

——. *Democracy and its Critics*. New Haven: Yale University Press, 1989.

Dasgupta, Partha. *An Inquiry into Well-Being and Destitution*. Oxford: Oxford University Press, 1993.

Diamond, Jared. *Guns, Germs, and Steel: The Fates of Human Societies*. New York: Norton, 1999.

Diamond, Larry. *Developing Democracy: Toward Consolidation*. Baltimore: Johns Hopkins University Press, 1999.

Drescher, Seymour. *Capitalism and Antislavery: British Mobilization in Comparative Perspective*. Oxford: Oxford University Press, 1986.

Dworkin, Ronald. "What is Equality? Part II: Equality of Resources." *Philosophy and Public Affairs* 10 (1981): 283–345.

Eichengreen, Barry, James Tobin, and Charles Wyplosz. "Two Cases for Sand in the Wheels of International Finance." *Economic Journal* 105, 428 (1995): 162–72.

Elster, Jon. *Sour Grapes*. Cambridge: Cambridge University Press, 1983.

——. ed. *Deliberative Democracy*. Cambridge: Cambridge University Press, 1998.

Elster, Jon and Rune Slagstad, eds. *Constitutionalism and Democracy*. Cambridge: Cambridge University Press, 1988.

Falk, Richard. *The End of World Order*. New York: Holmes and Meier, 1983.

FAO (United Nations Food and Agriculture Organization). *The State of Food Insecurity in the World 1999*. www.fao.org/news/1999/img/sofi99-e.pdf

Farer, Tom J. "The United States as Guarantor of Democracy in the Caribbean Basin: Is There a Legal Way?" *Human Rights Quarterly* 10 (1988): 157–76.

——. "A Paradigm of Legitimate Intervention." In *Enforcing Restraint: Collective Intervention in Internal Conflicts*. Edited by Lori Fisler Damrosch. New York: Council on Foreign Relations Press, 1993.

Feinberg, Joel. "The Nature and Value of Rights." *Journal of Value Inquiry* 4 (1970): 243–51.

Finger, J. Michael and Philip Schuler: "Implementation of Uruguay Round Commitments: The Development Challenge." World Bank Research Working Paper 2215, 1999. http://econ.worldbank.org/docs/941.pdf

Frankfurt, Harry. *The Importance of What We Care About*. Cambridge: Cambridge University Press, 1988.

Fried, Charles. "The Lawyer as Friend: The Moral Foundations of the Lawyer–Client Relation." *Yale Law Journal* 85 (1976): 1069–89.

Galston, William. *Justice and the Human Good.* Chicago: University of Chicago Press, 1980.

Gewirth, Alan. "The Basis and Content of Human Rights." In *Human Rights. Nomos*, vol. 23. Edited by J. Roland Pennock and John W. Chapman. New York: New York University Press, 1981.

Gibbard, Alan. *Wise Choices, Apt Feelings.* Cambridge, MA: Harvard University Press, 1990.

Giving USA 2001. Indianapolis: AAFRC Trust for Philanthropy, 2001.

Glendon, Mary Ann. *Rights Talk: The Impoverishment of Political Discourse.* New York: The Free Press, 1991.

Goodin, Robert E. "What is So Special about Our Fellow Countrymen?" *Ethics* 98 (1988): 663–86.

Gould, Stephen Jay. "The Moral State of Tahiti – and of Darwin." *Natural History* 10 (1991): 12–19.

Gourevitch, Philip. *We Wish to Inform You that Tomorrow We Will be Killed with Our Families.* New York: Picador, 1998.

de Greiff, Pablo. "Trial and Punishment, Pardon and Oblivion: On Two Inadequate Policies for the Treatment of Former Human Rights Abusers." *Philosophy and Social Criticism* 12 (1996): 93–111.

Griffin, James. *Well-Being.* Oxford: Clarendon Press, 1986.

Guinier, Lani. *The Tyranny of the Majority.* New York: The Free Press, 1994.

Gutmann, Amy and Dennis Thompson. *Democracy and Disagreement.* Cambridge, MA: Harvard University Press, 1996.

Habermas, Jürgen. *Moralbewusstsein und kommunikatives Handeln.* Frankfurt: Suhrkamp, 1983.

——. *Erläuterungen zur Diskursethik.* Frankfurt: Suhrkamp, 1991.

——. "Kants Idee des Ewigen Friedens – aus dem historischen Abstand von 200 Jahren." *Kritische Justiz* 28, 3 (1995): 293–319.

——. *Between Facts and Norms.* Cambridge, MA: MIT Press, 1996.

Hardin, Garrett. "Living on a Lifeboat." *BioScience* 24, 10 (1975): 561–8.

——. *Living within Limits.* Oxford: Oxford University Press, 1993.

——. "Lifeboat Ethics: The Case against Helping the Poor." In Aiken and LaFolette, *World Hunger and Marality*, 1996.

Harrison, Lawrence E. and Samuel P. Huntington, eds. *Culture Matters: How Values Shape Human Progress.* New York: Basic Books, 2001.

Hart, H. L. A. "Are There Any Natural Rights?" *Philosophical Review* 64 (1955): 175–91.

——. *The Concept of Law.* [1961] Oxford: Oxford University Press, 1994.

Hayner, Priscilla B. *Unspeakable Truths: Confronting State Terror and Atrocity.* New York: Routledge, 2001.

Held, David. *Models of Democracy.* Palo Alto: Stanford University Press, 1990.

Hertel, Thomas W. and Will Martin: "Would Developing Countries Gain from Inclusion of Manufactures in the WTO Negotiations?" 1999. www.gtap.agecon.purdue.edu/resources/download/42.pdf

Herz, John H. ed. *From Dictatorship to Democracy.* Boulder: Westview Press, 1982.

Hesse, Carla and Robert Post, eds. *Human Rights in Political Transitions: Gettysburg to Bosnia*. New York: Zone Books, 1999.
Hobbes, Thomas. *Leviathan*. [1651] Edited by C. B. Macpherson. Harmondsworth: Penguin, 1981.
Höffe, Otfried. *Demokratie im Zeitalter der Globalisierung*. Munich: Beck Verlag, 1999.
Hoffmann, Stanley. "Delusions of World Order." *New York Review of Books* 39, 7 (1992): 37–43.
——. *The Ethics and Politics of Humanitarian Intervention*. Notre Dame: University of Notre Dame Press, 1996.
Hohfeld, W. N. *Fundamental Legal Conceptions*. New Haven: Yale University Press, 1919.
Hume, David. *A Treatise on Human Nature*. [1737] Edited by L. A. Selby-Bigge. Oxford: Oxford University Press, 1973.
——. *An Enquiry Concerning the Principles of Morals*. [1751] Edited by Jerome B. Schneewind. Indianapolis: Hackett, 1983.
Huntington, Samuel P. *The Third Wave: Democratization in the Late Twentieth Century*. Norman: University of Oklahoma Press, 1991.
International Panel of Eminent Personalities: *Rwanda: The Preventable Genocide*, July 7, 2000. www.visiontv.ca/RememberRwanda/excerpts.doc
Kagan, Shelly. *The Limits of Morality*. Oxford: Oxford University Press, 1989.
Kant, Immanuel. *Kants gesammelte Schriften*. Volume 5, ed. Königlich Preussische Akademie der Wissenschaften. Berlin: Georg Reimer, 1913.
——. *Kants gesammelte Schriften*. Volume 6, ed. Königlich Preussische Akademie der Wissenschaften. Berlin: Georg Reimer, 1914.
——. *Kants gesammelte Schriften*. Volume 8, ed. Königlich Preussische Akademie der Wissenschaften. Berlin: de Gruyter, 1923.
——. *Kant's Political Writings*. Edited by Hans Reiss. Cambridge: Cambridge University Press, 1970.
Kesselring, Thomas. "Weltarmut und Ressourcen-Zugang." *Analyse und Kritik* 19, 3 (1997): 242–54.
Kreide, Regina. "Armut, Gerechtigkeit und Demokratie." *Analyse und Kritik* 20, 3 (1998): 245–62.
Kritz, Neil J., ed. *Transitional Justice: How Emerging Democracies Reckon with Former Regimes*, 3 vols. Washington, DC: US Institute of Peace Press, 1995.
Lam, Ricky and Leonard Wantchekon. "Dictatorships as a Political Dutch Disease." Working paper, 19 January 1999. Economic Growth Center, Yale University, Center Discussion Paper 795. http://econpapers.hhs.se/paper/wopyalegr/
Landes, David. *The Wealth and Poverty of Nations: Why Some Are so Rich and Some so Poor*. New York: Norton 1998.
Lefort, Claude. *Democracy and Political Theory*. Minneapolis: University of Minnesota Press, 1988.
Linz, Juan J. and Alfred Stepan. *Problems of Democratic Transition and Consolidation: Southern Europe, South America, and Post-Communist Europe*. Baltimore: Johns Hopkins University Press, 1996.

Lipton, Michael. "The 2015 Poverty Targets: What Do 1990–98 Trends Tell Us?" Unpublished paper, Poverty Research Unit at Sussex University, March 2001.

Locke, John. "An Essay Concerning the True Original, Extent, and End of Civil Government." [1689] In *John Locke: Two Treatises of Government*. Edited by Peter Laslett. Cambridge: Cambridge University Press, 1960.

Luban, David. "Just War and Human Rights." In *International Ethics*. Edited by Charles Beitz et al. Princeton: Princeton University Press, 1985.

MacIntyre, Alasdair. *After Virtue*. Notre Dame: Notre Dame University Press, 1981.

Mackie, J. L. "Can There Be a Right-Based Moral Theory?" *Midwest Studies in Philosophy* 3 (1978): 350–9.

Malamud-Goti, Jaime. *Game without End: State Terror and the Politics of Justice*. Norman: University of Oklahoma Press, 1996.

Malthus, Thomas Robert. *An Essay on the Principle of Population.* [1798] Harmondsworth: Penguin, 1982.

Mandle, Jon. "Globalization and Justice." *Annals of the American Academy* 570 (2000): 126–39.

Manin, Bernard. *Principles of Representative Government*. Cambridge: Cambridge University Press, 1997.

Margalit, Avishai and Joseph Raz. "National Self-Determination." *Journal of Philosophy* 57 (1990): 439–61.

Marshall, Geoffrey. *Parliamentary Sovereignty and the Commonwealth*. Oxford: Oxford University Press, 1957.

Marx, Karl. "The German Ideology." In *The Marx–Engels Reader*. Edited by Robert C. Tucker. New York: Norton, 1978.

Meyer, Lukas. "More Than They Have a Right To: Future People and Our Future-Oriented Projects." In *Contingent Future Persons: On the Ethics of Deciding Who Will Live, or Not, in the Future*. Edited by N. Fotion and J. C. Heller. Dordrecht: Kluwer, 1997.

Milanovic, Branko. "True World Income Distribution, 1988 and 1993: First Calculation Based on Household Surveys Alone." *The Economic Journal* 112 (2002): 51–92 (http://www.blackwellpublishers.co.uk/specialarticles/ecoj50673.pdf).

Mill, John Stuart. *On Liberty*. [1859] Indianapolis: Hackett, 1978.

Miller, David. "Justice and Global Inequality." In *Inequality, Globalization and World Politics*. Edited by Andrew Hurrell and Ngaire Woods. Oxford: Oxford University Press, 1999.

——. "National Self-Determination and Global Justice." In *Citizenship and National Identity*. Cambridge: Polity, 2000.

——. "Two Ways to Think about Justice." *Politics, Philosophy, and Economics* 1 (2002): 5–28.

——. "National Responsibility and International Justice." Forthcoming in *The Ethics of Assistance: Morality and the Distant Needy*. Edited by Deen Chatterjee. Cambridge: Cambridge University Press.

Minow, Martha. *Between Vengeance and Forgiveness*. Boston: Beacon Press, 1998.
Murphy, Liam. "Institutions and the Demands of Justice." *Philosophy and Public Affairs* 27 (1999): 251–91.
——. *Moral Demands in Non-Ideal Theory*. Oxford: Oxford University Press, 2000.
Nagel, Thomas. "Poverty and Food: Why Charity Is Not Enough." In *Food Policy: The Responsibility of the United States in the Life and Death Choices*. Edited by Peter Brown and Henry Shue. New York: The Free Press, 1977.
——. *Mortal Questions*. Cambridge: Cambridge University Press, 1979.
Nickel, James. *Making Sense of Human Rights*. Berkeley: University of California Press, 1987.
Nielsen, Kai. "World Government, Security, and Global Justice." In *Problems of International Justice*. Edited by Steven Luper-Foy. Boulder: Westview Press, 1988.
Nino, Carlos. *Radical Evil on Trial*. New Haven: Yale University Press, 1996.
Nozick, Robert. *Anarchy, State, and Utopia*. New York: Basic Books, 1974.
——. *The Examined Life*. New York: Simon and Schuster, 1989.
Nussbaum, Martha. *The Fragility of Goodness*. Cambridge: Cambridge University Press, 1986.
——. *The Therapy of Desire*. Princeton: Princeton University Press, 1994.
Nussbaum, Martha and Amartya K. Sen, eds. *The Quality of Life*. Oxford: Oxford University Press, 1993.
O'Neill, Onora. "Lifeboat Earth." *Philosophy and Public Affairs* 4 (1974): 273–92.
——. *Faces of Hunger*. London: Allen and Unwin, 1986.
Parfit, Derek. *Reasons and Persons*. Oxford: Oxford University Press, 1984.
Philpott, Daniel. "In Defense of Self-Determination." *Ethics* 105 (1995): 352–85.
Plato. *The Republic*. Translated by G. M. A. Grube. Indianapolis: Hackett, 1974.
Pogge, Thomas W. *Realizing Rawls*. Ithaca: Cornell University Press, 1989.
——. "The Effects of Prevalent Moral Conceptions." *Social Research* 57 (1990): 649–63.
——. "O'Neill on Rights and Duties." *Grazer Philosophische Studien* 43 (1992): 233–47.
——. "An Egalitarian Law of Peoples." *Philosophy and Public Affairs* 23 (1994): 195–224.
——. "Eine globale Rohstoffdividende." *Analyse und Kritik* 17 (1995): 183–208.
——. "Three Problems with Contractarian-Consequentialist Ways of Assessing Social Institutions." *Social Philosophy and Policy* 12 (1995): 241–66.
——. "Creating Supra-National Institutions Democratically: Reflections on the European Union's Democratic Deficit." *Journal of Political Philosophy* 5 (1997): 163–82.

——. "Group Rights and Ethnicity." In *Ethnicity and Group Rights. Nomos*, vol. 39. Edited by Will Kymlicka and Ian Shapiro. New York: New York University Press 1997.

——. "Gleiche Freiheit für alle?" In *John Rawls: Eine Theorie der Gerechtigkeit*. Edited by Otfried Höffe. Berlin: Akademie Verlag, 1998.

——. "A Global Resources Dividend." In *Ethics of Consumption: The Good Life, Justice, and Global Stewardship*. Edited by David A. Crocker and Toby Linden. Lanham, MD: Rowman and Littlefield, 1998.

——. "On the Site of Distributive Justice: Reflections on Cohen and Murphy." *Philosophy and Public Affairs* 29 (2000): 137–69.

—— ed. *Global Justice*. Oxford: Blackwell Publishers, 2001.

——. "Rawls on International Justice." *Philosophical Quarterly* 51 (2001): 246–53.

——. "Human Rights and Human Responsibilities." In *Transnational Politics and Deliberative Democracy*. Edited by Ciaran Cronin and Pablo de Greiff. Cambridge, MA: MIT Press, 2002.

——. "Relational Conceptions of Justice: Responsibilities for Health Outcomes." In Sudhir Anand, Fabienne Peter, and Amartya Sen, eds.: *Health, Ethics, and Equity*. Oxford: Clarendon Press, 2003.

Press and Information Office of the Federal Government, *The Basic Law of the Federal Republic of Germany*. Wiesbaden: Wiesbadener Graphische Betriebe GmbH, 1979 (also at www.rewi.hu-berlin.de/jura/proj/dsi/Gesetze/gg.html).

Rachels, James. "Killing and Starving to Death." *Philosophy* 54 (1979): 159–71.

Rawls, John. *A Theory of Justice*. Cambridge, MA: Harvard University Press, 1971.

——. "Social Unity and Primary Goods." In *Utilitarianism and Beyond*. Edited by A. K. Sen and B. Williams. Cambridge: Cambridge University Press, 1982.

——. "Justice as Fairness: Political not Metaphysical." *Philosophy and Public Affairs* 14 (1985): 223–52.

——. "The Law of Peoples." In *On Human Rights*. Edited by Stephen Shute and Susan Hurley. New York: Basic Books, 1993.

——. *Political Liberalism*. New York: Columbia University Press, 1993.

——. *The Law of Peoples*. Cambridge, MA: Harvard University Press, 1999.

Raz, Joseph. "On the Nature of Rights." *Mind* 93 (1984): 194–214.

——. *The Morality of Freedom*. Oxford: Clarendon Press, 1986.

——. *Practical Reason and Norms*. Princeton: Princeton University Press, 1990.

——. *Ethics in the Public Domain*. Oxford: Clarendon Press, 1994.

Reddy, Sanjay and Thomas W. Pogge. "How *Not* to Count the Poor." Unpublished working paper, 2002. www.socialanalysis.org.

Reichel, Richard. "Internationaler Handel, Tauschgerechtigkeit und die globale Rohstoffdividende." *Analyse und Kritik* 19, 3 (1997): 229–41.

Report of the Independent Inquiry into the Actions of the United Nations during the 1994 Genocide in Rwanda. December 15, 1999. www.ess.uwe.ac.uk/genocide/Rwanda.htm

Rome Declaration on World Food Security. 1996. www.fao.org/wfs/

Rorty, Richard. *Contingency, Irony, and Solidarity*. Cambridge: Cambridge University Press, 1989.

——. "Who are We? Moral Universalism and Economic Triage." *Diogenes* 173 (1996): 5–15.

Rosenblum, Nancy, ed. *Obligations of Citizenship*. Princeton: Princeton University Press, 2000.

Ross, Michael L. "The Political Economy of the Resource Curse." World Politics 51 (1999): 297–322.

——. "Does Resource Wealth Cause Authoritarian Rule?" Lecture, Yale University, April 4, 2000. www.yale.edu/leitner/pdf/ross.pdf

Rotberg, Robert and Dennis Thompson, eds. *Truth v. Justice*. Princeton: Princeton University Press, 2000.

Sachs, Jeffrey D. and Andrew M. Warner. "Natural Resource Abundance and Economic Growth." Development Discussion Paper 517a, October 1995. www.hiid.harvard.edu/pub/pdfs/517.pdf

Scanlon, Thomas M. "Rawls' Theory of Justice." Reprinted in *Reading Rawls*. Edited by Norman Daniels. New York: Basic Books, 1974.

——. "Preference and Urgency." *Journal of Philosophy* 72 (1975): 655–69.

——. *What We Owe to Each Other*. Cambridge, MA: Harvard University Press, 1999.

Scheffler, Samuel. *Boundaries and Allegiances*. Oxford: Oxford University Press, 2001.

Schumpeter, Joseph. *Capitalism, Socialism, and Democracy*. [1943] New York: Harper, 1984.

Sen, Amartya K. *Poverty and Famines*. Oxford: Oxford University Press, 1981.

——. *Commodities and Capabilities*. Amsterdam: North-Holland, 1985.

——. "Population: Delusion and Reality." *New York Review*, September 22, 1994: 62–71.

Shimazu, Naoko. *Japan, Race and Equality: The Racial Equality Proposal of 1919*. London: Routledge, 1998.

Shue, Henry. *Basic Rights*. [1980] Princeton: Princeton University Press, 1996.

Simmons, A. John. *Moral Principles and Political Obligation*. Princeton: Princeton University Press, 1979.

Singer, Peter. "Famine, Affluence and Morality." *Philosophy and Public Affairs* 1 (1972): 229–43.

Slote, Michael. *Goods and Virtues*. Oxford: Oxford University Press, 1983.

——. *From Morality to Virtue*. Oxford: Oxford University Press, 1992.

Tan, Kok-Chor. *Toleration, Diversity, and Global Justice*. University Park: Pennsylvania State University Press, 2000.

Taylor, Charles. *Sources of the Self*. Cambridge, MA: Harvard University Press, 1989.

Teitel, Ruti. *Transitional Justice*. Oxford: Oxford University Press, 2000.

Thucydides. *The History of the Peloponnesian War*. Harmondsworth: Penguin, 1986.

Tobin, James. "A Proposal for International Monetary Reform." *Eastern Economic Journal* 4 (1978): 153–9.

Tuck, Richard. *Natural Rights Theories*. Cambridge: Cambridge University Press, 1979.

——. "The "Modern" Theory of Natural Law." In *The Languages of Political Theory in Early-Modern Europe*. Edited by Anthony Pagden. Cambridge: Cambridge University Press, 1987.

Tugendhat, Ernst. *Vorlesungen über Ethik*. Frankfurt: Suhrkamp, 1993.

UDHR (*Universal Declaration of Human Rights*). In *Twenty-Four Human Rights Documents*. New York: Columbia University Center for the Study of Human Rights, 1992.

UN Convention on the Law of the Sea. 1982. www.un.org/Depts/los/convention_agreements/texts/unclos/closindx.htm

UNCTAD (United Nations Conference on Trade and Development). *Trade and Development Report 1999*. New York: UN Publications, 1999.

UNDP (United Nations Development Programme). *Human Development Report 1995*. New York: Oxford University Press, 1995.

——. *Human Development Report 1996*. New York: Oxford University Press, 1996.

——. *Human Development Report 1997*. New York: Oxford University Press, 1997.

——. *Human Development Report 1999*. New York: Oxford University Press, 1999.

——. *Human Development Report 2000*. New York: Oxford University Press, 2000. www.undp.org/hdr2000/english/HDR2000.html

——. *Human Development Report 2001*. New York: Oxford University Press, 2001. www.undp.org/hdr2001/

Unger, Peter. *Living High and Letting Die: Our Illusion of Innocence*. Oxford: Oxford University Press, 1996.

Unger, Roberto. *Democracy Realized: The Progressive Alternative*. London: Verso, 1998.

UNICEF (United Nations Children's Fund). *The State of the World's Children 2002*. New York: UNICEF, 2002. www.unicef.org/sowc02/pdf/sowc2002-eng-full.pdf

UN Millennium Declaration, General Assembly Resolution 55/2, 2000. www.un.org/millennium/declaration/ares552e.htm

USDA (United States Department of Agriculture). *U.S. Action Plan on Food Security*. 1999. www.fas.usda.gov/icd/summit/pressdoc.html

USDS (United States Department of State). *US Commentary on the Law of the Sea Convention including the 1994 Amendments*. 1994. gopher://gopher.state.gov:70/00ftp:DOSFan:Gopher:07%20Treaties%20and%20Legal%20Issues:01%20Releases%20-%20Statements:9410%20Law%20of%20the%20Sea

Waldron, Jeremy. "Special Ties and Natural Duties." *Philosophy and Public Affairs* 22 (1993): 1–30.

Wallerstein, Immanuel. *The Capitalist World Economy*. Cambridge: Cambridge University Press, 1979.

——. *The Politics of the World-Economy*. New York: Cambridge University Press, 1984.

——. *After Liberalism*. New York: New Press, 1995.

——. *The Essential Wallerstein*. New York: New Press, 2000.

Walzer, Michael. *Just and Unjust Wars*. New York: Basic Books, 1977.

——. "The Moral Standing of States." *Philosophy and Public Affairs* 9 (1980): 209–29.

——. *Spheres of Justice*. New York: Basic Books, 1983.

Wantchekon, Leonard. "Why do Resource Dependent Countries Have Authoritarian Governments?" Working paper, Yale University, December 12, 1999. www.yale.edu/leitner/pdf/1999-11.pdf

Wellman, Carl. "A New Conception of Human Rights." In *Human Rights*. Edited by E. Kamenka and A. S. Tay. New York: St Martin's Press, 1968.

——. *A Theory of Rights: Persons under Laws, Institutions, and Morals*. Totowa: Rowman and Allanheld, 1985.

Wellman, Christopher. "A Defense of Secession and Political Self-Determination." *Philosophy and Public Affairs* 24 (1995): 142–71.

Weschler, Lawrence. *A Miracle, a Universe: Settling Accounts with Torturers*. New York: Pantheon, 1990.

WHO (World Health Organization). *The World Health Report 2001*. Geneva: WHO Publications, 2001. www.who.int/whr/2001

Williams, Bernard. *Moral Luck*. Cambridge: Cambridge University Press, 1981.

——. *Ethics and the Limits of Philosophy*. Cambridge, MA: Harvard University Press, 1985.

——. *Shame and Necessity*. Berkeley: University of California Press, 1993.

——. *Making Sense of Humanity*. Cambridge: Cambridge University Press, 1995.

Wolf, Martin. "Broken Promises to the Poor." *Financial Times*, November 21, 2001, p. 13.

Wollheim, Richard. *The Thread of Life*. Cambridge, MA: Harvard University Press, 1984.

World Bank. *World Development Report 1999/2000*. New York: Oxford University Press, 2000. www.worldbank.org/wdr/2000/fullreport.html

——. *World Development Report 2000/2001*. New York: Oxford University Press, 2001. www.worldbank.org/poverty/wdrpoverty/report/index.htm

——. *World Development Report 2002*. New York: Oxford University Press, 2001. http://econ.worldbank.org/wdr/structured_doc.php?sp=2391&st=&sd=2394.

Index